THE ACTOR AND THE TEXT

Cicely Berry

REVISED EDITION

Foreword by Trevor Nunn

Virgin BOOKS

To the memory of my husband
Harry Moore

This edition first published in Great Britain in 2000 by
Virgin Books
Thames Wharf Studios
Rainville Road
London W6 9HA

Reprinted 2003, 2006

Revised edition first published in Great Britain in 1993 by
Virgin Books
an imprint of Virgin Publishing Ltd

Reprinted 1996, 1997

First published as *The Actor and His Text* in 1987 by
Harrap Ltd, and reprinted in 1988 and 1991

A catalogue record for this book is available from the British Library

ISBN 0 86369 705 4

Printed and bound in Great Britain by
Mackays of Chatham plc, Chatham, Kent

Contents

Foreword

This book will be used by actors and directors of every kind—amateur, professional, occasional and obsessional. Cicely Berry is irresistible; a potential administrator who writes everything down on the back of crumpled envelopes; a departmental head who convulses herself and me in her own self-deprecating laughter. But fueling these contradictions is an explorer's obsession, a radical's fervour and a philosopher's generosity; she is a voice teacher with a mission.

Her uniqueness and authenticity have made her work a fundamental part of the RSC's achievement. Although she is an immensely successful teacher of all the practical necessities of vocal technique, she dislikes the development and appearance of technique for its own sake.

Her mission is to expand the awareness of language, its roots, its possibilities of meaning, its physical seat and vibration, its associations, its weight and texture and colour. More than a teacher, she is a director, an analyst, a critic, a sociologist and above all, a restless and dissatisfied enquirer.

Her work demands, and is given, an unusual amount of trust from campaign-hardened professional actors and time-constrained directors, all of whom would quickly dispense with her methods if she did not so palpably stretch and improve all who came under her influence.

This book is full of the essential Berry, her responses to language—ancient and modern, heightened and prosaic—her missionary zeal, her reciprocal requirement for seriousness and dedication. But, gentle reader, try as you work through these chapters to hear her shrieks of laughter and her intense, private whispers as she looks full into your eyes and you will glimpse that ingredient that makes her an inspirational teacher, her humanity, or perhaps I should say, her love.

—Trevor Nunn

Acknowledgments

The author would like to thank the following for their kind permission to print the poems and extracts included in this book:

Penguin Books Ltd. for all the Shakespeare quotations from the plays (with the exception of *Titus Andronicus*), taken from the New Penguin Shakespeare, edited by T.J.B. Spencer (General Editor), and Stanley Wells (Associate Editor).

Hodder and Stoughton for 'The Sonnets', printed from the edition edited by W.G. Ingram and Theodore Redpath.

Methuen for the quotations from *Titus Andronicus*, printed from The Arden Shakespeare, edited by Richard Proudfoot (General Editor) and J.C. Maxwell.

The Oxford University Press for *Song* by John Donne, and three verses from his *Valediction: Forbidding Mourning*, printed from the edition edited by H.J.C. Grierson, first published in 1933.

Ernest Benn Ltd. for the quotation from *The Duchess of Malfi*, by John Webster, printed from the New Mermaids Edition, edited by Philip Brockbank and Brian Morris, this play edited by Elizabeth M. Brennan.

Vizetelly and Co. for the quotation from *The Country Wife*, by William Wycherley, printed from the Mermaid series, edited by W.C. Ward.

Methuen for: the extract from *The Sons of Light*, by David Rudkin, 1981 edition; the extract from *Lear*, by Edward Bond, first published in 1972; the extract from *Soft Cops*, first published in 1986; the extract from Part Two of 'The War Plays' (*The Tin Can People*), by Edward Bond, 1985 edition; the extract from *Sus*, by Barrie Keeffe, 1979 edition; the poem *Questions of a Studious Working Man*, by Bertolt Brecht, taken from 'Tales from the Calendar', translated by Michael Hamburger, published 1981; the two poems: *To the Audience and On Leaving the Theatre*, by Edward Bond, from 'Theatre Poems and Songs', 1978 edition.

Signet Books, by arrangement with New Directions Books and Tennessee Williams, for the extract from *A Streetcar Named Desire*, by Tennessee Williams, first published in 1947.

Penguin Modern Playwrights—8 for the extract from *Dingo*, by Charles Wood, first published in 1969.

The Society of Authors, on behalf of the Bernard Shaw estate, for the extract from *Man and Superman*, Penguin edition, published in 1946. The play was first published in 1903.

Penguin Books for the poem *A world in each human being*, by Gunnar Ekelof, translated by Ann Draycon, taken from 'Poetry of the Committed Individual', edited by Jon Silkin, 1973 edition; and for the poem *vending machine*, by Hans Magnus Enzensburger, translated by the author, taken from the Penguin Book of Socialist Verse, first published in 1970.

New Directions Books for the poem *Constantly risking absurdity*, by Lawrence Ferlinghetti, taken from the selection of poems 'Endless Life', first published in 1981.

Faber and Faber for the poem *Musee des Beaux Arts*, by W.H. Auden, taken from his Collected Shorter Poems; and for thirteen lines from *East Coker*, by T.S. Eliot, taken from the 1936 edition of his poems.

W.M. Dent for the poem *The Force that through the Green Fuse drives the Flower*, by Dylan Thomas, from the collected poems, published 1952.

Anchor Books for the excerpts from *L'Allegro, Il Penseroso*, and *Samson Agonistes*, by John Milton, from the edition of his works edited by John T. Shawcross.

Introduction

This book is about ways of working on the speaking of text. Much has been written about the voice and the sound we make, and about articulation and verbal clarity, but little on how we bring all this to bear on the specific speaking of text; and so I want to bring the two together in a practical way.

For it seems to me there is so often a gap between the life that is going on imaginatively within the actor in order to create the reality of the character he is playing, and the life that he gives the text which he finally has to speak. It is as if the energy and excitement that an actor feels when working on a part is not released fully when he commits to words, when he is bound by the language set down.

And this is true of all kinds of text, both modern and classical, though the problems are different and the gap is more apparent in the speaking of heightened or poetic text where there is a certain size to the language, and where the expectations of the listener are often an inhibiting factor — i.e., these texts have been heard before. But whatever the style of the writing, the actor has to find the right energy for that particular text; if his energy becomes too inward and controlled the words become dull; if he presses too much energy out the words will be unfocused and the thought will be generalized. Either way the result is that the speaking of text or dialogue is too often not as alive or remarkable as the imagination that is feeding it.

I do believe that work on Shakespeare is the surest way of learning about text, and for these reasons: because it demands such a complete investment of ourselves in the words; because it is so rich and extraordinary we are forced to be bold and even extravagant and so perhaps discover more possibilities within our own voice than we are aware of; because, in a very practical sense, the connection between the physical and verbal life of the characters is totally apparent and palpable; and lastly because, and this is particularly important for the modern actor, the structure of the thought demands both courage and discipline.

The main part of this book, then, deals with the speaking of Shakespeare and with the challenge of classical text — and it is practical. Having worked in a company for over twenty years where the focus is to a great extent on Shakespeare, I think there are things we have discovered together — practical ways of working on the text — which help us into the language and are useful. These have always been in the area of relating acting method to practical direct speaking. I would like, therefore, to set down what I have learnt.

However, I think it would be limiting if we left it there as an end in itself, so I have made reference to modern writing, for this always feeds our response to Shakespeare, and vice versa. We are always lucky when we have an opportunity to work on both, for it is the interchange between modern and classical writing that enriches both and makes each more alive. Work on Shakespeare opens our awareness to language in modern writing by adding to the resonance of the words we speak, even when they are rooted in a modern reality. And work on modern text keeps our ears tuned to the colloquial rhythms of everyday speech, which need to be integrated into our speaking of verse. We should be always balancing the two for, in a sense, every piece of text we speak on a stage is heightened — it is performed — and we have to find its particular voice and place that particular language.

I think it is also important to say here that, as actors, we are able to be articulate through the language we bring alive; we therefore have a responsibility to that language.The care and life that we bring to it helps the hearers also to be articulate; and I think this has a special value for the present time when computer technology threatens to dehumanize communication, and when the term 'post-articulate' has become current. Therefore we must always be after the reaching out through words, and not a dulled, inward-looking speaking of dialogue. We have to honour a greater need, and that is to make what we say remarkable to the hearer. This is what Brecht was after. Now obviously this cannot apply to everything we do — mediocre dialogue in second-rate scripts, for instance — yet I do believe that the richer our experience of handling language, the more we can get out of the most banal of writing.

Now Voice is a difficult subject to write about — I know from my experience of teaching it that everyone responds to instruction in different ways. Each person recognizes what is happening with his own voice purely subjectively, and although the basic principles are common to everyone, how we interpret them for ourselves varies enormously with each individual. This becomes even more complex when we are dealing with text.

As we shall be talking a great deal about the image we have of our own voice and how this conditions the way we work on it, it is perhaps useful here to recap briefly on what I have already written in *Voice and the Actor**, about how we arrive at our voice. Briefly it is this: the voice

* First published by Harrap in 1973. Reprinted ten times.

which we arrive at is the most intricate mixture of what we hear, how we hear it, and how we unconsciously use it in the light of our personality, our physical make-up and our experience. That is to say, how we use our voice is conditioned by a) our environment and our attitude to that; b) our perception of sound and the accuracy with which we hear it (our ear), and this is also involved with our aesthetic pleasure in sound and consequent judgement of it; c) our individual physical make-up and agility, and our natural power; and d) our own wish and need to communicate. So we see it is very bound up with our formative years — whether we were encouraged to speak or not, what influenced us, etc. — and to break from our habits of speech is often a huge step to take. And it is important always to remember the subjective nature of the voice, for it helps us to work through the limitations we make for ourselves.

In *Voice and the Actor* I have covered the general aspects of voice production. However I will be adding to the exercises given there, for since writing it I have developed the work and I think the emphasis has slightly changed. But my starting-point here will be that exercises are already part of the actor's work, that range and flexibility are opened out, and the voice is in readiness, as it were, at whatever stage of experience you are as an actor, and with whatever background of voice work you have.

So, this book is not simply about making the voice sound more interesting. It is about getting inside the words we use, responding to them in as free a way as possible, and then presenting that response to an audience. It is about how to use the freedom we get in exercises when we are being real in speech. It is about making the language organic, so that the words act as the spur to the sound, and so that flexibility and range are found because the words require them.

Finally, two general points. I think we tend to use words as if they belong to either our reason or to our emotions, so that we make them either only literal and logical, or alternatively only emotional. We do not use them as our thoughts in action, which are always shifting and changing, and are the result of both thought and feeling.

Secondly too often the imaginative process becomes ordinary at the moment of speaking. I think this is because we are tentative and do not know how far we can go, or because we do not know how to explore the language boldly enough without being unreal. I want, in this book, to set out the possibilities as I see them, which I hope will give us the confidence to trust in ourselves and in the text.

One last point: I felt the word *actor*, as referring to both male and female, was correct. At the time of writing I chose to use *he* rather than *he/she*, believing it to be less cumbersome. I now regret this, and I apologize to those whose feelings may be offended.

Part 1

Attitudes to Voice and Text

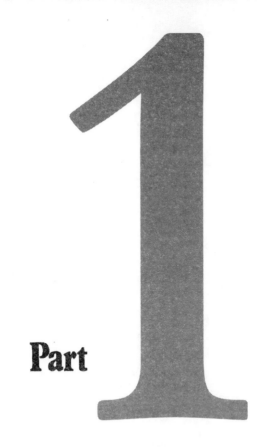

Chapter 1

SOUND AND MEANING

In this chapter I want to focus on two things:

1 The attitudes we have to our own voice: how we think of our own sound, and how this affects our work as an actor. And then:

2 The practical application of exercises: that is to say I want to clarify the aims of the voice work we do, so that it gives maximum support to the words we speak.

Ideally, I suppose, every actor wants to know that his voice is carrying what is in his mind and imagination directly across to the audience. He wants it to be accurate to his intention and to sound unforced. He wants to know that he is carrying the listener with him for, in the end, it is the voice which sets up the main bond between him and his audience. Certainly this is true of Western theatre. He knows that the audience want to be let into his character, and that this will happen to a large extent through his voice and speech. Above all, he wants it to be interesting.

This sounds simple enough, but many things get in the way. For, paradoxically, often the more truthful he wants to be and the more he wants to fill the text — i.e., the more possibilities he sees within the character — the more difficult it is to be simple, and to release the words directly and without pressure. Depending on the actor, this tension between himself and the text can make him over-explain, be over-emphatic, or over-charge the speaking with emotion — all qualities which come between him and the direct and simple sharing with his audience. Yet, equally, it is no good saying: let the words speak for themselves and just rely on the text. This is a platitude which has no meaning when you are on stage performing to several hundred people; and in any case it is misleading, for words have to be filled with your own experience or they will be flat and lack commitment, and so be uninteresting. Yet all these over-statements which come out of an anxiety to present are a matter of balance, of judging the precise amount of energy needed for the text you are working with and the space you are working in. And I feel strongly that we tend to work on voice as an end in itself, and somehow do not see that work through clearly enough to the specific speaking of text and, further, to our commitment to language.

Therefore we have to work at language as well as voice; we have to practise it, in a sense, to get more adept at feeling its weight and movement. Just as, in everyday life, how a person uses language (or does not use language) is part of the essence of that person, so the actor has to be ready for the dialogue to take us into the world of the character — he has to be able to pick up the resonances of the character through the words given in the script. He must touch the character through the language. Yet also we have to allow that language to bear on our own experience so that it is real for us, and this asks for a continual blending of our own truth with the truth of the character. And so I think we have to keep reassessing our attitudes to language — never taking it for granted — for this is our commitment; and each piece of writing asks for a different connection between the actor and his audience, a different style of speaking perhaps.

1 ATTITUDES TO VOICE

First, I want to look at the factors which hold us back from making the text as rich and alive as possible. This may seem negative, but I think there are certain attitudes and ways of working by which we are conditioned, which take our attention away from the right verbal focus, and I think by simply stating them it will help us to re-think that focus.

Now of course each actor is at a different stage of development and has different concerns, but I think the factors that hold us back are common to us all. They manifest themselves differently because each actor's personality and make-up is different, but the causes remain similar. Sometimes the adjustment that is needed is to do with the perception of language; sometimes it is technical; more often than not it is a mixture of both.

I think these inhibiting factors fall roughly into five areas — the order is not important:

(a) The reliance we put on our own sound

To a large extent I think we are trapped in our own sound and sound pattern. This is because our voice has evolved with us, and is therefore a complex mix of background, physical make-up and personality, and the interactions of one upon the other. And because of this we quite involuntarily make a statement with our voice. This statement has a great deal to do with class, education and cultural background, and therefore with what we expect of ourselves. Here I do not mean accent — we can work on that quite specifically and get beyond limitations of dialect — what I mean is something more, something we feel inside. We are used to our own voice in a quite palpable way, and I think it quite unconsciously forms the way we think about language and use it.

It is curiously difficult to work on our own voice both boldly and creatively, because it means we have to let go of our own patterns. Let me explain: given that our voice is our sound presence, and is the means by which we commit our private world to the world outside, it is tied up with how we think of ourselves — our self-image — and with the image of ourselves we wish to present. It is therefore bound absolutely to our own self-confidence, and so is particularly sensitive to both criticism and to feelings of unease. This is true even in our everyday life: we find our voice changes according to how we feel our status to be at any given moment. It is also true that we are quite strongly affected by criticism of our voice, even to the point of it inhibiting our wish to talk. None of this happens particularly consciously, or necessarily at a very deep level; nevertheless, the voice is extremely sensitive to our own ego.

The important point I think is this: we are more strongly aware of our own sound than we realize, and that sound is strongly bound to our emotional state, and to our self-esteem. Yet, because we hear the sound via the bone conduction in our own heads, and also because we hear it subjectively in the sense that it is tied up with our perception of our voice and how we would like it to sound, and also to how we feel at the time, we seldom hear it accurately. We obviously never hear it in the way we hear someone else's voice — we are aware of this when we hear ourselves on tape, but even then we listen subjectively. It certainly seldom tallies with how others hear us; but then, they are only listening from the outside!

For the actor, all this takes on a slightly different emphasis — for the voice is part of his job, and a skilled part. He has to train his voice and to begin to know it objectively. Yet it is still part of his private means of communication, and is still subject to his confidence. So how he uses his voice in a job is bound up with how he feels about that job, and how confident he is in it. Now part of the actor's business is to know how he is presenting himself: just as he has a persona which he objectively needs to use, and for which he is often cast, so he needs to rely on the vocal qualities in which he feels sure and confident. Certainly, when you do not feel easy with a particular part it is difficult to find your authentic voice in it — your vocal stresses. So we tend to hold on to the sound which feels familiar, and in which we have confidence; and this happens at all stages of an actor's life, regardless of how much flexibility and range he has acquired. We tend to limit ourselves to what we know. I suppose this is how in the end vocal mannerisms develop — seldom consciously, but rather because we hold on to a quality of sound or inflection which we recognize from inside, and we start to repeat that and 'firm it up', as it were. We ourselves do not hear it as a mannerism.

So when an actor is working on a part, he needs to discover and experience feelings while he is speaking, while at the same time he must know what effect his voice is having. He needs to know his voice both subjectively and objectively at the same time: he needs that third eye, or perhaps ear. Now when we make adjustments to how we speak, the difference we hear inside our heads is often much greater than it sounds to the listener. Small differences seem big. Yet the actor has got to feel true to his sound, for, just as a writer cannot take the words back once they are in print, so an actor, once he has committed himself to speech, either in rehearsal or in performance, feels he has said something both about himself and about his work which cannot be retracted. This is part of the pressure an actor has to deal with and which is not fully understood by those who are not actors. Even in the early days of rehearsal, once you are speaking the part you are already making decisions about it — you are taking yourself along the path. Therefore, when being bold either with an inflection or in response to a word, or in the very manner of speech, we can quite often feel we are doing too much and the result will not be quite true. Our concern, then, is often to make the voice behave in the way in which we feel comfortable, to be in control of it, and to some extent plan it. This prevents us exploring a text as creatively as we could however flexible the voice is in exercise.

Obviously none of this is wrong, for we need confidence and we need to be able to trust in our own voice — yet this reliance on our own sound, without realizing it, gives the words a secondary importance. And this is reinforced by the fact that we hear the sound in our own heads more dominantly than the words, and this is a very important point. It is always interesting, for instance, when you have been working on a part for some time and know it well, to then whisper a part of the text through — you notice quite freshly what the words are actually doing, their movement, weight, and length and they take on a new focus and layer of meaning.

The crucial thing for us to notice is this: that we frequently get over our intention by loading the sound with meaning, and this overlays and dominates the words. (And this again is tied up with our subconscious emotional response to the sound of our voice — in everyday life we so often transmit our needs in the tone that we use.) So often, when I have been listening to a performance, I have made a mental note, 'sound v. words'; and to me it simply means that I, the listener, am receiving the sound of the voice, perhaps full of 'meaningful' inflection, but am not being made to notice the words. I therefore am not being interested by the argument, and so I am not fully engaged. Technically it could be that the speaker is not finding the correct muscular pressure for the consonants, and certainly this is often the case; but it is never just that, for it always has to do with the speaker's commitment to language and a right sense of its importance. You could also say that the actor is not thinking specifically enough and therefore not pointing the phrases adequately, but I think that is an easy solution and not necessarily true. I think it is to do with not having the right focus — the right balance between words and sound — for it is the meaning that must always dictate the sound, and not the other way round. It is through the words that we will find the possibilities of the sound.

I think this over-consciousness of sound dulls our response to words, and somehow lets us off the hook of thinking accurately through them.

(b) How the actor works

This second reason is to do with how the actor works. Each actor has his own way of working, and therefore of finding the reason for the words he has to speak, of relating them both to his own experience and to the motive of the character, in order to make them authentic. The way he does this will vary according to the text he is speaking, but he is continually probing and asking himself: 'why these words'. When he has come as near as he can to the answer, he is ready to say them in performance. But somehow he very often stays with the reasons in his head, without quite springing the energy of the thought into the words. In a sense, the words are by-passed, and they become slightly less important than the thought, instead of being the thought in action. So the actor remains just behind the words — a metaphorical half inch — and not quite on them. This is not a big problem, but a very common one. And what is difficult is to judge exactly the right energy needed, for somehow, to be that much more positive in speech is a balance we resist, for it is tied up with our own taste and our wish not to be crude. However, what is important is that the energy of the thought and the word coincide.

Obviously this is partly to do with how we use our voice. Nevertheless, the time taken to get to this point of being 'on' the words will vary according to the material we are working. If, for example, we paraphrase a Shakespeare speech in order to clarify the meaning, we know that we will miss important clues into the character which lie precisely in the choice of language, though this could be a necessary and valid stage in our preparation. In Shakespeare the motive of the character and the way the character expresses himself coincide in a positive way. Whereas in a great deal of modern work the actor needs to play the sub-text against the spoken text, so there has to be a different kind of focus on the words. Also, different styles of production ask for different kinds of concentration. But, whatever the style, and however naturalistic, language is always a positive choice, and as such it is special, and must create interest in the hearer.

Perhaps what we should hold on to is this: that the words must be a release of the inner life, and not either an explanation of it or a commentary on it, otherwise we start to present the reason for the language and not the discovery of the thought. This does not stop us being able to have a perspective on the language when we wish.

I would like to put this another way: in our concern to get the motive right, we sometimes think the thought slightly before we say it — we plan our thinking to an extent — and so we do not live through the thought as it happens. The result is that the speaking becomes what I call passive, and not active, in that we are presenting the result of a thought and not the thought itself. We are then at one remove from the words, and there is no possibility of either ourselves or the listener being surprised by them. They cannot take us anywhere. And, to tie this up with what I said earlier, I think we do this to keep control over what we are speaking, because we do not quite have the courage to live at the moment of speech. We make the language behave, instead of staying free to our basic primitive response to it — primitive in the sense of being less consciously organized, and less culturally based. This of course does not mean that we should be uncontrolled; we must be clear and organized as to the motive and reasoning of the character, but the speaking should be free to the moment. And this is not as difficult as it sounds, as we shall see. You must forgive me if I say the same thing in more than one way. As I have said, to talk about voice is always subjective, and each person interprets what is said in a slightly different way according to his skill and experience and nature, and although we are reaching after the same skill, that skill can be found in different ways. And, as all teachers know, the moment when someone understands a point totally for themselves has nothing to do with how often that point has been made, but just to do with the moment that person is ready to receive it.

(c) Attitude to words

The third factor I think has to do with our attitude to words. We tend to think of them as springing from somewhere around the neck up. That is to say we are curiously unaware of their physical nature, and think of them mainly in terms of expressing reasons and ideas and of colouring them with feelings, and not in terms of our physical self being expressed through them and involved in them.

For language, as well as being highly sophisticated, is also primitive in essence. We may have technological jargon of every kind, we have legal language, language of sensibility and emotion allied to literature and art. We have the bloated language of the media and of much political speaking. We also have highly sophisticated slang which communicates social patterns and change, often subversively and always with wit. Yet words evolved out of noises which were first made to communicate basic needs; they were in fact signals. And we still have that sense memory within us — that resonance if you like. For they still act as signals and can arouse quite basic and primitive responses in us, which are totally subjective. We know we can still be stirred by words spoken in public, without quite knowing why we are stirred. I am not talking about rhetorical resonances which are rhythmic and of a different and more public kind; I am talking about the physical response which we have to words which touch our inner thoughts and feelings, where the association of the word itself can evoke a response separate from the feeling.

For instance, if there is something in our life about which we have a deep feeling, perhaps of regret or shame, it is possible to look back upon the event after a time without seemingly feeling upset. However, were we to tell someone about it, the act of putting the feeling into words — finding the words associated with the feeling and being precise about it — can in itself be upsetting, and we may break down in the telling. Most of us have something in our lives which we find painful to talk about, a condition or event, where the act of committing this to words makes us not quite in control of our physical self. It can 'choke' us up. Now actors know well what it is to be vulnerable: they lay themselves open to criticism whenever they go on stage, and therefore to the possibility of being hurt; and this is an awareness they use as they reach into the study of a character. But I think that awareness is not always allowed to inform the speaking, because we feel we must be in control. It is of course not necessarily a sad experience that can affect us physically in this way. We get feelings of elation and joy through words too, and they can arouse us sexually and you cannot get more physical than that. It is simply easier to make the point on a serious note first; we recognize it more readily.

To put it in another form: if we genuinely own up to something and admit that we have been wrong, the more serious we are about it the more effort the words require. When we finish we feel a sense of relief, but not only that, I think we feel physically different; there is almost a chemical change, and we say we have 'got something off our chest'. The point being that the words have been the instrument of change within us.

Practically, this seems to me one of the most important points to keep in mind: that words change both the situation, the speaker and the listener. After words are spoken, nothing is quite the same again. I remember Peter Brook saying words to that effect during rehearsals of *The Dream* (one of so many things that he said which informed my attitude to work); and suddenly I realized how important it was to think about them in this way, for then the energy is handed from one character to the next, and the words become an active force not for yourself alone. I think in our anxiety to fill the text with our own meaning, we often become too involved with what we are saying for ourselves, and how we are saying it; we overplay our own feelings and our own responsibility, so that we do not let the words go, let them free to change the situation and provoke a response.

Words are the opposite of silence, and as such make a positive stand. We must recognize that there is an element of challenge always present in the words:

> The worst is not,
> So long as we can say 'This is the worst'.
>
> Edgar — *King Lear*

Recognizing these two factors, 1) that words have a physical root, and, 2) that they are an active force, gives the speaker another dimension. They are also very practical notions to hold on to.

But I would make a further point: if we are truly to make the words active, it asks for a commitment to the work beyond a personal commitment, which is to do with seeing theatre as a serious political force in the context of the society we live in.

Words spring from many layers of consciousness: from the ordinary management of our everyday lives, to the unguarded expression of deep feeling. We must be ready for their shifts.

(d) How we present language

The fourth point I want to make is partly technical, and is to do with how we present language. It ties up with what I have already said about being 'on' the words. The cause, however, is different. It is this: because words are part of our everyday living we tend, even in performance, to keep them at an energy level which we recognize. This of course does not mean that we are not aware of projecting to an audience — obviously we speak louder so that they can hear — but in a subtle way we still keep the words at an energy level with which we are comfortable. In fact we increase the sound energy, the volume, but do not increase the verbal energy to balance with it. Now the energy required to share with a large number of people is only partly to do with volume, but it is all to do with how we fill the words themselves. And this is not done just by greater sharpness but by carrying the intention through the vibrations of the vowels and the consonants, being aware of the physical movement of the words and making them reach. We tend to reduce their possibilities to our everyday expectation of them — anything else sounds slightly false to our ears — instead of giving them the room that they need, and this will vary with each space you work in.

An actor may have found all the right feelings and motives, he may be working from the gut if you like, but if he transmits these only naturalistically it will seldom be enough. We are obviously influenced in this by television, where the more naturalistic the actor appears the better, though even this requires to be presented and needs great skill, but of a different kind. In all live performance there is something more that has to be done to make the language telling to the audience. This is of course apparent in heightened language, but I believe it to be true of naturalistic writing as well. To fill another character we need to open ourselves to all the possibilities of the language, and this has to reach an audience not just by being loud enough, but by being filled with purpose. The making of the words themselves has to be perceived.

(e) An over-educated response

This last point may seem obvious, but I think it is crucial, and I think it underlies what is unimaginative in the end result of speaking: it is to do with an over-educated response to words. We learn dialogue from a printed page, which is in itself a cerebral process. We know that to make it our own we have to repeat it until it is physically 'on the tongue'; we have got to get round the words. However, I think that because we see lines on the printed page first, the residual effect is that we keep them within that connotation. Our eyes take in a grammatical set of words — a sense clump — and we make a judgement on them from a cultural and sense point of view, so that our initial response to them is a 'read' one and not an intuitive one. I think this puts a subtle pressure on us to make 'good sense' and not to say it 'wrong'. Perhaps it makes us plan how we are going to say it. The important point is that it makes it difficult for us to live through the words as they happen, because we begin to feel out of control of the sense.

I know from my experience in working on Shakespeare with groups of schoolchildren — mainly 15 to 18-year-olds — that those who are classed as low ability readers get a stronger, clearer and more immediate response to the physical nature of the words and images, and are more deeply moved by them, than do the more sophisticated and highly educated 'A' Level students. They get closer to the sense that a character can be possessed by the words, and as it were, driven by them. And in the prison where I work quite frequently I have had quite extraordinary reactions to the underlying force of the imagery from men who know little or nothing of the literary values of Shakespeare. And this to me is an important point for actors to grasp: the fact that people understand words at a much simpler level than we have come to expect — a more intuitive level. They will also pick up the gaiety which is there. So, we have to find ways to get them not only on our tongue, but to make them part of our whole physical self in order to release them from the tyranny of the mind.

All these points are quite simple, and we know them in our heads, but it is often difficult to get the right perspective on them. For what is always working against the actor, that prevents him from taking time with the language even when working on his own, is the fact that most of the time he feels under pressure to present some kind of result, under pressure to be interesting; and so he becomes concerned with getting to the end of what he has to say, with all the meaning that he wants it to contain, without allowing himself to discover the thought in action through the words as they are spoken. This is often an unreasonable pressure that we put on ourselves. Nevertheless we have to interest our director, our fellow-actors and the audience. So what we frequently do, and this happens to actors at all levels of experience, is get caught up in the idea of how best to put the text over, and this makes us lose contact with the text itself. For it inhibits the less conscious responses, and it is those responses which are often the most interesting, for they come from a deeper current within us. Words are so often much rougher and more anarchic than we allow them to be.

This feeling that we need to present and be interesting, even at early stages of rehearsal, makes us press in some way. Each actor will press differently according to his inclination and his pattern of working. The actor whose pattern it is to emphasize the logic of the character, will tend to be didactic and overweight the stress of the words. Technically this will make him press out the consonants and reduce the vowels to equal short weight and length. The speaking then becomes emphatic, which at once reduces the possibilities within the text by keeping it at a totally logical level. It is literal and allows for no ambiguity, and therefore no richness of texture. In other words it is less interesting. At the other end of the scale, the actor who is attracted by the emotional quality and mood of a character will find a poetic and romantic line, and the thoughts will more often than not become generalized. He presses out the mood, and we are then not put in touch with how the character thinks — how he ticks — which is in fact what the audience wants to know. The words are then dulled by the mood. Then there is the actor who responds in totally the opposite way: in his concern with the truth of the motive he delays his commitment to the words for as long as possible, and holds back from them in rehearsal as if distrusting them. This way, it is much more difficult for him to find a true release of thought through them, for he is denying something of the nature of the thought. And whilst I respect enormously the desire to be truthful, if he holds back in this way he will not find the life-force which the words must be, even when they are expressing an oblique or negative thought — 'The worst is not, So long as we can say "This is the worst" ' — Edgar again. If we hold back from the words, we are not being quite truthful.

Now I have obviously over-simplified these attitudes of working, but I suspect we will recognize them in ourselves to some degree or other. And it is important to look at them objectively for they can limit our work in rehearsal, and it is the choices we make there that we bring into performance.

It is difficult to find an extravagance in language, a music which is perhaps beyond our everyday usage, and I think the answer has always to be through some form of physical release: I am not talking about large movements, but simply an awareness that the words are themselves a movement — and this is quite subtle. It would seem more appropriate to express large emotions through dance and song than through the words and inflections that we use every day, so we must now look at our attitudes to the practical work that will help us through to this freedom.

2 THE PRACTICAL MEANS

I want to look now at how we prepare our voice through exercise and see how we can connect that work more organically to our response to words. I think that when the voice is not interesting enough, it is rarely to do with it not being good enough, but simply that it is not being given the right stimulus.

Again, what I am going to say will seem simple, but the deeper we take it the more important it will be: we have to make the breath and the muscular formation of the words the means by which the thought is released. The thought needs to be spoken, that is the choice, so breath and verbal movement are part of that need. Whatever work we do on breathing and articulation must be towards this end.

Like any interpretive artist, actors have to work at their craft because they are always being faced with the challenge of new work, and because they want to continue to develop and perhaps do more ambitious parts. Because every job presents different challenges they have to renew ways of exploring character and character relationships, of relating to the narrative and style of each particular production; they have to keep alive to different ways of working and the problems that different spaces may bring. Most actors, for instance, keep up some form of basic movement work. All actors, I think, realize the importance of voice and to what extent they are dependent on it, so they do exercises on relaxation, on breathing and resonance, power and clarity, according to what they need at any particular time. All these exercises are necessary and good. However, unless this work connects organically with an ever-fresh and developing response to language, it remains a technical accomplishment, which makes the voice stronger and more resonant, but does not necessarily make the speaking more interesting, for it is not necessarily feeding the sense of freedom with the text that he is really after.

For perhaps we work vocally at too conscious a level, and we must look to see how exercises can feed us in a deeper way than we are accustomed. Exercises should make us ready for the intuitive response.

Plainly, freedom with the text comes from knowing what you are saying — i.e., knowing well the character, motive and action. But, because we are so afraid of not making sense, we end up only making sense — literal sense — and so we put a strait-jacket on the language, for we do not hear what is happening under its surface. When we are over-concerned with our logical, conscious thought, we simply do not hear what the language is doing; and here I mean structure not only of the rhythm and phrasing, but the structure of the words themselves — the dynamic of each word. We have to train ourselves to respond to words in a less obvious and stated way, so that their very movement contains our feeling.

And this kind of response demands our whole attention: we have to be physically as well as imaginitively prepared. So I want to clarify our attitude to the work in three areas.

(a) **Relaxation.** Obviously this is of vital importance, for, in a sense, relaxation is resonance. If we have muscular tension in the neck, the shoulders or the back, firstly we cannot breathe properly, and secondly our resonators cannot work fully. So we need to make sure that our body is in a good alignment for all this to be free, yet ready for action. But I do think that we must keep our desire for relaxation in its right perspective: to work at it as an end in itself is fruitless, for it unconsciously makes us feel that there is something wrong with our psyche if we are tense, and this in itself creates anxiety. It is also important to realize that there are times in one's life when one is tense, and you have to live through it. This is of course not to say that we should not consciously look for it, and many actors find great benefit from work in the Alexander Technique which teaches a conscious awareness of bodily alignment, and through this a freeing of physical tension in both movement and stillness. But relaxation of itself is not a virtue, for we have to come to terms with the fact that there is a tension which we require in acting which is a positive and a good one, for it is to do with the wish to communicate. Also, some people have a kind of tension in their personality, which is a quality that perhaps is necessary to their work. Too much relaxation can be dulling. What is important is to find where our energy lies, and that is always with the breath. It is breath that gives us our strength, and when we feel strong tension becomes unnecessary. I suppose what I am really saying is: do not worry about tension — work on it but do not worry about it. Find your strength, your breath.

(b) **Breath.** We know we need a good supply of breath to give the voice power, resonance and flexibility. We know we need its power when working in large spaces. We know we need it when working on classical text where the thoughts are long and often span a number of lines; where, if we break that span we do not quite honour the meaning, or cannot quite twist the pay-off line in the way we want to get the full comedy value out of the speech. But I think we have to see more than this when we are working. We have to see the breath not simply as the means by which we make good sound and communicate information; but rather we have to see it as the physical life of the thought, so that we conceive the breath and the thought as one. We need to be able to encompass one thought with one breath. In everyday life we do not run out of breath in the middle of an idea — or seldom — so, even though the lengths of thought in a text are infinitely variable, this is what we should aim for. Unless we recognize that the breath and the thought are one, no amount of breathing exercises will give purpose to the breath, will make it organic to what we are saying.

The further we go in getting this integration of breath and thought — and by thought I mean the utterance of a character charged with whatever feelings he may have — we begin to experience how the thought itself is moving, and the quality of the thought becomes active. We also see that how we share the breath is how we share the thought. If we waste the breath, we disperse and generalize the thought; and, conversely, if we hold on to the breath in some way, we reduce the thought by holding it back and locking it into ourselves. But, more important than this, we perceive that how we breathe is how we think; or rather, in acting terms, how the character breathes is how the character thinks. The breath must encompass the thought, no more or less is needed: that is the precise energy of the thought.

If we think of breath in this way, and providing our capacity is good, we will always have enough. This is, of course, a little simplistic, and we obviously have to work at it as any athlete has to work at his supply of breath. We have to get to the point where the thought will control the breath: I think we often run out of breath on a long phrase for no other reason than that we are afraid we will not have enough.

I do believe that when we find this integration of thought and breath, when they are rooted down one with the other, the voice takes on a quite different and surprising energy, and the speaking becomes effortless. For, and this is what is important, we have made the thought our own physically through the breath, and so we do not have to press out our emotional and intellectual intentions on top of the text. We actually think differently because we are open to the thought in this way. And because we have made the thought our own in a quite specific way, we are at liberty to be open to the possibilities of the words, to let them free, and to be extravagant with them if that is required, without 'doing' anything with them.

Let us look for a moment at the following ten lines of *Othello*, just at how the speech breathes. The lines come from Act III, Scene 3, near the end of the central scene between Othello and Iago, during which Iago has worked so successfully on Othello's hidden doubts and jealousy that Othello believes Desdemona to have been unfaithful. And he is prepared to kill her for this.

Othello: O, blood, blood, blood!
Iago: Patience, I say: your mind perhaps may change.
Othello: Never, Iago. Like to the Pontic sea,
Whose icy current and compulsive course
Ne'er feels retiring ebb, but keeps due on
To the Propontic and the Hellespont,
Even so my bloody thoughts with violent pace
Shall ne'er look back, ne'er ebb to humble love,
Till that a capable and wide revenge
Swallow them up. Now, by yond marble heaven,
In the due reverence of a sacred vow
I hear engage my words.

The long sentence from 'Like to the Pontic sea' to 'Swallow them up' consists of about six phrases which are all part of the whole thought, and it would be possible to speak them naturalistically making sense of each phrase, and break the speech up accordingly. In this way Othello would be explaining his feelings to Iago. However when we look further, we see that the structure and rhythm of the passage is totally related to the surge and current of the sea — there is more than grammatical sense here. For the whole thought becomes the current in which he is caught, and the specific words and phrases are like the waves. If we honour each one of these small phrases, yet ride the whole sentence on one breath, we will come close to the elemental nature of that thought. That is the skill we need, yet without ever losing the spoken impulse, for it should not sound rhetorical. The point is, there is a parallel between the actor reaching down for that breath, and Othello reaching for that thought: his feelings are released, and that release happens by means of the breath. The inevitability of the thought, and the small phrases rocking within it, allow us into the movement and passion of the character. He is thus not merely describing his feelings to Iago: he is discovering them and releasing them for himself. And it is breath that enables their release.

Now obviously this is an extreme example, for you would not be contemplating those lines unless you were preparing them as an actor, but it is often easier to understand a point through a difficult example, as the need is more apparent and you can see the principal underlying it. It works for the wit of Rosalind, the urgency of a Messenger speech from *Antony and Cleopatra*, and for the pragmatic philosophy of Ulysses in *Troilus and Cressida*. It works for long speeches in Shaw, in Rudkin and in Bond. The breath needed in this passage is deep and needs preparation as does the thought, for you have to reach down within yourself to find the image of the sea, the current within yourself. And Othello is moved by the current of his own passion.

When the breath works for you in this way, it takes the words down to a physical level, deeper than the intellect, and it allows us to be unemphatic. The passion is then allowed to come through the language, with its enormous variety of sounds, rather than through syllabic pressure.

(c) **Muscularity.** The message is similar with muscularity exercises which we do to achieve clarity, projection and placing of tone. These are of course very necessary, but we should never do them only as technical exercises, but always with the purpose of exploring the substance of the sounds; this will then relate to the substance of the meaning. Articulation exercises — the old kind of 'patter' exercises — will make the tongue and lips move more quickly, and for that purpose are good, but they will not necessarily enhance our use of words. For each word has its own energy and substance within its context, and this is the awareness we must grow to. Exercises are important to make us agile of speech, so that we can go as quickly as the thought takes us; and just as we need unlimited breath, so we need sureness in placing the word, and some actors need more conscious work in this area than others. But all these exercises must be done with this awareness: that we release the thought, itself a physical activity, through the physical energy of the word. The words are the means by which we articulate thought, words are movement, and we have to find the precise energy for that movement.

To see what I mean, let us look at the following lines of Cordelia: *King Lear*, Act IV, Scene 4. The scene comes roughly three-quarters of the way through the play, after Lear has been rejected by his two eldest daughters, has been exposed to the storm, and has been sighted wandering near the cliffs at Dover. His youngest daughter, Cordelia, now Queen of France, comes with her army to find him. At the beginning of the scene Cordelia talks to her doctor (the numbers are referred to on page 99):

Cordelia: 1 Alack, 'tis he! Why, he was met even now
2 As mad as the vexed sea, singing aloud,
3 Crowned with rank fumiter and furrow-weeds,
4 With hardokes, hemlock, nettles, cuckoo-flowers,
5 Darnel, and all the idle weeds that grow
6 In our sustaining corn.
[*To soldiers.*
A century send forth;
7 Search every acre in the high-grown field
8 And bring him to our eye.
[*To Doctor.*
What can man's wisdom
9 In the restoring his bereavèd sense?
10 He that helps him, take all my outward worth.

Speak those lines through for yourself out loud, firmly but unhurriedly. Notice the different weight and substance of the words: how light 'hemlock, nettles, cuckoo-flowers' against the more solid 'sustaining corn'; how limitless 'mad as the vexed sea' — the image is immeasurable; and how strong the sure 'Search every acre of the high-grown field'; the depth of sensibility in 'What can man's wisdom in the restoring his bereaved sense', against the simple command of the last line — 'He that helps him, take all my outward worth'. In these ten lines the speech has profound changes of substance and weight, yet it has but one drive, one motive, one action.

Now this weight and substance comes precisely from the different lengths of the vowels, and sometimes their movement; and also from the variable times the consonants need to fulfil their vibrations. For example, the vowels are short in the words 'alack' and 'hemlock', long in 'sea' and 'weeds', and even longer, because they are dipthongal, in 'crowned' and 'grow'. The time the consonants take to speak varies according to whether they are unvoiced or voiced, plosive or continuant, and how many there are. For example, the end consonants take less time in the words 'vexed', 'hardokes', 'rank', than they do in 'sustaining corn' or 'search', and they are longer still in 'weeds', 'field' and 'bereaved'. These are negotiable, but as you see, the interaction of length between vowels and consonants is limitless, for the length of the consonant affects the length of the vowel. And further, you will see that the weight and substance of the words coincide with the meaning in a remarkable way. In literary terms, of course, this is called 'onomatopoeia', but I believe it is not helpful for the actor to put a label on it in this way. I would even say it was destructive, in that it leads him to be descriptive with the words rather than feel their essential impulse, the need to speak them. It puts a kind of remove between himself and the words.

So when we do exercises for muscularity (or articulation) it is this awareness we are preparing for: the perception of the length and movement of the vowels, and the length and vibration of the consonants, for it is this that keeps the language always active and muscular. Now what is difficult is to find all this and swiftness too — for speech must go at the speed of thought, and we must always be slightly ahead of the listener. If we do exercises only for rapidity, the consonants become over-explosive, the vowels clipped and of the same length, and the speech is flat, and this is what happens when we are acting and going only for speed. This, therefore, is what takes all our energy and focus, to find swiftness, but never at the expense of the quality of the language.

This sense of the substance of the sounds is very helpful to those working from their own dialect. I feel strongly that it is not important for an actor to iron out his own regional variations, for often you iron out the vigour of the speech in the process; what is important is to become aware of the energy of the words — particularly the consonants — and fill them out.

Now the awareness of the room the sounds need helps us to adjust to different spaces. When we are working in a small space at a naturalistic level, and fairly quiet and quick, we must still honour the energy needed for the consonants at that level, or they will drop away and become difficult to catch, and so the language will become less active. When working in a large space it takes longer for the consonant vibrations to reach out. The answer is never to push them out explosively, for that makes the speech clipped and not easy to hear, but always to feel the room necessary for the vibrations to be complete.

All this will help us to find, not just the literal meaning, but the meaning which is transmitted through the very sound of the words. I worked on *King Lear* in a German translation with a group of actors in Hamburg, and I remember particularly this Cordelia speech and how we worked on it. Its whole nature changed because of the didactic sound of the German language, and how difficult it was for those German actors to free themselves from the functional meaning of the words in order to find the quality of the thought, and how the thought moves and changes through the speech. We sang out and danced through the list of weeds — 'üppigem Erdrauch und Furchenkraut, mit Ampfer, Schierling, Nesseln, Kuckucksblumen' — to take those words beyond a functional list, and to make them relate to the tactile nature of the images themselves.

Where we have got to then is that the words themselves are the journey to be lived through. We should not worry about getting to the end: if the thought is whole and the breath has encompassed it, the end is there anyway. I do not really like talking about a 'journey', as that implies something mystical, and what I am saying is entirely practical. If we can be totally direct, perhaps that is enough.

Once you can be behind each word as you say it, neither pressing it or describing it, each word having its own room — its own stillness if you like — then the language becomes active and interesting. Then you can be as swift as you like, as swift as the thought will take you: for it is always exciting when an actor is swift yet seeming to take all the time in the world. And in fact, it is only when we load the speech too much with conscious intention that it becomes slow and difficult to follow.

So the actor must always be questioning his response to language — practising it if you like. For words are the actor's tools, as colour and brush-strokes are the painter's, and we have to be constantly sharpening our focus on them to find new textures and colours.

To sum up quite practically: through breath and verbal muscularity we must be so free that there is no sense of pressing the sound out. We must not, through lack of trust either in ourselves or in the text, over-control the language. We must first allow the words to act upon us — this asks for inner stillness — and then we must touch them out, let them free. This freedom in the words will in no way negate our individuality as a performer. We need to make the listener remark: the audience must not only hear the words but realize them fully. We have to be continually balancing our need to be truthful with a way of presenting that truth to an audience through the style of the language.

None of this is particularly difficult or complicated as we shall see: it is just a matter of focusing the energy that is already there.

Chapter 2

HEIGHTENED VERSUS NATURALISTIC TEXT

I know that many actors find it difficult to work within the structure of dramatic verse. I am of course talking of those who would like to but simply do not feel comfortable with it. This can be true of those with a good deal of acting experience, as well as those just starting out in the theatre, though obviously at a different level.

I would put the reasons for this as follows, though they will apply in different ways to each actor. The first is quite simply to do with practice. There is less opportunity to work in classical text than in modern, and you have to get to grips with it before you begin to see how it works, so you can go with it.

Secondly, it has to do with a feeling that poetic writing is in some way less than real — for one thing there are an awful lot of words! — and it is therefore more difficult to equate it with our own truth as a modern actor. What we are failing then to see is that poetry contains a fierceness and a reality perhaps at a different temperature than that of naturalistic writing. To quote from the American Beat poet, Ferlinghetti:

> the poet like an acrobat
> climbs on rime
> to a high wire of his own making. . .
> For he's the super realist
> who must perforce perceive
> taut truth
> before the taking of each stance or step. . .

And again to quote — Edith Sitwell: 'poetry is a suppressed scream'. The point is, poetic writing gets at truth in a different way from that which is naturalistic. We must find the common ground.

For the actor whose main experience has been in modern work, perhaps a good deal of television and film, often the qualities that work well for him in those areas — intensity of thought and emotion, and perhaps an under-stated way of expressing these — seem to work against him when speaking heightened or poetic text, where the language is formal and we need to be verbally explicit, and where our feelings and thought have to be released at the moment of speech. It is not that the inner concentration should be less; it is simply geared differently. It is not that the actor should for a moment sacrifice his individuality to a generalized poetic form; rather he must gather his genuine response and release it through the discipline of the structure — and when this happens it can be very powerful. Conversely, I believe that an awareness of form and of how thoughts drive through a text is an essential part of our preparation of modern work.

Thirdly, I think there is often a cultural resistance in that poetic writing seems to be to do with educated speech and speech patterns, and so has class overtones, and this is therefore alienating to anyone who has regional differences of speech, or whose background is working-class. It can feel a serious betrayal of one's background to use a formal speech of a different class, not because you cannot do it, but because it does not seem fitting to one's own outlook — and this is a political point. Perhaps it feels over-elaborate. Now the accent to me is not important, for, although we do not know precisely how Elizabethan English was pronounced, we do know that it was nothing like today's RP (Received Pronunciation) and that the vowels were longer and more open, the final 'r's' were pronounced, and it was probably much closer to present-day Warwickshire speech. This ought to give us a kind of freedom, for, as we shall see, it is the vigour in the language that is crucial, and not an accepted set of vowel sounds. And this goes for all verse text, both classical and modern: it is the vigour of the text that is surprising and earths it. So often a regional accent in Shakespeare gives it a new life. The resistance I think comes from a feeling that the language does not belong to you in the same way as modern writing.

Fourthly, we have to be open to different speech patterns. Modern speech patterns are very often downward, and so in a sense introvert: but there is a different music in heightened speech which is to do with an ongoing energy, and so we need to be conscious of an upward movement. This applies to modern text as well. And this is not just a matter of using upward inflections — that is merely technical and will become automatic and ultimately boring — it is feeling a physical impulse always which impels you from one line to the next, one thought to the next, and this makes for a different cadence.

And lastly, I think we just do not know enough about how formal language works, and therefore, by simply stating its terms, we shall start to be at ease with it. We will take up all these points again, but first let me define what I mean by 'naturalistic' and 'heightened'.

I am taking heightened text to mean writing which is built on a rhythmic structure, where there is compression of imagery, and where we understand as much through the logic of the imagery as through the factual reasoning. And I am taking naturalistic writing to be prose, where the structure of the story is built on a logical progression of ideas, where the dialogue is rooted in everyday speech patterns, and where imagery is more incidental than essential.

Now this of course is very loose, and is immediately open to contradiction. For poetic writing is often naturalistic in sound: there are passages in Shakespeare and the Jacobeans that strike our ears as being totally modern, where the spareness and directness of a line can make us catch our breath in surprise at its contemporary ring. I think of lines from *Coriolanus*, or the Nurse in *Romeo and Juliet*. There is a good deal of prose in verse drama, but it is always highly shaped and has its particular cadence. Eliot's verse moves in and out of colloquialisms.

Then there is a huge amount of dramatic prose writing, from Restoration comedy to Shaw and Coward, which is highly shaped in style, and though not verse, is certainly not naturalistic. It seems as though the ideas are there before they are expressed, so the dialogue seems often to do with a discussion of ideas and motives rather than a discovery of them; it feels calculated. I am not quite sure about this, but it seems as if we have to enter objectively into a way of thinking and presenting ideas before we can get to grips with a character. By this I do not mean go only for the style — this would be empty and false — but we do have to come to terms with a way of presenting dialogue which has as much to do with style and effect as with reality; and I suppose its style is its reality. It does, however, depend on an ear for shaping phrases, on finding out how verbal comedy works, and often on a literary enjoyment of language. It is not ordinary, and it is conscious; it is in a sort of way public. This applies mostly to comedy, though there are serious plays — those of Galsworthy or Maugham for instance — where the dialogue is more literary than spontaneous.

Modern naturalistic prose writing ranges from the kind of gentle lyricism of Tennessee Williams to the ironic understatement of Brecht, from the tough spare writing of Barrie Keeffe to the wordy heightened language of Rudkin . . . full of oblique imagery. All good modern writing has very specific rhythms and contains heightened iterative imagery, and needs as careful handling as verse. The rhythms are all-important: the dialogue of Beckett and Pinter has its own cadences which allow for silence; and Brenton, Barker, Caryl Churchill have their own particular music.

Almost as soon as you have made some kind of definition between formal and colloquial text you want to contradict it. Even so it helps us to pin-point the differences, and only by recognizing the differences do we begin to be aware of style, and so of how we speak and how we present that style. To an extent all writing is heightened, for through the style we apprehend part of the meaning: the audience must therefore be able to recognize the style. In being naturalistic, or 'real', it is easy to throw away too much: the audience then loses the resonance.

What I want to deal with briefly here is the contrast between the heightened poetic text of Shakespeare and the Jacobeans, and the naturalistic modern text of the last forty or so years. Because the contrast is sharp, we will learn more, and it will enable us to deal better with other areas of writing. What is also important is that it will make us assess our ways of working on text: for the writing itself makes for methods of acting.

Let us look for a moment at the function of poetry: we know it is understood on many levels. It is understood at the logical level of subject matter and argument, but also at the less conscious level of the association of words with both social and cultural experience: and of words with sounds.

In the two passages we have already looked at we have seen how the nature of the image is part of the expression of the character: for Othello, there was no other image than the sea which could have conveyed the size — the enormity — of his inner turmoil of spirit. For Cordelia, her images of the healing properties of nature are totally to do with the way she looks on life: they are a compression of her spiritual state. The images are not a description of how they feel: they are an essential part of their expression. They are therefore not poetic elaboration, not there for an effect. They are necessary, and part of the vigour of the language. Let us look at some other examples. This first is again from *Othello*, and is to do with choice of vocabulary. In Act III, Scene 3, Iago, dropping the seeds of suspicion into Othello's consciousness, says:

Iago: Good name in man or woman, dear my lord,
Is the immediate jewel of their souls.
Who steals my purse, steals trash; 'tis something, nothing;
But he that filches from me my good name
Robs me of that which not enriches him
And makes me poor indeed.

The reasoning is clear, but there is something about the use of words 'filch' and 'trash', with their implications of underhand and dirty activity, which sets the emotional position of the lines. They tell us as much about Iago's inner life — where he lives — as they do of his manipulation of Othello. He could have used two other words, but these two are both implicitly in opposition to 'good name'; and what is more, they both sound ugly. We are therefore receiving information through choice and sound of words.

Next, from *The Tempest*, is to do with an atavistic response to words, Act III, Scene 2.

Caliban: Be not afeard; the isle is full of noises,
Sounds, and sweet airs, that give delight and hurt not.
Sometimes a thousand twangling instruments
Will hum about mine ears; and sometimes voices
That, if I then had waked after long sleep,
Will make me sleep again; and then, in dreaming,
The clouds methought would open, and show riches
Ready to drop on me, that when I waked
I cried to dream again.

This is simply a passage about listening to the sound of a place — Caliban's awareness of the life of the island. But in describing it, he makes us aware of something beyond ourselves, or a past that is contained in each place and which is separate from our life in it. And which we have to listen for.

If we look at the last part of the play which the Mechanicals perform to Theseus and his Court, in the last scene of *A Midsummer-Night's Dream*, we will learn something about rhythm and sound. The reasoning is patently absurd, but there is something so true in the rhythm and the sound that the effect is both comic and moving.

O wherefore, nature, didst thou lions frame,
Since lion vile hath here deflowered my dear?
Which is — no, no, which was — the fairest dame
That lived, that loved, that liked, that looked with cheer.

Come tears, confound:
Out sword, and wound
The pap of Pyramus.
Ay, that left pap,
Where heart doth hop.
Thus die I — thus, thus, thus.

[*He stabs himself.*

Now am I dead,
Now am I fled;
My soul is in the sky.
Tongue, lose thy light;
Moon, take thy flight;

[*Exit Starveling as Moonshine.*

Now die, die, die, die, die. [*He dies.*

The argument is naive, in opposition to the sophistication of the Court and the lovers. The fact that it is a play is a device to remind us that we too are at a play: the play itself is therefore a sophisticated metaphor. The Mechanicals believe in it totally, and though there is an absurdity in the argument, there is at the same time a dignity in the utterance born out by the rhythm. This strong rhythm, with the combination of the long vowels in the short lines, and the last line with its long repeated monosyllables — which can be taken as a three-beat or a five-beat line — makes us apprehend something of the nature of death and time in a particular way, which we cannot quite explain. It also tells us something of the character of Bottom, who can give himself so completely to the simplicity of the story and the words — his basic reasoning, again in contrast to the Court. He cannot hurry those words because the rhythm will not let him. We are being given information, through the rhythm and sound, of the nature of Bottom and the fabric of his life.

We see that poetry is made up of two elements: the formal and the colloquial. It mixes both, moving easily from one to the other. The formal has its origins in magic and religion, where the rhythmic element was strong, and this plays an important part in our atavistic verbal memory. The rhythm is a powerful ingredient, for we still chill to passages which have a strong rhythmic drive, and this can be to some extent irrespective of meaning. The colloquial element comes from its ear to everyday speech, which was present in ballads and the passing down of stories in verse form; and this story element informs us how to present language. Every poet finds his own form, his own mixture if you like, but, however heightened the language, it is there for the purpose of putting us in touch with a deeper reality. That is why there can be no sense of it being removed from our everyday life — whatever our speech pattern — and why we cannot afford to take any word for granted.

To go on with this point, let us look at a short passage from Eliot's *Four Quartets*. In all Eliot's writing, plays and poems alike, there is constantly a wonderful mixing of the colloquial with the formal. From 'East Coker', Part III:

> O dark dark dark. They all go into the dark,
> The vacant interstellar spaces, the vacant into the vacant,
> The captains, merchant bankers, eminent men of letters.
> The generous patrons of art, the statesmen and the rulers,
> Distinguished civil servants, chairmen of many committees,
> Industrial lords and petty contractors, all go into the dark,
> And dark the Sun and Moon, and the Almanach de Gotha
> And the Stock Exchange Gazette, the Directory of Directors,
> And cold the sense and lost the motive of action.
> And we all go with them, into the silent funeral,
> Nobody's funeral, for there is no one to bury.
> I said to my soul, be still, and let the dark come upon you
> Which shall be the darkness of God . . .

I think it is useful to listen to this for a moment, and to hear how it shifts. How easily it moves from the formal rhythm of the first line, with its repetition of the word 'dark' with its long, weighty vowel — and with that repetition the implications of cold and death which we pick up on later— into the breezy lists of sets of people; and then back again to the chill of 'all go into the dark', and on into 'And cold the sense and lost the motive of action'. Throughout his writing Eliot juggles the rhythm so that the colloquial is always knocking against our deeper consciousness.

It is useful because it makes us ready for the shifts within a character, when thoughts take on a darker turn. I think of the Nurse's line at the end of Act I, Scene 5 of *Romeo and Juliet*. Capulet has opened his house to the notables of Verona, Romeo has gatecrashed the revels with his friends, there has been much dancing, and there has been the first meeting between him and Juliet. After all the noise, the house is suddenly cleared of revellers, and Juliet and the Nurse are left alone:

Juliet: Come hither, nurse. What is yond gentleman?
Nurse: The son and heir of old Tiberio.
Juliet: What's he that now is going out of door?
Nurse: Marry, that, I think, be young Petruchio.
Juliet: What's he that follows here, that would not dance?
Nurse: I know not.
Juliet: Go ask his name. — If he be marrièd,
My grave is like to be my wedding bed.
Nurse: His name is Romeo, and a Montague,
The only son of your great enemy.
Juliet: My only love, sprung from my only hate!
Too early seen unknown, and known too late!
Prodigious birth of love it is to me
That I must love a loathèd enemy.
Nurse: What's this, what's this?
Juliet: A rhyme I learnt even now
Of one I danced withal.

[*One calls within:* 'Juliet'.

Nurse: Anon, anon!
Come, let's away. The strangers all are gone.

Romeo and Juliet, I.5.

The music of the last line embodies a whole world of feeling, of the emptiness in the house which has been full of people.

One last passage, from *Coriolanus*, Act II, Scene I. It is a speech of Brutus, in a scene where he and Sicinius — the two Tribunes of the people — comment on how the people come to look at Coriolanus as he goes to seek the patrician's vote that he be made Consul. The people come out to cheer him, but the Tribunes both know that Coriolanus despises the people.

Brutus: All tongues speak of him and the blearéd sights
Are spectacled to see him. Your prattling nurse
Into a rapture lets her baby cry
While she chats him. The kitchen malkin pins
Her richest lockram 'bout her reechy neck,
Clambering the walls to eye him. Stalls, bulks, windows
Are smothered up, leads filled, and ridges horsed
With variable complexions, all agreeing
In earnestness to see him. Seld-shown flamens
Do press among the popular throngs and puff
To win a vulgar station. Our veiled dames
Commit the war of white and damask in
Their nicely gawded cheeks to th'wanton spoil
Of Phoebus' burning kisses. Such a pother
As if that whatsoever god who leads him
Were slily crept into his human powers
And gave him graceful posture.

Coriolanus, II.1.

How dense the description is! Every window and roof-top is full of people, that even the rich women who do not like to be in the sun, and the priests ('flamens') who seldom show themselves in public, are all jostling for a place to see Coriolanus.

What is wonderful is the sense of suppressed outrage that we get through the energy of the particularly muscular language: the way the last word of one line kicks into the next line, and the last word of one thought impels us into almost the middle of the next thought. So we get an accumulation of images and details all of which feed his frustrated anger: and all he can say to cap it is 'such a pother . . .' It is all undercut by the word 'pother' which is suddenly homely and a little absurd, and underlines the impotence of his position. What we have to recognize is that there is a pleasure at being that articulate, but the pleasure is not to do with being elaborate and poetic, it is to do with release of feeling, and the ability to be explicit about it . . . 'All tongues speak of him . . .'

Taken that naturalistic writing depends on sounding as much like ordinary speech as possible, with its ear to colloquial speech patterns, the content of the writing will not be ordinary, for of its very nature it is expressing through character and situation an emotional/social issue — a point of view of modern life — so the language is special to the situation and defines the attitude. Therefore the cadences and rhythms into which the speech patterns fall may have a poetry to them. And sometimes, as in Bond's 'War Plays', the writing is in a verse form: in this case it is to do with the pointing within each line (here I mean pointing in the way that we point psalms) and is nothing like the conscious verse form of Fry. It can, as in Brecht, shift into a kind of ballad form, 'sprecht-gesang', but the vocabulary is of every day. The content of the language may be strange or violent, and the events of the play may impel the characters into heightened language which will shock, but it is still recognizable in everyday terms.

So now I want to look at three passages from plays written within the last ten years. The writing in each case has a very particular style.

The first is a speech of Gower from Rudkin's *The Sons of Light*. It is rhythmically quite colloquial, but the language itself is not, and that is what is shocking.

Gower: (songless, stunned) They have divided me. They clamped me to a wheel, my face to Heaven, arms out, legs wide. Brought whitehot blades: to ease between my hides: along my arms, calves, sides, to slit me, long and parallel and deep. Here, here here; here, here; here, here, here . . . 'Search more,' Holst said. With the redhot piercing tips of hooks, the wall of my belly, the flesh of my breast: deeper: deeper . . . the flesh ripped out of me. 'Look!' they said, 'we can see his beating heart!' And the King said 'That? An heart? Is that what breaks in a man?' 'Caress him more,' Holst said: 'search more.' Everywhere that I was rent and gouged, with seething oil and spitting pitch and wax they larded me. So . . . So . . . So . . . My legs raised up before me, up, over my face, to bend me like a hoop: there — into me . . . with a searing implement, opening me and pumping into me such scalding shocks — How could I endure this? I was fixed. . . Why am I in so many pieces? To each of them that worked upon me, each an arm or leg of me: to jerk, wrench, strain, each toward his own crossquarter with each his part of me. But I would not undo, they could not even split my fork. As last Holst said, 'we must ease him with saws.' Holst hagged me, most careful: and while he sawed me through my armpits and my groin, I uttered not one cry. Why was that? I came apart quite easy then. (Pause)

Poor King of Love. To find a soldier blemished. And have to toil so hard and long unstitching me. That I should make him weep, over whatever blemish Gower's was, in a beloved soldier. Poor King . . . To make Him grieve . . . Poor King of Love . . .

The Sons of Light, Part Two.

It is the natural, almost comforting quality of the rhythm, which heightens the cruelty of the content, and it is the unexpectedness of the word which has to be allowed for in the same way as for classical text.

Rudkin's writing is wordy and filled out — cumulative. Bond writes in a much sparer way, as if finding the feeling and analysing it at the same time. It brings no comfort, simply makes us ask questions of ourselves, for only by doing that will there be hope.

Here is a speech near the end of Bond's *Lear*, after he has been disposed by his daughters and treated most cruelly by them. His journey in the play has been violent and tortuous, but this speech has great spiritual calm. It is very simple, but needs most careful pointing and poising.

Lear: (to the audience). A man woke up one morning and found he'd lost his voice. So he went to look for it, and when he came to the wood there was the bird who'd stolen it. It was singing beautifully and the man said 'Now I sing so beautifully I shall be rich and famous'. He put the bird in a cage and said 'When I open my mouth wide you must sing'. Then he went to the king and said 'I will sing your majesty's praises'. But when he opened his mouth the bird could only groan and cry because it was in a cage, and the king had the man whipped. The man took the bird home, but his family couldn't stand the bird's groaning and crying and they left him. So in the end the man took the bird back to the wood and let it out of the cage. But the man believed the king had treated him unjustly and he kept saying to himself 'The king's a fool' and as the bird still had the man's voice it kept singing this all over the wood and soon the other birds learned it. The next time the king went hunting he was surprised to hear all the birds singing 'The king's a fool'. He caught the bird who'd started it and pulled out its feathers, broke its wings and nailed it to a branch as a warning to all the other birds. The forest was silent. And just as the bird had the man's voice the man now had the bird's pain. He ran round silently waving his head and stamping his feet, and he was locked up for the rest of his life in a cage.

Lear, III.2

Now of course this is rich with the resonances of all that has happened to Lear in the play, and it is such a great play. What I want you to notice is how simple the language is, yet how precisely placed. It has, as in all Bond's writing, a very clear rhythm, which must be observed, or the full meaning will not be realized.

The third example is the final speech of Pierre from *Soft Cops* by Caryl Churchill. It is the last speech in the play. It is Civil Service jargon which, because he has been faced with a truth and a situation with which he cannot quite cope, he cannot get quite right.

Pierre: The trouble is I have to make a speech. Later on. In front of the minister. He's going to lay the foundation stone. I'm always a little nervous at these official — I shall just explain quite simply how the criminals are punished, the sick are cured, the workers are supervised, the ignorant are educated, the unemployed are registered, the insane are normalized, the criminals — No, wait a minute. The criminals are supervised. The insane are cured.

> The sick are normalized. The workers are registered. The unemployed are educated. The ignorant are punished. No. I'll need to rehearse this a little. The ignorant are normalized. Right. The sick are punished. The insane are educated. The workers are cured. The criminals are cured. The unemployed are punished. The criminals are normalized. Something along those lines.

Its irony comes from the breakdown of thought within the familiar pattern of rhythm, and the twisting of cliched word patterns. And it is very powerful.

These three examples require a very sharp focus on the text: the language is active – we cannot throw it away.

But I would like to look back for a moment at the forties and fifties when styles of acting changed quite radically. In the US it was the new realism of the writing of Williams, Miller and Odets, among others, which started the movement of change. This coincided with a new impulse and style of acting which grew out of the Group Theatre, with great directors and teachers such as Berghof, Kazan and Clurman; and from this movement came the strong film actors, Brando and Malden and so on. The acting style, as we all know, was labelled Method acting, and this was the American version of Stanislavsky's acting philosophy. The accent was on finding the character, and they developed very thorough techniques to explore the physical and psychological make-up of a character — the objectives, motivation, sense memory — everything which contributed to an intensified life within the fourth wall. So in a sense, to be verbally explicit was the least important consideration. The physical and sensory skills of the actor were developed wonderfully, but the verbal skills were neglected sometimes to a perverse degree.

It is interesting to notice that, in quite a lot of acting training in the US, Voice and Speech have been taught as two separate subjects, and that there is a 'stage' speech taught, and I think this has something to do with the fact that American actors have difficulty in finding their voice in Shakespeare. There is often a kind of awkwardness, and they either use a slightly English accent, or they fail to find a muscular firmness. Is it because they have not found a central emotional root to the language? Certainly some of the best Shakespeare I have heard there has been in a strong mountain dialect of West Virginia. But that is by the way.

What the American Group Theatre brought was a whole new outlook, and an extremely important one, for the quality of acting that came out of it was rich. It certainly had an influence here, for it made us question the long tradition of acting based on verbal skills and rhetoric to the exclusion often of an inner reality — acting which was often unrooted, and perhaps shallow.

In this country I suppose it was Osborne who finally broke the stranglehold of class, and so brought a realism into the theatre — an aggressive realism. Not that there had not been plays about the working-class before, but somehow they had been out of the mainstream. Osborne made the language real; it had a tough rhetoric about it, and after that one could not go back to the kind of language good behaviour which had been the norm in the theatre until then. It made obsolete a kind of upper class, educated stance on language: it was anti-class, wordy, challenging and on the offensive. You could say like Shakespeare!

It was a different realism to the American one: the focus was very much on language. There was always a movement, a discovery in the language, though the discovery often happened through an evasion of feelings, or touching obliquely on feelings. As with Beckett or Pinter, the evasions came through word games, rhythm games, oblique silences. The silences were just as much a part of the text as the words, and the games were through ladders of words often.

Now, as in America, a lot of this was happening sub-text, but our sub-text was possibly less psychologically orientated and more to do with telling a story: perhaps more European, and so had its affinity with Sartre and Genet. But here I would say that translations are seldom quite so verbally satisfactory; the underlying scheme of thought which emerges through the vocabulary of any play is more difficult to find. The associations of the language which make us aware of the precise mode of thought are just not there; we can only guess at it, and we are totally dependent on the translation.

Two more pieces of text — three actually, but two from the same play. First from Tennessee Williams' *Streetcar Named Desire* (1947) poetic, hesitant, full of the past.

Here Blanche is talking to her sister Stella, trying to persuade her that her husband Stanley is totally wrong for her, and that she should leave him. The whole of the writing of *Streetcar* is drenched in the past, which we see through Blanche's eyes. Later, we come to doubt her veracity. She cannot come to terms with the present, represented by Stanley, or the social and economic reality by which he lives, and to which she has come for refuge. She is eventually destroyed because she cannot cope with the real world. Stanley accidentally overhears the following:

SCENE 4

Blanche: Suppose! You can't have forgotten that much of our bringing up, Stella, that you just *suppose* that any part of a gentleman's in his nature! *Not one particle, no*! Oh, if he was just — *ordinary*! Just *plain* — but good and wholesome, but — *no*. There's something downright — *bestial* — about him! You're hating me saying this, aren't you?

Stella: [coldly] Go on and say it all, Blanche.
Blanche: He acts like an animal, has animal's habits! Eats like one, moves like one, talks like one! There's even something — sub-human — something not quite to the stage of humanity yet! Yes, something — ape-like about him, like one of those pictures I've seen in — anthropological studies! Thousands and thousands of years have passed him right by, and there he is — Stanley Kowalski — survivor of the stone age! Bearing the raw meat home from the kill in the jungle! And you — *you* here — *waiting* for him! Maybe he'll strike you or maybe grunt and kiss you! That is, if kisses have been discovered yet! Night falls and the other apes gather! There in front of the cave, all grunting like him, and swilling and gnawing and hulking! His poker night! — you call it — this party of apes! Somebody growls — some creature snatches at something — the fight is on! *God*! Maybe we are a long way from being made in God's image, but Stella — my sister — there has been *some* progress since then! Such things as art — as poetry and music — such kinds of new light have come into the world since then! In some kinds of people some tenderer feelings have had some little beginning! That we have got to make *grow*! And *cling* to, and hold as our flag! In this dark march toward whatever it is we are approaching . . . *Don't — don't hang back with the brutes*!

These next two passages are from Charles Wood's *Dingo*: 1967: sharp, savage, impressionistic. The characters are simply what they say. As Wood says at the beginning:

Set in the Whole of the Western Desert during the Second World War against the Germans. All of it, from a small bit of it.

ACT I, SCENE 1

A sangar made of stones.

Mogg *and* **Dingo** *are dressed in khaki gone yellow trousers/shorts with webbing equipment, battle order, faded almost white, and boots scuffed white, hair bleached white.*

Legs where you can see them through tatters and between short skirt of **Mogg***'s shorts, and his hose tops/puttees are deep black brown, red, splashed with gentian violet.*

Faces are burned, bloated, splashed with gentian violet. Arms likewise. They lie prone and look over the sangar.

Mogg: You've got a bloated face and your limbs are bloated up.
Dingo: And you Jack.
Mogg: So have I.
Dingo: Gentian violet.
Mogg: I think it attracts the flies.
Dingo: Like cake.

Mogg: Don't make me laugh.
Dingo: I shall shortly piss gentian violet.
Mogg: Then piss some over me.
Dingo: The thing about fighting a desert war . . .
Mogg: We agreed not to talk about it.
Dingo: I must state it for them.
Mogg: Piss some over me because my sores are lifting up their flaming lips.
Dingo: The thing about fighting in the desert is that it is a clean war — without brutality. And clean limbed — without dishonourable actions on either side.
Mogg: They say.
Dingo: And there are no civilians.
Mogg: Except me — I'm a civilian.
Dingo: What am I then?
Mogg: Try as I may — I can't see you standing for a number eight bus picking your nose with the edge of your paper.
Dingo: Or barbarity.
Mogg: I've never stopped being a civilian.
Dingo: Or frightfulness.
Mogg: No refinements.
Dingo: I think you are a civilian.
Mogg: I can't deny that — I find the climate most exhilarating.
Dingo: Characteristic of a civilian.
Mogg: You'll find the climate most exhilarating.
Dingo: Take for instance the shit beetle – a more exhilarative sight . . .
Mogg: And I find excitement bubbling within me . . .
Dingo: . . . you never shat.
Mogg: . . . at the nearness of the enemy.
Dingo: Characteristic of a civilian.
Mogg: Or a soldier.
Dingo: When did we last brew up?
Mogg: The inevitable brew up.
Dingo: Thumbs up.
Mogg: Desert fashion — the old brew up.
Dingo: You take the old benzina.
Mogg: Take the old sand.
Dingo: Take the old brew can.
Mogg: Sand.
Dingo: Benzina.
Mogg: And you take the old dixie.
Dingo: Water.
Mogg: In the old dixie.
Dingo: Benzina.
Mogg: On the old sand.
Dingo: Light the old benzina.

[*A flash, and they have gone, into their hole.*

And almost at the end of the play, Act III, Scene 3, after some time in a POW camp, awaiting release by the Allies:

Dingo: I want to go home to my wife who cries, she has cried since the day I went away, she cried because I went away — she cried all the time I was in the drill hall down the road, she cried when I moved to Wembley Stadium, a twopenny bus ride, she cried all weekend I was at home, she has cried since 1939 . . . she doesn't cry because I'm suffering, because I'm not, she doesn't cry because I'm shot at . . . she cries because I've gone away, and she won't stop crying and she will go out of her mind and be put in hospital for ever,
which she did,
which is where she is today in 1967 . . .
The thing I blame that bastard for more than anything is that he has taken away my sorrow, like the lads on that bloody ridge, the first time I knew it was gone, like we tossed the Eyetie prisoners over the ledge to their death, British soldiers did this at Keren, we did . . . I did, over.
That's what I blame the bastard for more than anything, chopping off, more like wearing away, rubbing down my compassion to not a thing, it is nothing. Alamein, Alamein, Alamein . . .
What was this wailing, it was the wailing of my wife — it was the wailing of myself, it was the wailing of all that I have seen die and it was nothing.
It is such a pity this war was not fought for them . . . I might have kept my compassion, I might not have felt guilty, which I don't, because everybody will say it was fought for them.
It was not. It was fought for all the usual reasons.

[*During the singing the* COMIC *speaks out of the darkness.* DINGO *stays sitting downstage spotlit.*

Churchill (Comic): Is this the West Wall?
Do you wish to visit the men's room, Prime Minister?
Mogg: And there'll be memorials won't there? What about a few for the living, memorials for us.
Churchill (Comic): Are all my generals here?
Comic: I'm here your captain.

[*The* COMIC *faces upstage and hitches his coat for pissing.*

Churchill (Comic): Gentlemen I would like to ask you all to join me in this task. Let us all urinate on the West Wall of Hitler's Germany.
This is one of those operations connected with this great conflict which must not be reproduced graphically. . .
Dingo: Am I a fool, are we fools that comedians are sent to lead us?

All the pieces of modern text we have looked at have modern speech rhythms: and the speaking is private and not public. The last two writers are very different: one is searching the character through a logical sequence of thoughts; the other is very stylized, there are a lot of jumps, and the character exists from what is spoken. In all of them there is a specific choice of vocabulary, and we cannot afford to miss a word.

So what is the practical difference for the actor working in modern and in classical text. I think one point is this: in modern text there is a kind of introvert awareness of feeling and thought, a consideration of motive in and around the text, so that therefore what happens between the words is as important as what is spoken and must be as accurate. This includes silence, for silence is a positive verbal choice. So the actor's concentration must be on the feelings and motives around the word, as much as on the word itself. The actor working in Chekhov, the obvious example, has to make his imaginitive leap into the character, but what he feels and what he says do not necessarily coincide, and we understand him by what he chooses not to say as much as by what he says. Each character works off what is said to him yet keeps his private motive intact.

In the discipline of poetic text we have to release our feeling through the structure of the speech; we therefore have to know the structure in order to fit the two together. There is a size to the imagery which we have to be able to enter into. There is a pleasure in the music: there is so often humour in the interplay of sounds, assonance and alliteration, and a meaning beyond the grammatical sense which audiences pick up on, and which is not far removed from our pleasure in nursery rhymes. And, most important, we should not explain — this reduces it, and the audience has too many signals to pick up.

So the thought and feeling must seem instinctive and must be let go unambiguously with the words, for there is no time for naturalistic consideration: it is always explicit. When, within the character, there is consideration of feeling or ambiguity of thought, these are expressed in the choice of word itself and the rhythm of the speech, and happen with it. Ambiguity is always communicated either to another character or to the audience: the choice of the word is its sub-text. And I think on the whole we are afraid of ambiguity. The way the language happens always begs the question: which comes first, the thought or the word.

And because the speech is direct, it is the physical movement of the thought. So, when Peter Quince introduces the play of Pyramus and Thisbe to his audience, he gets lost in his desire to please, and to be good enough for their standards: his embarrassment is implicit in the coil of the speech:

Quince: If we offend it is with our good will.
    That you should think we come not to offend
But with good will. To show our simple skill,

> That is the true beginning of our end.
> Consider then we come but in despite.
> We do not come as minding to content you,
> Our true intent is. All for your delight
> We are not here. That you should here repent you
> The actors are at hand, and by their show
> You shall know all that you are like to know.
>
> *A Midsummer-Night's Dream*, V.1.

The actor playing Quince does not have to demonstrate that he is out of his usual pattern — it is there in how he shapes his thought: all the more touching because the speech is obviously prepared, its shape is formal.

And this immediacy, this kind of innocence of communication, untinged by reluctance or embarrassment at being articulate, has to be grasped. And I think it is difficult for a modern actor to trust the text sufficiently to allow this to happen. Whatever we imagine of the character, it has to be made apparent through the language itself. We can invent only what it allows us to invent.

As I have said already, this reluctance at sounding formal is partly to do with work in television and film, where you have to be concerned with the behaviour of the character and the need to seem as 'real' as possible — like the person next door. This of course requires its own concentration to put over one's persona, but the language itself is secondary.

But I think there is something more. We live at a time when people are less articulate about their feelings. As we become more educated in the sense that we have more information, we become less in tune with our instincts, and so our response to words becomes only literal: we stop feeling the emotional life of the language. In Elizabethan times, for instance, because the majority of people were not literate they relied much more on verbal communication: stories, information, whole histories of families were passed on by word of mouth. Complicated pneumonics were often used to do this, and these latter probably contributed to an ear for word games and rhymes: it was to do with a whole fabric of life. Today, our dependence on the media — where so much of the talk is there to fill out time in a knowing way — on machines, on the speeding up of life that technology produces, on urbanization, the breakdown of family units, the breakdown of community involvement: all these factors contribute to less real verbal communication between people. This is manifested in extreme forms by cases of youngsters who are unable to communicate their ordinary needs through speech, not because there is anything medically wrong, but simply because they have not been talked to and so are unable to negotiate a simple conversation. Perhaps they have never been told a story or a rhyme. How can they express anything so complicated as their feelings. There are also cases of youngsters who find it hard to distinguish between different sounds in the language because they have constantly heard speech through electronic means and lack enough physical experience of speech.

All this is perhaps extreme, and what has it to do with acting? I think it makes for a climate where text which is verbally explicit is not so believable in today's terms, and is therefore harder for the actor to fill — we feel awkward with its music. It is also perhaps the reason why so much of the important dramatic writing in the last thirty years has been related in some way to the difficulty of communicating with other people, where words, though still a choice, are there to hide rather than discover.

I want to go at a tangent for a moment. It is interesting to note that a good political speaker has a skill with the same structures of speech that we find in dramatic verse, only he happens to use prose. He is aware of the emotive power of rhythm, of the patterns of sound and their repetition, and of the building up of the form of a speech — all based on the old figures in rhetoric. All this he uses to reinforce his argument for his own purposes of manipulation and persuasion. There is an excellent book by Max Atkinson called *His Master's Voice* which analyses the art of political speaking: I think it is interesting for us in that it gives an insight into the effect of words spoken in public, and how the form of a speech can rouse an audience quite apart from its content. It is both an education and a warning!

Now it is quite difficult to work on text as such, partly because such work can never be wholly relevant until you are totally committed to a part and know just what intricacies are there that you want to convey. At the same time many actors are reluctant to work on the text itself, and I think this comes from a belief that if the voice is free and working well, and the thinking behind the character is true, the speaking will come right, and that perhaps if you work at it too much you will lose the spontaneity. I can understand this, but it should not be true: it seems to me that it is an essential part of the preparation that you discover how the speeches work both rhythmically and in terms of imagery; only then will you be free to be instinctive. To explore the structure of a part should feed the imagination not lessen its importance.

So what have we got to do? I think there are quite specific ways of working on poetic text to make us alert to the metre and pattern of the verse, to the structure of the speeches, to the tactile nature of the language, and the energy which impels one line into the next line, and one speech into the next.For modern text, we have to sense when it needs heightening and be absolutely accurate to the words, giving them in such a way that they cannot be missed, particularly when performing in a small space which so often misleads us into being casual.

We can do a lot of good work in feeding this sensibility to the shifts between heightened and naturalistic rhythms by working on poetry: for there we have to find the talking voice of the poet — the ballad-maker — through the specific form in which he is writing. We can practise handling lines without having to be involved in character and interpretation. When working on Shakespeare and the Jacobeans it is useful to use metaphysical poetry and the Shakespeare sonnets as a parallel source of work, and become familiar with the thought structures. Equally, modern poetry — Auden, Eliot, Hopkins, Yeats, Brecht, Bond — serves to help us deal with the colloquial mode while keeping the exactness of the form.

Because language at its best can evoke a response from both the actor and the listener, responses beyond the implications of the story or the character, it puts a particular responsibility on the actor to present it in a way that allows this to happen. We have to notice it (Brecht again). Thus to feel and be is not enough; the language must be given room. Yet this presenting must in no way be untrue, external: it is not public in that it is not simply for effect, but there is enjoyment in being articulate — like playing a brilliant game of snooker or tennis! Even in soliloquies there is a sense of sharing. There is a constant balancing of the formal with the colloquial, and the balance is different with each play.

The difference is always in the timing of thought and word, and with having an attitude to the work which is beyond the personal.

We are in a special way the guardians of the language, and we are able to be articulate through the language we bring alive. This care helps the hearers also to be articulate. We must always be after this reaching out through words. You may say that this cannot apply to mediocre dialogue, but the richer our experience of words, the more we can bring to the most banal of scripts.

When reading all this, speak out loud as much of the texts given as possible.

Part 2

Shakespeare – Setting out the Rules

Chapter 3

METRE AND RHYTHM

So now to business and to Shakespeare. I do believe that with Shakespeare, more than any other writer, you have to speak the text out loud and feel the movement of the language before you can begin to realize its meaning — to read it on the page is just not enough. We have to feel so easy with its structure that it becomes a strength and not an impediment.

How then do you find your way into the text, using all your drive, all your inhabiting and understanding of character, and yet do it through a precise attention to the word, the image, the rhythm and wonderfully shaped expression? How do you feel this language knocking around inside you, as it were, and know that only those words will do at that moment, that no paraphrase could work so well or be so clear?

Now obviously volumes have been written on the structure of the writing, the use of rhetoric, etc., but these do not cover the physical involvement of the actor speaking the text and his need to make it coincide with his motive. So now in this chapter I want to set out the requirements as practically as possible — the rules of metre and form — all the properties, as I see them, that have to be honoured. I do stress that rules are open to each person's interpretation, but you do have to know them in order to choose how to use them, and indeed know whether they can be broken.

Then in chapter 5 we will look at the ways in which we can work at all these points, and the exercises which may be useful.

The cornerstone is the metre.

The bulk of Shakespeare is written in verse, and that verse takes the form of iambic pentameters. Because the rhythm of the iambic pentameter is very like ordinary speech rhythms, a lot of the time we observe the metre instinctively — or accidentally — and it easily falls into a naturalistic speech pattern. We can always make it make sense. And because of this we are often inexact about the precise beat, and so lose something very valuable which it gives us, and that is the sense of continuum through the line, for it provides the emotional pulse of the speech.

We have to know, therefore, the function of the metre: why it is there at all, and would it be as good in prose.

We know that this form, the iambic pentameter, was evolved by the Elizabethan dramatists as being as near to ordinary speech as possible, yet having a definite pulse to drive the writing forward. It was therefore not artificial or elaborate in the way much of the writing had been up till then, with complex verse structures and rhyme. Shakespeare developed the form, and used it with a greater freedom than any other writer of the period: he was able to make it as formal or as colloquial as he wished.

The beat is absolutely firm, and there is something palpably exciting about its pulse. Because it is so close to everyday speech, it is organic to the thought, and when the rhythm breaks or jumps in any way it means there is something dramatic happening, either within the action of the play or with the feeling and behaviour of the character.

The Elizabethan audience must have been so attuned to this pulse that they would have picked up immediately on the dramatic nature of the writing by the way the beat was behaving. The quality of their listening must have been different: more focused on the word. I suppose their response to the beat would have been as instinctive as a modern audience listening to Rock or Reggae or Jazz: we know when it is consistent with the message, we very often pick up on the humour in the rhythm, and we know when it is broken. The more attuned people are, the finer the differences they perceive. For the Elizabethan audience, the beat held the tension and the attention.

If the metre is the rule by which we should work (and this delicate point we will discuss later), the actor must start to think and feel in that pulse; for when the rhythm breaks within the text it does so because the character, to a large or small degree, is at odds with his natural rhythm. And so the metre is there to help the actor find the impulse.

So I am going to set out the basic definitions of the metre, and then list the variations we can expect to find. To some this will be familiar, but it is important to go back to this basic structure and start from a common point. Once we have got this fixed in our heads we will discover the possibilities of movement within the line, and great freedom and delight from the interchange of sense and rhythm. We just have to make ourselves ready to hear it.

The definition of the metre is as follows:

An IAMBIC FOOT consists of two syllables, the first unstressed and

> the second stressed — i.e., short-long, which we mark thus: ◡ —
> e.g., the word 'alike'
> or the two words 'our scene'
>
> A PENTAMETER consists of five strong beats, or feet, per line.
>
> So an IAMBIC PENTAMETER is one line consisting of five beats in short-long rhythm. And this equals 10 syllables.

So a regular line — in this case the first line of the Prologue from *Romeo and Juliet* — works like this:

Two households, both alike in dignity. . .

If you read this one line aloud, you will notice at once that it is not satisfactory to read it to the metrical rule. The syllables of the first two words are long and take time to speak, whereas the syllables in the second half of the line are short, and this alters the weight of stress you can put on them. Nor would you give full stress to the final syllable of 'dignity', though the stress is implicit and gives an open-ended quality to the word which has no final consonant.

We see at once how the stress changes according to the length and quantity of the syllable.*

Now let us look at the whole of the Prologue and see how the basic metrical structure works. It is a straight piece of narrative spoken direct to the audience, and is therefore useful to us at this point:

Two households, both alike in dignity
  In fair Verona, where we lay our scene,
From ancient grudge break to new mutiny.
  Where civil blood makes civil hands unclean.
From forth the fatal loins of these two foes
  A pair of star-crossed lovers take their life;
Whose misadventured piteous overthrows
  Doth with their death bury their parents' strife.
The fearful passage of their death-marked love
  And the continuance of their parents' rage,
Which, but their children's end, nought could remove,
  Is now the two hours' traffic of our stage;
The which if you with patient ears attend,
  What here shall miss, our toil shall strive to mend.

* See *Voice and the Actor.* Harrap 1973.

Make sure you have the meaning clear, then read it through carefully out loud twice. First, naturalistically, only caring about making sense. Then, keeping the sense in your mind, but reading it for the metre, tapping the metre out gently with your hand.

You will notice two things which are at the core of rhythmic structure: i) the combination of stress with length of syllable varies the movement of the line, and ii) the metre stress does not always lie with the sense stress. The permutations made by these two factors are endless, and therefore are endlessly interesting. Further, and this is most important, an awareness of the metre subtly enhances the meaning.

Here are notes on what you are likely to find:

Line 1 First two words very full with long vowels. 'Two' — a long vowel but unstressed, and needing weight as the information is important. The vowel is open-ended without a final consonant so it is more variable.

The second syllable of 'households' is unstressed but holds weight because of the length of the vowel and the quantity of the consonants 'lds' which take time to speak. This gives the whole word substance — important, as indeed the word 'households' implies not only the house, but the family, the servants, and all the activity which takes place in a house, down to the linen cupboards.

Second half of the line: sharp consonants and short vowels giving a sense of evenness and balance. The stress is regular — i.e., the sense fits with the metre, though the final word 'dignity' is not straightforward in that the first syllable possibly takes extra weight, for the last syllable is short and cannot be fully stressed, yet it has to hold up into the next line.

Line 2 Regular stress; vowels open and long — even the unstressed vowels are quite long — the consonants are all continuants, so the line flows and is liquid and has a sense of ease. The sense and the metre coincide.

Line 3 The sound contrasts with the last line, and the metre is broken here for you have to stress 'break' in order to make sense even though it is in an unstressed position. I think you also have to stress 'new', though not as harshly. The juxtaposition of the strong stresses on 'grudge' and 'break', with their very hard sounds, is quite brutal, and makes a small shock within the line.

'mutiny' goes quite quickly to make up for the extra stresses within the line, and, as with 'dignity', you cannot lay full stress on the final syllable, yet it has to lie open to the next line.

Line 4 This is an even line, weighing up the two concepts of 'blood' and 'hands'. There is a certain weight on 'makes' even though it is in an unstressed position, because it is an active word — i.e., it implies the action of the blood influencing the hands. There is also a certain weight on the first syllable of 'unclean'.

Line 5 This is a regular line; the stresses coincide with the long vowels, except for 'two', and with the sense. The consonants are continuant, with 'f' repeated; and 'From' has a certain weight, as it is taking us on to a new stage of the story.

Line 6 Again regular, the stress coinciding with the sense and long, open vowels.

However, there is a certain weight on the unstressed 'crossed' which qualifies the meaning of the whole word; and there is a sharpness at the end of the line which makes it sound definite — the final consonants are sharp and clean.

Line 7 This line rocks, partly because of the four-syllabled 'misadventured', which is regular in stress but filled with a quantity of hard consonants separating the short vowels; and partly because of 'piteous' with its short first vowel in the stressed position and the long second syllable in an unstressed position — this contains two vowels given in the space of one. The devoiced consonants 'p', 't' and 's' make it sharp and spitting.

The whole line is comfortless. It is awkward to speak.

Line 8 Here the rhythm breaks: 'Doth' needs stress, and it holds up for a moment so that it leads us to 'death'. This is pointed up by the repetition of the consonants and the gentle sliding of the vowels.

There is an inverted stress on 'bury', which jogs us and gives the word prominence. The consonant is hard.

Line 9 This line is smooth: the vowels are open and mostly long; the shorter vowels such as 'death' and 'love' are given length by their final continuant consonants. It is smooth in contrast to the preceeding line, and is the start of the sestet — it is beginning to sum up. Both the syllables of 'death-marked' need weight and a certain length, and this is allowed for by making 'of their' short and unstressed. 'love' needs as much weight and length as possible: it has to embrace 'death-marked' and also to balance with 'rage' at the end of the next line.

Line 10 A little bumpy. 'And' I think takes the weight at the beginning to serve the cumulative needs of the story. 'continuance' is full and a little clumsy, with two vowels crammed into the last syllable, yet all coming to rest on the word 'rage', with its long vowel and continuant voiced consonant — rather hard.

Line 11 This line rocks to make the argument clear, not to shock us. 'Which' takes the stress, again having a cumulative effect, and it somehow holds us ready for the way the information in the line is balanced.

'nought' takes most of the stress from 'could', so you get 'end' and 'nought' stressed together, underlining the finality of each word.

'remove' is regular in stress, and has a final voiced continuant which softens it and takes us over into the next line.

Line 12 Very regular and even — long vowels and repeated 'OW' sounds.

Straight, unemotive information, and its evenness endorses the sense of time the line contains. Though 'two hours' takes a fairly equal stress and the vowels are long, 'traffic' is short and makes up for the time taken. It is, however, an unexpected word, it contains a sense of business in more senses than one, and its sharpness makes us remark it.

Line 13 A perfectly regular line — a kind of relief, bringing us back to the ordinary.

Line 14 Again regular: with the exception of 'miss' which is sharp, the vowels are long and ringing, giving it a concluding sound. 'miss' is lifted to throw up the comfort of 'mend'.

You will notice too the difference between lines which are predominantly monosyllabic, and those with words of two or more syllables. Line 12 consists of monosyllables except for the word 'traffic', and that gives it additional pointing. The last line contains only monosyllables, which adds to its sense of conclusion.

These are just notes: there is more we could pick upon, but I do not want to overload at the moment. You will probably have noticed other points. What is marvellous is that the passage, seemingly quite straightforward, has so much going on rhythmically under the surface. It is one piece of information, starting with 'Two households' and not coming to rest until 'strive to mend'; yet within that unity of thought each line has a different movement. How you make that movement work for you is a matter of individual choice. I remember working on this particular passage with a group of 17-year-olds in Newcastle, and they were just astonished at what the language was doing.

You may feel that you would have found much of this instinctively, and I daresay that is true. But I feel strongly that we should be as fully cognisant of the structure as possible, for that is what gives it its vigour. To pretend that it is incidental is both to cheat it, and to be unaware of the choices.

You will notice that the passage — which happens to be a sonnet — is printed with spaces within the lines. And this brings us to the next important thing we have to notice in the line structure, and that is the break which occurs within the line, and which we call the caesura.

A caesura. Because of the length of a five-beat line, there is nearly always a break within the line, in most cases after the second or third stressed syllable. Sometimes this break coincides with a full-stop or a colon, and so with a break in thought. But more often, as in the passage we are looking at, it is simply a poise on a word — i.e., the word holds and lifts for a fraction of a moment before it plunges into the second half of the line. This poise is necessary for the ear of the listener in that it allows a space, a still moment, for us to clock the key word in the line, and so be ready for the information in the second half of the line — to throw it up as it were. Now the quicker we are speaking, the more the shape needs to be observed. Very often, when we do not understand a speech, it is because this shaping has not been attended to. Now this gives even more variety of movement to the line. If you read the Prologue again, observing the spaces, you will see the value of those poises; you may also feel that some are not necessary, and that there is a value in certain lines being given totally smoothly. It is all negotiable. So let us see what the caesura does in those lines — again notes:

Line 1 It allows us to hook our minds on households'.

Line 2 The same with 'Verona'.

Line 3 It stresses the ugliness of 'grudge', and also the break in metre with two stressed words coming together.

Line 4 This is open to negotiation — you may choose to feel it after 'blood' to make the weighing of the two concepts of 'blood' and 'hands' clear. You may choose to have two. I have put it before 'unclean', as I think it helps to make the word active rather than merely descriptive.

Line 5 There is hardly a break in this line; you could almost manage without one. However 'forth' is lifted to impel us to 'fatal loins'; and 'loins' takes time to speak because of its diphthong and two continuant consonants, so a caesura is implicitly contained within it. Also 'fatal loins' is a large concept for us to take in, and therefore needs space. There is of course alliteration in the line, which is continued into the next.

Line 6 The caesura comes after 'lovers', so we can both look back at the packed image, and also prepare for the enormity of the action we are being led to.

Line 7 A full, weighty line, with the caesura probably after 'misadventured' — but this is negotiable.

Line 8 As we have already seen, this line rocks, and the break comes after 'death' to allow us to take in the information.

Lines 9 & 10 The concepts in these two lines are antithetical to each other, yet rhythmically they are steady, and I think this points up the fatal movement towards death which is contained in the thought. They possibly hold no caesuras, and the rhythm moves inexorably to the next line.

Line 11 'Which' holds up slightly as we have seen to prepare us for 'children's end' where the caesura is, emphasizing the finality of 'nought'. And we feel that the previous two lines have been rhythmically leading us to this point.

Line 12 A regular line, defusing emotionally, with a slight caesura after 'traffic', to bring us down to earth and everyday matters, and consequently the fact that we are watching a play. 'traffic' is such a sharp word that it almost works its own caesura.

Line 13 A regular line, really without a break, though I have included a possible one.

Line 14 A slower rhythm, with the caesura after 'miss', to point up the plea for the audience's tolerance towards the players. This final couplet rounds the whole thought off, and emphasizes the invitation to participate in the whole event. As with all Shakespearean sonnets, the last two lines contains the summing up of the whole argument.

This then, is the basic form of the iambic pentameter: five strong beats, ten syllables to a line, with usually some break or poise within the line. And it is on this basic form that variations are made, variations which are always to do with the state of the character, and it is therefore important that we get the sound of the regular beat clearly in our heads, so that we can pick up immediately on the irregularities.

Because the Prologue is a passage spoken direct to the audience, its function chiefly to inform, it is possible to be more objective about the speaking of it. When inside a character, however, what you do then becomes subjective and the possibilities much more variable, and in constant flux according to the moment. So here are two other passages from the same play, both in iambic pentameters, but with very different movements. I will just mark the stress and the possible caesuras. The first is Romeo — it is smooth and gentle in sound. Notice the value of the vowels, their openness and length, and the quality of the consonants:

Romeo: He jests at scars that never felt a wound.

[Enter Juliet above.

But soft!   What light through yonder window breaks?
It is the East,   and Juliet is the sun!
Arise, fair sun,   and kill the envious moon,
Who is already sick and pale with grief
That thou her maid art far more fair than she.
Be not her maid,   since she is envious.
Her vestal livery is but sick and green,
And none but fools do wear it.   Cast it off.
It is my lady.   O, it is my love!
O that she knew she were!   II.2.

Two things: I did not mark a caesura in the first line — it is the second half of a couplet, the first line of which ends the previous scene; it therefore depends on how that previous line is treated. And the last line is short — only three beats.

The other passage is Juliet's second soliloquy. It is interesting because, as in most of the early plays, the rhythm is strong and uncomplicated — naive in a way — and so when it breaks it does so quite sharply. Again I have marked only the metre stress, so you will see clearly where metre and stress are in counterpoint. There are several things to notice:

The first word breaks the rhythm immediately: the first syllable of 'Gallop' has to be stressed.

This then sets up a kind of gallop in the rhythm of the whole, which is related to the racing of her blood, and the whole speech alternates between being quite violent and calm.

In quite a few other lines the first stress is inverted, thus making the first word remarkable.

This happens notably on 'Hood my unmanned blood . . .' where the stress of the whole line is inverted until the last beat, so that the rhythm is underpinning her sexual arousal, and 'unmanned' becomes very specific.

> Rhythmically the speech works up to 'And when I shall die', 'die' being a euphemism of 'come'. After this point the speech is calmer and more reasoned.
>
> Certain lines are over-full: words such as 'Towards' and 'runaways' have to be fitted in to less than their syllabic count.
>
> Names subtly change their stress: for instance, 'Romeo' sometimes has full weight, and other times is subservient to the sense stress.

When you read this through aloud to discover the rhythm, you will notice just how much the length and weight of syllables is negotiable, and how much play there is within the lines.

Juliet: Gallop apace, you fiery-footed steeds,
Towards Phoebus' lodging! Such a waggoner
As Phaëton would whip you to the West
And bring in cloudy night immediately.
Spread thy close curtain, love-performing night,
That runaway's eyes may wink, and Romeo
Leap to these arms untalked of and unseen.
Lovers can see to do their amorous rites
By their own beauties; or, if love be blind,
It best agrees with night. Come, civil night,
Thou sober-suited matron, all in black,
And learn me how to lose a winning match,
Played for a pair of stainless maidenhoods.
Hood my unmanned blood, bating in my cheeks,
With thy black mantle till strange love grow bold,
Think true love acted simple modesty.
Come, night. Come, Romeo. Come, thou day in night;
For thou wilt lie upon the wings of night
Whiter than new snow upon a raven's back.
Come, gentle night. Come, loving, black-browed night.
Give me my Romeo. And when I shall die,
Take him and cut him out in little stars,
And he will make the face of heaven so fine
That all the world will be in love with night
And pay no worship to the garish sun.

O I have bought the mansion of a love,
But not possessed it; and though I am sold,
Not yet enjoyed. So tedious is this day
As is the night before some festival
To an impatient child that hath new robes
And may not wear them. . .

III.2.

I think from the actor's viewpoint the variations on this basic form are of two kinds:

1: Those to do with the number of syllables or beats in a line. These variations alter the movement of a line, and therefore its emotional colour: there is always a reason for them. However, for our purposes, their effect is more often subliminal in that they are part of the motive and texture of the whole thought, and do not substantially alter the style of speaking. But, of course, there are exceptions.

2: Those which are used more consciously and purposefully to dramatic effect, such as the broken or split lines, rhyme and rhyming couplets. The last two are not in a sense variations, rather an increased stylization in the writing — the form at its most heightened.

1a: The feminine endings. Now of the first kind, the most common is the FEMININE ENDING. This is simply when the line ends with an extra unstressed syllable, giving it 11 syllables instead of 10. The line still has five regular feet, but the extra syllable makes it slightly fuller, as thus:

Farewell — Thou are too dear for my possessing,
And like enough thou know'st thy estimate:
The charter of thy worth gives thee releasing;
My bonds in thee are all determinate . . .

Sonnet 87.

As you see, the feminine ending is on alternate lines. The whole of the rest of the sonnet is in feminine endings, and is worth reading to get the sound in your mind. I think they have the effect of making the thought itself ironic. I think when they occur within the text of a play they have the effect of making the line more pliant, and often give a quality of working through the thought, sometimes giving it a haunted and unfinished sound as though leaving the thought in the air: the effects are different. On the whole they are interspersed within a speech. I think it is true to say that they occur less frequently in plays such as the histories where action is more definite, perhaps swifter and less considered. All we have to do is feel their movement and use it. But certainly, when there are several consecutively, they point up the next regular line, which then appears stronger and more definite.

Here are some examples. In this first one, the first three lines have feminine endings, and therefore 11 syllables; the fourth ends on a stressed beat:

Katherina: A woman moved is like a fountain troubled,
Muddy, ill-seeming, thick, bereft of beauty,
And while it is so, none so dry or thirsty
Will deign to sip or touch one drop of it.

Taming of the Shrew, V.2.

In this speech of Katherina's they seem to point up the discovery and consideration of her thought: as the speech goes on she becomes surer and these endings become scarcer. They are then clues into the way the thoughts are shaped.

Hamlet: To be, or not to be — that is the question;
Whether 'tis nobler in the mind to suffer
The slings and arrows of outrageous fortune
Or to take arms against a sea of troubles
And by opposing end them. To die, to sleep —
No more — and by a sleep to say we end
The heartache and the thousand natural shocks
That flesh is heir to. 'Tis a consummation
Devoutly to be wished. To die, to sleep —
To sleep — perchance to dream. Ay, there's the rub.

Hamlet, III. 1.

Obviously there is much going on in this speech, but you see how the short sharp word 'rub' is pointed up by either the previous unstressed final syllables or by softer more continuant sounds.

In this last example, the speech itself is troubled and broken up: the thoughts splintered and emotionally charged, and almost seem to be there in spite of the metre. The weak endings of lines 1, 4 and 5 point this up.

Leontes: Ha'not you seen, Camillo —
But that's past doubt, you have, or your eye-glass
Is thicker than a cuckold's horn — or heard —

For to a vision so apparent rumour
Cannot be mute — or thought — for cogitation
Resides not in the man that does not think —
My wife is slippery. . .

The Winter's Tale, I.3.

This last example from *As You Like It* is different — the form is used to heighten the formality of the moment, yet giving it a delicate quality; but we also have short lines of three or four beats and also an amount of repetition as in a prayer. To Silvius, Orlando and Phebe the moment is to do with making a vow of love and is almost religious. The short lines need to be observed; they ask for some movement or moment from the actor. Rosalind breaks the intensely romantic sequence by speaking in prose on:

'Why do you speak too "Why blame you me to love you?" '
and then from 'Pray you no more of this . . .' on to the end of her speech. She undercuts the romanticism and puts it into her practical perspective.

Phebe: Good shepherd, tell this youth what 'tis to love.
Silvius: It is to be all made of sighs and tears,
And so am I for Phebe.
Phebe: And I for Ganymede.
Orlando: And I for Rosalind.
Rosalind: And I for no woman.
Silvius: It is to be all made of faith and service,
And so am I for Phebe.
Phebe: And I for Ganymede.
Orlando: And I for Rosalind.
Rosalind: And I for no woman.
Silvius: It is to be all made of fantasy,
All made of passion, and all made of wishes,
All adoration, duty and observance,
All humbleness, all patience, and impatience,
All purity, all trial, all observance;
And so am I for Phebe.
Phebe: And so am I for Ganymede.
Orlando: And so am I for Rosalind.
Rosalind: And so am I for no woman.
Phebe: [*to Rosalind.*
If this be so, why blame you me to love you?
Silvius: [*to Phebe.*
If this be so, why blame you me to love you?
Orlando: If this be so, why blame you me to love you?
Rosalind:
Why do you speak too 'Why blame you me to love you?'

Orlando:
To her that is not here, nor doth not hear.
Rosalind:
Pray you no more of this, 'tis like the howling of Irish wolves against the moon . . .

As You Like It, V.2.

There is an incredible lightness here: the syllables are light and short and the stress is ambivalent to an extent. 'wishes', 'observance', 'Phebe', 'love you' are feminine endings; but, for instance, 'fantasy' and 'woman' both end on stressed syllables, yet you would not give those words that stress — indeed it would be absurd to stress the final syllable on 'woman', and perhaps Rosalind is already breaking with the metre there anyway. However, the consciousness of the possibility of stress is there in both cases, and it has to be given room. The same applies to the two names 'Ganymede' and 'Rosalind', though I think the end syllables here carry more weight, and in any case the names would be cared for. There is also the sound pun on 'here' and 'hear'. This does not alter the metre but informs the movement of the line.

Now we do not want to be pedantic about any of this, but you have to honour the formality of the rhythm or the particular intensity of the thought is not fulfilled. We have to know the mathematics of the lines so that we can tune into the quality of the thought. In this case it is to do with the purity of idealized love.

1b: Short lines. And this brings us nicely on to the other important variation to do with the quantity of a line, SHORT LINES: when there are fewer than five beats in a line in an otherwise regular passage. And I would say that there is always a reason for the missing beat, that there is a demand within the situation or within the character for silence. It may be that a movement is needed, or that the thought needs time to settle between characters, or that the thought overwhelms the speaker for that moment. You will find this occurs somewhere in most of the plays — you must always look for the reason.

Here are some examples from *Othello*: In Act III, Scene 3, Iago's speech beginning line 407, the first line

I do not like the office.

contains only three beats; and further on

I could not sleep.

contains only two; and

One of this kind is Cassio.

contains three or four, depending on how you pronounce 'Cassio'. These short lines seem to point to the fact that Iago is giving Othello time to absorb the implications of what he is saying. They are calculated: he is keeping Othello on the hook, and he is observing the effect he is having. Later in the scene Othello's

> O, blood, blood, blood!

has quite a different purpose: the three beats indicate an overcharging of emotion. And Iago's last line, the final one in the scene,

> ◡ — ◡ — ◡ —◡
> I am your own for ever.

indicates the winding up of the scene; its simplicity underlines both the irony of the lie, and his relief at the success of his hard work.

Other examples include Isabella in *Measure for Measure*, contemplating alone Angelo's proposition that she should sleep with him in exchange for her brother's life:

Isabella: . . . I'll to my brother.
Though he hath fall'n by prompture of the blood,
Yet hath he in him such a mind of honour
That, had he twenty heads to tender down
On twenty bloody blocks, he'd yield them up,
Before his sister should her body stoop
To such abhorred pollution.

II.4.

and Brutus in *Julius Caesar*, when he is contemplating the assassination of Caesar:

Brutus: . . . And, since the quarrel
Will bear no colour for the thing he is
Fashion it thus — that what he is, augmented,
Would run to these and these extremities;
And therefore think him as a serpent's egg
Which, hatched, would, as his kind grow mischievous,
And kill him in the shell.

II.1.

In both these it is the enormity of the thought that requires time and space. The silent beats are filled.

1c: Over-full lines. There are, too, OVER-FULL lines, where there are extra syllables within the line, and where some fitting in has to be done, often by running two unstressed syllables together. We have already had two examples of this:

And by opposing end them. To die, to sleep

and

Though he hath fall'n by prompture of the blood,

and I have indicated the elisions that can be made. Now obviously sometimes this is simply an awkwardness in the writing: but most often full lines happen because of a density of thought that prevents the language running smoothly, and as such is an indication of the state of the character. It happens with Leontes in *Winter's Tale* for instance, also with Othello and Ulysses, and at some point in most of the plays. You just have to beat the metre out firmly and negotiate how the sense best fits; that is why it is so important to be confident about the beat. In this way we also find whether a final 'ed' on a word is pronounced or not: and it is also a guide as to the pronunciation of names. However, always the rules are there to be handled, and partly you have to do what sounds right to you.

1d: Long lines. Occasionally you will find a six-beat line, as in Ulysses' famous speech, 'Time hath, my lord, a wallet at his back . . .' you will find one six-beat and one seven-beat line. Here is the middle section of it:

Ulysses: For time is like a fashionable host,
That slightly shakes his parting guest by th'hand,
And with his arms outstretched, as he would fly,
Grasps in the comer: the welcome ever smiles,
And farewell goes out sighing. O, let not virtue seek (6)
Remuneration for the thing it was;
For beauty, wit, (7)
High birth, vigour of bone, desert in service,
Love, friendship, charity, are subjects all
To envious and calumniating time . . .

Troilus and Cressida, III.3.

Perhaps he gets lost in his own oratory; certainly there is a great wryness there.

2a: Split lines. Now to the second kind of variation, those to do with a heightening of style. First the SPLIT LINE. These occur in most of the plays at some point, but frequently in the later ones. They are simply when one line is split between two or more characters, yet keeping the iambic pentameter intact. Now these are not heightened in poetic form as is the rhyming couplet for instance, yet they are still very much to do with a heightened style of speaking, for they are to do with the actor's sense of the rhythm of the whole, and the ability to pick up on the individual rhythm of the actors he is working with. For the line must have the same continuum as if spoken by one person, yet each actor has to fill it with his own motive and energy: and always it is one character sparking a response from another. However, what is important is that the speaker of the first or middle part of the line has to give it out so that it can be taken on by the next speaker. It has to be poised, and cannot be just naturalistic.

Now there are many examples you can find. In some places they are used no more than to give a quickening to the scene and a sharpness of verbal exchange, but always they give a sense of a shared experience as we shall see. In the summit meeting between Antony, Caesar and Lepidus in *Antony and Cleopatra*, Act II, Scene 2, for instance, there are a number of split lines in the scene pointing up the common political interest and the way they are bargaining. But very often they are used to more dramatic effect, as in that central scene between Othello and Iago where the thoughts are so dovetailed that they are almost breathing together.

In the following section of that scene, if you read it through for the metre, you will see how Othello breaks the rhythm three times: on 'I am bound to thee for ever', 'Not a jot, not a jot' which half fits in but does not quite, and 'I will not'. It is as if he wants to finish the exchange, but the interesting thing is that Iago persists and each time brings it back on to an even beat. You feel the awful irony from the inevitability of the rhythm, particularly in the last line.

Iago: . . . But Ī am mūch to blāme,
I hūmbly dō beseēch you ōf your pārdon
For tōo much lōving yōu.
Othello: I am bound to thee for ever.
Iago: I sēe this hāth a līttle dāshed your spīrits.
Othello: Not a jot, not a jot.
Iago: . . . In fāith, I fēar it hās.
I hōpe you wīll consīder whāt is spōke
Comes frōm my lōve. But Ī do sēe you're mōved.
I ām to prāy you, nōt to strāin my speech
To grōsser īssues, nōr to lārger reāch
Than tō suspīcion.

Othello: I will not.

Iago: Should you do so, my lord,
My speech should fall into such vile success
Which my thoughts aimed not at. Cassio's my worthy friend.
My lord, I see you're moved.

Othello: No, not much moved.
I do not think but Desdemona's honest.

Iago: Long live she so! And long live you to think so!

Othello, III.3.

We sense how Iago manipulates Othello by how he manipulates the rhythm.

In this next exchange between Leontes and Camillo in *Winter's Tale* it is a reverse situation. Leontes' jealousy is already implanted, and he pushes Camillo into corroborating it by forcing him to repeat what he says. The rhythm pushes it:

Leontes: . . . How came't, Camillo,
That he did stay?

Camillo: At the good queen's entreaty.

Leontes: 'At the Queen's' be't. 'Good' should be pertinent;
But, so it is, it is not. Was this taken
By any understanding pate but thine?
For thy conceit is soaking, will draw in
More than the common blocks. Not noted, is't,
But of the finer natures? By some severals
Of headpiece extraordinary? Lower messes
Perchance as to this business purblind? Say.

Camillo: Business, my lord? I think most understand
Bohemia stays here longer.

Leontes: Ha?

Camillo: Stays here longer.

Leontes: Ay, but why?

Camillo: To satisfy your highness, and the entreaties
Of our most gracious mistress.

Leontes: Satisfy?
Th'entreaties of your mistress? Satisfy? . . .

The Winter's Tale, I.2.

The rhythm only breaks once on 'Ay, but why', when Camillo needs time to find an answer, and for the same reason there is a moment after 'Ha'. But as you see the rhythm of Leontes' speech is jagged and fits uneasily.

In this next section from *Macbeth*, the split lines make it very exciting. Beat it through lightly to see how it works: 'When' comes so quick, and 'Ay' can take as long as you want. The suspense in the way the thoughts are poised between the two characters makes its own music. And always the split line heightens the sense of people sharing a situation but from a different viewpoint: they are listening to each other and to the situation.

Macbeth: I have done the deed. Didst thou not hear a noise?
Lady Macbeth: I heard the owl-scream and the cricket's cry.
Did you not speak?
Macbeth: When?
Lady Macbeth: Now.
Macbeth: As I descended?
Lady Macbeth: Ay.
Macbeth: Hark!
Who lies i'the second chamber?
Lady Macbeth: Donalbain.
Macbeth: [*looks at his hands.*
This is a sorry sight.
Lady Macbeth: A foolish thought, to say a sorry sight.

Macbeth, II.2.

They are absolutely in tune with each other.

In the whole of the first scene of *Hamlet* there is a very strong feeling of shared experience, of something going on under the surface and of questions being asked. If you read it through just noticing how lines are broken and picked up by the next speaker you will become aware of a very particular music:

Francisco: For this relief much thanks. 'Tis bitter cold,
And I am sick at heart.
Barnardo: Have you had quiet guard?
Francisco: Not a mouse stirring.
Barnardo: Well, good night.
If you do meet Horatio and Marcellus,
The rivals of my watch, bid them make haste.

You feel the moments of watchfulness when the lines are short. Further on in the scene, after the Ghost of Hamlet's father has appeared a second time, Horatio speaks to it: and the speech which was begun in a very even rhythm, is now interspersed with short lines as he hopes for an answer. The section ends with a split line between him, Marcellus and Barnardo — Marcellus' last 'Tis gone' rounds it off rhythmically. Each part of the line has to be kept in the air for the whole to have its effect:

Horatio: . . . In the most high and palmy state of Rome,
A little ere the mightiest Julius fell,
The graves stood tenantless and the sheeted dead
Did squeak and gibber in the Roman streets. . . . etc . . .

[*Enter the Ghost.*

But soft, behold, lo where it comes again!
I'll cross it, though it blast me.

[*He spreads his arms.*

Stay, illusion.
If thou hast any sound or use of voice.
Speak to me.
If there be any good thing to be done
That may to thee do ease and grace to me,
Speak to me.
If thou art privy to thy country's fate,
Which happily foreknowing may avoid,
O, speak!
Or if thou hast uphoarded in thy life
Extorted treasure in the womb of earth,
For which, they say, you spirits oft walk in death,
Speak of it.

[*The cock crows.*

Stay and speak. Stop it, Marcellus.
Marcellus: Shall I strike it with my partisan?
Horatio: Do, if it will not stand.
Barnardo: 'Tis here.
Horatio: 'Tis here.

[*Exit the Ghost.*

Marcellus: 'Tis gone.

Now partly this form holds excitement for the listener because of its artificiality. We get pleasure from the fulfilling of the rhythm of a line started by one character and finished by another: we wonder how it will be solved, not consciously, but we are aware of a pattern that has to be rounded off. This awareness heightens the irony which may be there — as in the word 'satisfy' in the section from *Winter's Tale*, or in this exchange between the Queen and Guildenstern in *Hamlet*:

Queen: Thanks, Guildenstern and gentle Rosencrantz.
And I do beseech you instantly to visit
My too much changèd son. — Go, some of you,
And bring these gentlemen where Hamlet is.
Guildenstern: Heavens make our presence and our practices
Pleasant and helpful to him!
Queen: Ay, Amen.

Hamlet, II.2.

And in the final lines of a scene in *Richard II* between Bushy, Bagot and Green, when, learning that Bolingbroke has landed in England with an army, and that the King's faction is in disarray, they decide to split to different parts of the country. We will look at the whole of the scene later because it is interesting rhythmically, but for now we will just look at the split line:

Bagot: Farewell at once, for once, for all, and ever.
Bushy: Well, we may meet again.
Bagot: I fear me, never.

[*Exeunt.*
Richard II, II.2.

But also this artificiality heightens the humour, serves the wit — because, as it were, they dance. Take these lines between Romeo and Mercutio:

Romeo: And we mean well in going to this masque,
But 'tis no wit to go.
Mercutio: Why, may one ask?
Romeo: I dreamt a dream tonight
Mercutio: And so did I.
Romeo: Well, what was yours?
Mercutio: That dreamers often lie.
Romeo: In bed asleep, while they do dream things true.
Mercutio: O, then I see Queen Mab hath been with you.

Romeo and Juliet, I.4.

Or later in the same play, the game on the line takes on a much bitterer note in this exchange between Paris, Juliet and the Friar:

Paris: Happily met, my lady and my wife!
Juliet: That may be, sir, when I may be a wife.
Paris: That 'may be' must be, love, on Thursday next.
Juliet: What must be shall be.
Friar: That's a certain text.

Romeo and Juliet, IV.1.

There are many more examples that you can find: look at the exchanges between Cleopatra and the Messenger for instance (*Antony and Cleopatra* Act II, Scene 5, and Act III, Scene 3); humour and irony are both there. I have taken time over the split line because it tells us so much about the energy of the writing: how it is always carried on from one character to another and when it breaks it does not drop, it is simply poised. The reason is always there in the movement of the thoughts: the rhythm tells us all we need to know about the situation.

Now you will have noticed the last examples are in rhyme, which leads us to just that point.

2b: Rhyme. There is nothing difficult about this: we simply have to be alert to it and use it, we have to allow it its artificiality.

I think perhaps the important thing to realize is that we must never underestimate what I call the 'nursery rhyme' element which appeals to all of us. And I mean by this that if you take any nursery rhyme and speak it through aloud but stop before the last line, you will feel just how much that last line is needed to fulfil both the sense — however crazy — and the pattern set up. And this is precisely what we have to be conscious of when using rhyme in Shakespeare — a sense of delivering up the rhyme to satisfy the ear of the listener. That is part of its purpose: either a delight in sound and meaning games, or, when used seriously, a tuning into a resonance of meaning through the sound.

In the early comedies, the verse passages slip in and out of rhyme a good deal: almost always it is in couplets, but in *Love's Labour's Lost*, for instance, the rhyme is often on alternate lines, making it a good deal more artificial and in a way literary, which is something the actor has to deal with. When, as we have seen in examples already given, the rhyme is split between two characters, this adds to the pleasure, and the possible irony. Now what is important to notice is just how vital the caesura becomes: the poise at some point in the line not only makes you able to point up the rhyme, but, vitally, it gets the listener ready to take in the rhyme — if we are not ready for the rhyme we miss its pleasure.

Here are three examples from comedies: the first two are conscious and playing literary philosophical games; the third, from *The Dream*, is quite different — though the rhyme heightens it, it feels colloquial and quite real. Here is a short passage from *Comedy of Errors* between Adriana and her unmarried sister Luciana. It sets up the debate about partnership in marriage, which occupies part of the thinking of the play.

Adriana: Neither my husband nor the slave returned,
That in such haste I sent to seek his master?
Sure, Luciana, it is two o'clock.

Luciana: Perhaps some merchant hath invited him,
And from the mart he's somewhere gone to dinner.
Good sister, let us dine, and never fret.
A man is master of his liberty.
Time is their master, and when they see time
They'll go or come. If so, be patient, sister.
Adriana: Why should their liberty than ours be more?
Luciana: Because their business still lies out o'door.
Adriana: Look when I serve him so he takes it ill.
Luciana: O, know he is the bridle of your will.
Adriana: There's none but asses will be bridled so.
Luciana: Why, headstrong liberty is lashed with woe.
There's nothing situate under heaven's eye
But hath his bound in earth, in sea, in sky.
The beasts, the fishes, and the wingèd fowls
Are their male's subjects, and at their controls.
Man, more divine, the master of all these,
Lord of the wide world and wild watery seas,
Indued with intellectual sense and souls,
Of more pre-eminence than fish and fowls,
Are masters to their females, and their lords.
Then let your will attend on their accords.
Adriana: This servitude makes you to keep unwed.
Luciana: Not this, but troubles of the marriage bed.
Adriana: But were you wedded, you would bear some sway.
Luciana: Ere I learn love, I'll practise to obey.
Adriana: How if your husband start some otherwhere?
Luciana: Till he come home again I would forbear.
Adriana: Patience unmoved! No marvel though she pause.
They can be meek that have no other cause.
A wretched soul, bruised with adversity,
We bid be quiet when we hear it cry.
But were we burdened with like weight of pain,
As much or more we should ourselves complain.
So thou, that hast no unkind mate to grieve thee,
With urging helpless patience would relieve me.
But if thou live to see like right bereft,
This fool-begged patience in thee will be left.
Luciana: Well, I will marry one day, but to try.
Here comes your man. Now is your husband nigh.

Comedy of Errors, II.1.

And of course it is the wrong Antipholus, so the trouble begins. The following from *Love's Labour's Lost* rhymes on alternate lines. The writing is particularly elegant, as is the whole play. Finally the King of Navarre and his lords admit they are in love, and ask Berowne to justify the breaking of their oath to forswear the company of women and give themselves up to study:

Berowne: O, if the streets were pavèd with her eyes,
  Her feet were much too dainty for such tread.
Dumaine: O, vile! Then, as she goes, what upward lies
  The street should see as she walked overhead.
King: But what of this? Are we not all in love?
Berowne: O, nothing so sure, and thereby all forsworn.
King: Then leave this chat, and, good Berowne, now prove
  Our loving lawful and our faith not torn.
Dumaine: Ay, marry, there; some flattery for this evil!
Longaville: O, some authority how to proceed!
Some tricks, some quillets, how to cheat the devil!
Dumaine: Some salve for perjury.
Berowne: 'Tis more than need
Have at you then, affection's men-at-arms! (etc.)

Love's Labour's Lost, IV. 3.

And there begins Berowne's wonderful speech about the qualities and effects of love. In *The Dream* there is a good deal of rhyme between the lovers at the beginning, but it is much more fluid: it is more part of the action than the debate of the characters. Here Helena is comforted by Hermia and Lysander because Demetrius loves Hermia and not her:

Hermia: Good speed, fair Helena! Whither away?
Helena: Call you me fair? That 'fair' again unsay.
Demetrius loves your fair. O happy fair!
Your eyes are lodestars, and your tongue's sweet air
More tuneable than lark to shepherd's ear
When wheat is green, when hawthorn buds appear.
Sickness is catching. O, were favour so,
Yours would I catch, fair Hermia, ere I go.
My ear should catch your voice, my eye your eye,
My tongue should catch your tongue's sweet melody.
Were the world mine, Demetrius being bated,
The rest I'd give to you to be translated.
O, teach me how you look, and with what art
You sway the motion of Demetrius' heart.
Hermia: I frown upon him, yet he loves me still.
Helena: O that your frowns would teach my smiles such skill!
Hermia: I give him curses, yet he gives me love.
Helena: O that my prayers could such affection move!
Hermia: The more I hate, the more he follows me.
Helena: The more I love, the more he hateth me.
Hermia: His folly, Helena, is no fault of mine.
Helena: None but your beauty. Would that fault were mine!
Hermia: Take comfort. He no more shall see my face.
Lysander and myself will fly this place.
Before the time I did Lysander see
Seemed Athens as a paradise to me.
O then, what graces in my love do dwell

That he hath turned a heaven unto a hell?
Lysander: Helen, to you our minds we will unfold.
Tomorrow night, when Phoebe doth behold
Her silver visage in the watery glass,
Decking with liquid pearl the bladed grass —
A time that lovers' flights doth still conceal —
Through Athens gates we have devised to steal. (etc.)

A Midsummer-Night's Dream, I. 1.

However, sometimes rhyme is used for more serious purposes, as in *Richard II*, where there are hints of it through the play, heightening the formality of the content. As here, in Gaunt's speech to the Duke of York:

John of Gaunt: Will the King come, that I may breathe my last
In wholesome counsel to his unstaid youth?
York: Vex not yourself, nor strive not with your breath;
For all in vain comes counsel to his ear.
John of Gaunt: O, but they say the tongues of dying men
Enforce attention like deep harmony.
Where words are scarce they are seldom spent in vain,
For they breathe truth that breathe their words in pain.
He that no more must say is listened more
Than they whom youth and ease have taught to glose.
More are men's ends marked than their lives before.
The setting sun, and music at the close,
As the last taste of sweets, is sweetest last,
Writ in remembrance more than things long past.
Though Richard my life's counsel would not hear,
My death's sad tale may yet undeaf his ear.

Richard II, I. 4.

It is interesting to feel the different quality and substance of the writing of these last two passages: same beat, both quite regular and with rhyme, yet the weight of the writing is quite different. For a series of perfectly balanced couplets, look at the Friar's speech to the audience in *Romeo and Juliet*, Act II, Scene 3. We shall be looking at it later to see how the thought is built on antithesis, but for now look to see how the rhyme helps to balance the thought, and how so often we need the caesura in the middle of the line to point up the end.

And the last point is this: when, because of the emotional intensity, the writing gets particularly heightened, it sometimes takes on a poetic form — we have already seen this in the short scene from *As You Like It*. But occasionally it takes on the form of a sonnet, and the most notable example of this happens at the first meeting of Romeo and Juliet. It is a perfect sonnet in that the argument is laid out quite objectively in the first half, the first eight lines; and in the second half, the last six lines, the feeling intensifies and the thought gets more complex. Both are resolved in the last couplet, where the thought and feeling are clinched together. Here the sonnet movement becomes an action, where they each put forward their thoughts in the first half; the pace then quickens as their exchanges become more passionate, and it is resolved in the taking of the kiss after the last two lines. There are then four more lines of verse, and it is broken by the Nurse's unrhymed line:

Romeo: If I profane with my unworthiest hand
  This holy shrine, the gentle sin is this.
My lips, two blushing pilgrims, ready stand
  To smooth that rough touch with a tender kiss.
Juliet: Good pilgrim, you do wrong your hand too much,
  Which mannerly devotion shows in this.
For saints have hands that pilgrims' hands do touch,
  And palm to palm is holy palmers' kiss.
Romeo: Have not saints lips, and holy palmers too?
Juliet: Ay, pilgrim, lips that they must use in prayer.
Romeo: O, then, dear saint, let lips do what hands do!
  They pray: grant thou, lest faith turn to despair.
Juliet: Saints do not move, though grant for prayers' sake.
Romeo: Then move not while my prayer's effect I take.

[*He kisses her.*

Thus from my lips, by thine my sin is purged.
Juliet: Then have my lips the sin that they have took.
Romeo: Sin from my lips? O trespass sweetly urged!
  Give me my sin again.

[*He kisses her.*

Juliet: You kiss by th'book.
Nurse: Madam, your mother craves a word with you.

Romeo and Juliet, I. 5.

It is interesting to notice the religious purity of the metaphor in the sonnet, but that as soon as the kiss is taken, the word play immediately has more licence.

So we have to be alert to rhyme and enjoy using it: for we must remember that pleasure in rhyme is a very basic instinct, which has nothing to do with class or education, simply with a delight in the turning of a word, as in children's rhymes, music-hall songs, etc. (One remembers the delight one had as a child at verses which led you to expect a particular rhyme, usually a rude word, only to find a different word was supplied. Some music-hall songs operate similar devices.) Sometimes Shakespeare turns rhyme to literary use and it becomes bookish, as is often the case in *Love's Labour's Lost* for instance, but on the whole it is quite down to earth and real, and we enjoy it for its inventiveness and wit. We also need to be alert to internal rhymes — that is rhymes which occur within one line; these are often quite subtle, and just have to be listened for. And now to the last variation:

2C: Final rhyming couplets. These are not the same as rhyme within a scene, for they are used quite purposefully to finish off a scene, or part of a scene or a soliloquy: and as such they have a quite specific function, for they carry us with a certain flourish into the next piece of action. They need care because they provide a formal ending to what may have been a free and naturalistic piece of writing; so again it is to do with style. They are a gesture in verbal terms, rather like a music-hall comedian who lifts the end of his act with a song or a drum-roll. And they have a double function: firstly they should quicken our pulse, our interest in the action, for there is always a certain elation to them; and secondly, their artifice makes us conscious of the actor playing a part, and so they remind us of the convention of the play. They also carry a sense of time moving on, and of making us ready for the next piece of action. The rhythm and rhyme of the couplet have to be honoured completely for all this to happen. Perhaps in their very artifice there is a coarseness, and I think this helps the actor to put them across.

They occur a good deal all the way through the plays. Here are a few examples. Hamlet, after he has been told of the appearance of the Ghost of his father, at the end of that scene has a short soliloquy:

Hamlet: My father's spirit! In arms! All is not well.
I doubt some foul play. Would the night were come!
Till then sit still, my soul. Foul deeds will rise,
Though all the earth o'erwhelm them, to men's eyes.

Hamlet, I. 2.

Indeed there are wonderful examples all the way through *Hamlet*, with Claudius, Gertrude and Ophelia, and they are particularly telling as the language in the play is very free and unbound — two of Hamlet's main soliloquies finish with the device. His speech which brings the closet scene to an end, during which he has killed Polonius, ends with one which contains a crude pun on the word 'grave'. He has a further line and a half afterwards, but it is the couplet which is final to the scene, and we feel the movement between the formal and the domestic:

Hamlet: I'll lug the guts into the neighbour room.
Mother, good night. Indeed, this counsellor
Is now most still, most secret and most grave,
Who was in life a foolish prating knave.
Come, sir, to draw toward an end with you.
Good night, mother.

Hamlet, III. 4.

Edmund, in *King Lear*, in mid-plot, having turned his father against his brother by lies — again this is quite coarse:

Edmund: A credulous father and a brother noble,
Whose nature is so far from doing harms
That he suspects none; on whose foolish honesty
My practices ride easy — I see the business:
Let me, if not by birth, have lands by wit;
All with me's meet that I can fashion fit.

King Lear, I. 2.

In *Romeo and Juliet* there is a split rhyming couplet between the end of one scene and the beginning of another. Although the two scenes follow obviously consecutively and fast, there is a humour in the way the couplet works to end one scene and begin another. Benvolio and Mercutio, unaware of Romeo's presence, are looking for him in the grounds of the Capulet household:

ACT II, SCENE 1:

Mercutio: If love be blind, love cannot hit the mark.
Now will he sit under a medlar tree
And wish his mistress were that kind of fruit
As maids call medlars when they laugh alone.
O, Romeo, that she were, O that she were
An open-arse and thou a poppering pear!
Romeo, good-night. I'll to my truckle-bed.
This field-bed is too cold for me to sleep.
Come, shall we go?
Benvolio: Go then, for 'tis in vain
To seek him here that means not to be found.

[*Exuent Benvolio and Mercutio.*

ACT II, SCENE 2:

Romeo: [*coming forward.*
He jests at scars that never felt a wound.

There are endless examples: some, as in *Henry V*, are intended to rouse our spirits and to put our minds on higher things, in this case patriotism:

Henry: . . . Let us deliver
Our puissance into the hand of God,
Putting it straight in expedition.
Cheerly to sea! The signs of war advance!
No King of England if not King of France!

Henry V, II. 2.

But, more often than not, they undercut the feeling and bring us down to basic thinking and practicalities — they always lead to action:

Pandarus: Go to, a bargain made; seal it, seal it, I'll be the witness. Here I hold your hand, here my cousin's. If ever you prove false one to another, since I have taken such pains to bring you together, let all pitiful goers-between be called to the world's end after my name; call them all Pandars. Let all constant men be Troiluses, all false women Cressids, and all brokers-between Pandars! Say, Amen.
Troilus: Amen.
Cressida: Amen.
Pandarus: Amen. Whereupon I will show you a chamber with a bed, which bed, because it shall not speak of your pretty encounters, press it to death; away!

[*Exeunt Troilus and Cressida.*

And Cupid grant all tongue-tied maidens here
Bed, chamber, and Pandar to provide this gear!

Troilus and Cressida, III. 2.

Always there is a sense, soliloquy or not, of provoking a response from the audience.

We have looked quite fully at the basic metre and its variations, and that is the starting point for all our study. Although we may seem to be jumping about, I think it is very good to look at a variety of examples in this way, for, without consciously making a point of it, we begin to be aware of the huge variety of movement and texture which is possible within a line, and therefore how the quality of each play is so different. Even if we do not know the particular play well, the points made will begin to seep into our subconscious, and they will interrelate between the plays.

Once the pulse is firmly established within your head, then you can be free to interpret. Always, while studying a part, go back at intervals to the metre, not to limit what you are doing with it, but to see what more shades of meaning are possible. Test your intention against the metre: small words which seem unimportant, in context of the stress take on a different shade of significance, and enrich the meaning — or rather shift the meaning. The more familiar you become with the metre, the less didactic you can be and so the ambiguities emerge.

Now it seems to me that so often directors and actors limit their choice by taking one of two definite lines of approach. One way is to go with the metre as much as possible, and, within the basic sense, accentuate its regularity. This accentuates a heightened emotional state, is rhetorical in essence, and is also very powerful. It is authoritarian and leaves no room for questions, and so people like it: it is how they think verse should sound. It is, quite crudely, a fascist approach. The second way is basically naturalistic, in that the conversational element is stressed, and the metre disguised as much as possible. I suppose this is what is called a popular approach, taken because it is felt to be more readily understood by a modern audience. But oddly, it does not necessarily make it easier to understand, for the meaning is so often made clear by the rhythm, and in the end it is both reductive and patronizing, for it ignores people's innate response to sound and language. And we may miss something so rich and deep within it. So we must work between these extremes by finding our own response to the language, bearing in mind the metre, the sense and the substance of the words themselves. As Peter Brook would say: there are a million ways of stressing one line. That is no exaggeration.

The metre is by far the most complex factor to explain, because it involves feeling it with your body as well as your mind. However, all other points hang on it: even the prose writing, by the very fact that it is the antithesis of the verse, and we have to be fully aware of the verse beat before we can appreciate the alternative music of the prose. So let us look rather more briefly at the other requirements, and then look at how they fit in to the structure of the whole.

Chapter 4

STRUCTURES, ENERGY, IMAGERY AND SOUND

1 ENERGY THROUGH THE TEXT

Perhaps the most useful thing to realize is this: there is in Shakespeare an energy which runs through the text which is not a naturalistic one; an energy which impels one word to the next, one line to the next, one thought to the next, one speech to the next, and one scene to the next. I would say that there is really not a full-stop until the end of the play; only places where the thought and action pause and change direction. This is the action of the text, and this informs the style of speaking.

Practically this means that actors have to be aware of a sense of continuum. There are many cliches for this: 'keep the ball in the air', 'pass the baton on', whatever. But it is more than that: it is to do with pursuing the thought, and knowing that whatever is said changes the moment and provokes the next thought, and requires more. For instance, falling inflections are usually given as a technical note, as something which is just wrong because it impedes audibility. They are certainly not right when they drop because at that moment you are dropping the energy, and the listener may lose the end of the thought; however, if the thought is being carried through to the end of the line or phrase, knowing that it is active and asking for a response or further thought, the inflection will not fall anyway. But this tendency to drop ends is to do with our modern style of speech which is laconic and understated, and so we have to attune our ears to a different style, a different music, one which is based on a desire to be articulate: both the habit and the expectation are different.

Now obviously we don't want upward inflections at the end of each line; that would be repetitive and false. But the sense of continuum we are after can come in many and subtle ways: by stretching or poising on a word so that it leads us to the next; by different weighting of syllables. And it is this subtlety that we have to practise. When we start on the exercises we shall see that this sense of movement through the word happens best when we are physically involved, and, one step further, when we perceive the thought as movement. I think this is the key.

The crucial thing is this: when we get the sense of one thought leading to another, the speeches become cumulative — i.e., they are not a series of statements which are end-stopped, they always build.

It seems to me that there are three kinds of energy that go through a speech, and which, in their interaction, give the specific movement of the thought. First, there is the ENERGY FROM WORD TO WORD, and for this let us look at Ophelia's soliloquy. To be clear, the choice of passage is arbitrary, for the qualities we are looking at can be found anywhere in the writing, only I am drawn to certain examples as perhaps being particularly clear. Here we find Ophelia alone, having encountered what she sees to be Hamlet's madness, and knowing that Claudius and Polonius have 'heard it all'.

Ophelia: O, what a noble mind is here o'erthrown!
The courtier's, soldier's, scholar's, eye, tongue, sword,
Th'expectancy and rose of the fair state,
The glass of fashion and the mould of form,
Th'observed of all observers, quite, quite, down!
And I, of ladies most deject and wretched,
That sucked the honey of his music vows,
Now see that noble and most sovereign reason
Like sweet bells jangled, out of time and harsh,
That unmatch'd form and feature of blown youth
Blasted with ecstasy. O, woe is me
T'have seen what I have seen, see what I see!

Hamlet, III. 1.

First read it through naturalistically for the sense; then tap the metre out gently — you will see it is quite regular except for line 10, where 'blasted' breaks the metre and so takes the emotional weight of the speech. The word pin-points her recognition of his state, and so the possibility of her own depths. (To quote from *Sonnet 65* of Hopkins:

O the mind, mind has mountains; cliffs of fall
Frightful, sheer, no-man-fathomed.

but that is by the way.) If you now read it, not in clumps of sense but word by word, you will see how one word informs the next, how the small joining words such as 'and', 'now', 'like', 'that' make the following word that much more telling, and so how the picture she paints is cumulative. So read it, just filling each word as it happens, yet keeping the overall sense in your mind, and find out just how much each word contributes.

Among other things you will notice:

Line 1 'what' takes on a specific quantative value, as if measuring the nobility of the mind;
How the first four words get us ready for 'mind';
'o'erthrown' becomes violent.

Line 2 the list of people with their attributes is cumulative.

Line 3 More elaborate: 'expectancy and rose' containing so much to do with what could be.

Line 4 The 'glass' even of 'fashion', and not only that the 'mould of form' — and not only that —

Line 5 'Th'observed of all observers'; the repetition of 'quite', the second taking the first even further, and coming to rest on the full word 'down'.

Line 6 'And I' — the antithesis of Hamlet — and this 'I' has to remain in our mind until we pick the main clause up again two lines on.
'most' is important; 'and' is cumulative to 'wretched'.

Line 7 A wonderful unexpected piece of information.

Line 8 Picks up from 'And I', and places us in time with 'Now . . . noble and most sovereign reason'.

Line 9 A metaphor here to keep the suspense of the whole, and to keep our minds on what has been in tune.

Line 10 'unmatch'd' is the sum of all so far; 'blown' has an odd resonance in context with 'youth'; the images lift us and the whole line suspends so that the following has full impact.

Line 11 The effect of 'Blasted' in contrast is violent and ugly; 'O, woe is me' — the two 'OH' sounds seem to gather all that has gone before.

Line 12 A regular line, contained. Notice the change of tense.

You will no doubt hear other things in it, for different words hit you at different times and suddenly become full. What matters now is that we learn of the energy that leads from word to word, that each small word has its place and adds to the meaning of the emotive word. Do not worry about the time it takes: once you find how active each word is you can let it go, but the awareness will remain.

One other thing about the speech as a whole: you will notice that the subject or matter of the speech is given in the first line; subsequently the thoughts are investigated and discovered around that subject, until the conclusion 'blasted with ecstasy'. And this shape, in variable form, is common throughout the writing. We will deal with this idea of structure in detail later, but it is something we should start to be aware of. Here the last line and a half are as a coda to the main part of the speech, as if Ophelia is bringing the predicament contained in it back to herself.

Next, let us look at the ENERGY FROM LINE TO LINE, which is something quite readily felt in the more formally poetic writing, particularly in the early plays. Practically it means that the line drives through to the final word, and that word then activates the following line. It impels the thought through regardless of punctuation. For instance, you would have to work quite hard to deny the line endings in the following:

Chorus: O for a Muse of fire, that would *ascend*
The brightest heaven of *invention*,
A kingdom for a stage, princes to *act*,
And monarchs to behold the swelling *scene*!
Then should the warlike Harry, like *himself*,
Assume the port of Mars, and at his *heels*,
Leashed in like hounds, should famine, sword and *fire*
Crouch for employment . . .

Henry V, I.1.

Indeed it would sound faintly ridiculous if you did not mark them. We need them pointed up, not just to satisfy our ear, but to serve up the extravagance of the thought, which will be undercut later. 'Ascend' points up the following line and makes it even more extravagant: 'invention' needs to be lifted, for it is that which is detailed in the next part of the speech. We need 'act' lifted because it feeds the next thought, and so on. A wonderful example to look at is the Chorus to Act IV in the same play, where you will hear very clearly the movement of the story through. Indeed, you can take it a step further, and by just speaking the last word in each line, you will get an impressionistic picture of the whole — this is often interesting to do within a character.

In *Henry V*, as in the other histories, the ends of the thoughts and the ends of the lines tend to coincide more, and so the issue is relatively simple. But in the more complex writing where the thoughts are convoluted, this is not so, and we have to be quite specific about our choices. We have to feel the impelling of the line forward as part of its pulse, and of how the thought unfolds. Still thinking only of line endings, look at this next passage:

Macbeth: If it were done when 'tis done, then 'twere *well*
It were done quickly. If the *assassination*
Could trammel up the consequence, and *catch*
With his surcease success — that but this *blow*
Might be the be-all and the end-all! — *here*,
But here, upon this bank and shoal of *time*,
We'd jump the life to come. But in these cases. . .

Macbeth, I.7.

We will look at this in more detail later, but for now read these lines twice through: first for sense only, quite naturalistically; then read them consciously lifting the words in italic, and notice how they open up and activate the next line. 'well' becomes active, in that it is measuring up the situation; 'assassination' has to be marked, for it is the first time Macbeth has put a name to the deed; 'catch' carries such immediacy, pointing up both the chance nature of an act and the moment of the action; 'here' confirms this sense of catching the moment and leads us to 'but here' and to 'time', the subject of this whole thought. As the speech progresses the line endings become less defined, and this reinforces the sense that his thoughts get out of control.

And thirdly, let us consider the energy from THOUGHT TO THOUGHT: the following passage is quite jagged, and the thoughts are palpably self-feeding.

It is a speech of Claudio from *Measure for Measure*, and in it he pleads with his sister for her compassion. Claudio is under sentence of death for fornication: and Angelo, the Duke's deputy who is enforcing the puritanical law, has made a bargain with Isabella that if she sleeps with him he will spare her brother's life. This thought is repugnant to her and her whole set of moral values: she tells her brother of the proposition, certain that he will repudiate the idea out of his own sense of honour. Claudio, however, does not, and here uses all his wits to appeal to his sister. In the early part of the scene he has begun to realize the weight of her intransigence which has been strengthened by her life within a religious order; so the speech is therefore not someone musing upon death, but someone thinking on the spot of all the reasons why he wants to live. It is therefore active, and acts on him as he speaks it, for he becomes overwhelmed at the thought of death.

Read it through first quite naturalistically, for sense only: then read it driving through to the words in italic, noticing on the way the joining words like 'and', 'but' and 'or' and how they change the direction of the thought and feed the cumulative power of the whole.

Claudio: Ay, but to *die*, and go we know not *where*,
To lie in cold obstruction and to *rot*;
This sensible warm motion to become
A kneaded *clod*; and the delighted spirit
To bathe in fiery *floods*, or to reside
In thrilling region of thick-ribbèd *ice*,
To be imprisoned in the viewless winds
And blown with restless violence round about
The pendent *world*; or to be worse than worst
Of those that lawless and incertain thought
Imagine *howling*, 'tis too *horrible*.
The weariest and most loathèd worldly life
That age, ache, penury, and imprisonment
Can lay on nature is a paradise
To what we fear of *death*. *Measure for Measure*, III.1.

This is a powerful argument requiring an answer. And it is interesting in that the length of thoughts varies a good deal — you may choose to break it up slightly differently. What I want you to feel is how one thought impels the next. Now read it one more time, being also aware of the line endings. Here are some of the things you will notice:

Line 1 'Ay but to die, and go we know not where': this is the subject of the speech, the departure point, and he goes on to explore the idea in relation to himself. It is what is beyond death that he is afraid of, so that 'where' takes on a larger meaning if we lift it — it starts our imagination working.

Line 2 Adds to the previous line, and brings us up short with 'rot'.

Line 3 'sensible warm motion' is the antithesis of 'kneaded clod', and so needs pointing up.
'become' — this is an active word: i.e., it does not merely serve the grammatical meaning; something has to happen in order that you become a 'kneaded clod', and it lifts us into that image.

Line 4 'the delighted spirit': this needs a moment for us to take in the image, and it also has to stay in our minds right down to 'pendent world'.

Line 7 'winds' — springs us into the next line.

Line 9 'worse than worst': this is a cumulative image, and we have to get its full implication. 'worst' becomes something quite positive, as if 'worst' was a definite state.

Line 12 'life', 'paradise', and 'death': these all need throwing up as they are in balance with each other.

Line 15 The speech ends with a short line, which is not filled by Isabella.

> The images become wilder and less specific as he gets caught up with his own fearful imaginings; it is self-feeding, and 'horrible' is the sum of them. The speech takes on a particular poignancy because of their close family knowledge of each other.

So all these different energies are going on within the speech, and the more we become aware of this life, the more the possibilities will open up. You will notice that when you read it for sense only it is the large emotive words that we tend to emphasize: but when you read it aware of this through energy, then each word takes its particular place in the whole, continually shifting the sense.

Now let us look at the ENERGY FROM SPEECH TO SPEECH: here is part of a scene from *Richard II*. We have already looked at its final couplet. In it the King's followers, Bushy, Bagot and Green, decide on their action in the face of Bolingbroke's power. It has a quite remarkable collective music.

Bushy: The wind sits fair for news to go for Ireland,
But none returns. For us to levy power
Proportionable to the enemy
Is all unpossible.
Green: Besides, our nearness to the King in love
Is near the hate of those love not the King.
Bagot: And that is the wavering commons; for their love
Lies in their purses, and whoso empties them
By so much fills their hearts with deadly hate.
Bushy: Wherein the King stands generally condemned.
Bagot: If judgement lie in them, then so do we,
Because we ever have been near the King.
Green: Well, I will for refuge straight to Bristol Castle.
The Earl of Wiltshire is already there.
Bushy: Thither will I with you; for little office
Will the hateful commons perform for us —
Except like curs to tear us all to pieces.
Will you go along with us?
Bagot: No, I will to Ireland to his majesty.
Farewell. If heart's presages be not vain,
We three here part that ne'er shall meet again.
Bushy: That's as York thrives to beat back Bolingbroke.
Green: Alas, poor Duke! The task he undertakes
Is numbering sands and drinking oceans dry.
Where one on his side fights, thousands will fly.
Bagot: Farewell at once, for once, for all, and ever.
Bushy: Well, we may meet again.
Bagot: I fear me, never.

Richard II, II.2.

Here we can hear so clearly how one speech provokes the next, as each character is both thinking his way through the situation, and feeling the others out. It is metrically quite tricky: at least three of the lines are irregular and rock a bit. This reinforces the feeling of insecurity, but as they become clearer of purpose the rhythm firms up, and, as we have already noted, it ends very formally with two rhyming couplets shared between them.

You will also notice the joining words 'besides', 'and', 'for', 'wherein', 'because', 'well', and how they facilitate the picking up of each others' thoughts, and shift them into a new direction.

Also what is interesting, and an area that we so often miss out on when we are acting Shakespeare, is their common vocabulary: because they are individually so plugged into the situation, there are common ladders of thought running through the scene, so that the language is picked up from character to character. This happens all through Shakespeare: the scene can be strongly emotional but the ladders will be there. Here of course the vocabulary is political, and I have picked out the ladders as I see them. You might pick out different ones:

wind — news — Ireland
none — returns — power
Proportionable — enemy
unpossible
nearness — King — love
near — hate — love not — King
commons — love
purses — empties them
fills — hearts — hate
King — condemned
judgement — them — we
we — near — King
refuge — Bristol Castle
Earl of Wiltshire — there
Thither — I — you
hateful commons — us
curs — tear — pieces
you — us
I — Ireland — Majesty
heart's presages — vain
We three — ne'er — meet
York — Bolingbroke
Duke — task
numbering sands — oceans dry
one fights — thousands — fly
Farewell — ever
may meet — never

To set these words down in this way is not to do with emphasis, quite the reverse: they would only be emphasized if they felt unfamiliar. And in any case, to be emphatic stops the possibilities, and these words accumulate meanings and pressures as they go. The three are not making statements, they are pursuing the possibilities of action, and through the argument they reach an uneasy conclusion. These ladders of thought are part of the through energy of the play.

So we have looked at the different energies going through a speech or series of speeches: it is, I know, difficult to switch from example to example, yet the advantage is that we begin to feel the elements in our bones and begin to be aware of the permutations within the line, so that in the end we do not have to work at them. But it would be a good thing to try it all out on something you know, to which you have a particular attitude as an actor, and find how this awareness of energy informs that text and character.

2 ANTITHESIS

This is really most important to come to terms with, for the writing is built on an extensive use of antithesis.

Briefly, it means the contrasting of two ideas by using words of opposite meaning in consecutive clauses, and the audience's understanding of a text hinges very much on how the actor deals with this. And of course sometimes the complexity of the thought obscures the antithetical words, and they have to be looked for. So again, not by emphasis but by awareness, the actor has to be in tune with this way of thinking, and he has to be able to lift these opposites so that they catch the attention of the hearer, for it is through this rhetorical device that the argument is presented. And this is what gives the writing so much vigour, because it is between extremes that a character operates and thinks.

A simple example is the beginning of *Sonnet 138:*

> When my love swears that she is made of truth
> I do believe her, though I know she lies. . .

The argument is built round those two extremes, 'truth' and 'lies', and the shades of truth that lie in between. It is a rich sonnet, full of puns, made richer by the extravagance of the initial thought.

Or there is this speech of Romeo where, after the initial concept — 'Here's much to-do with hate, yet more with love' — the opposites pour out in consecutive words: 'O brawling love, O loving hate', etc., and through them we are immediately in tune with the inner turmoil of youth.

Romeo: Alas that love, whose view is muffled, still
Should without eyes see pathways to his will!
Where shall we dine? O me, what fray was here?
Yet tell me not, for I have heard it all.
Here's much to-do with hate, but more with love.
Why then, O brawling love, O loving hate,
O anything, of nothing first create!
O heavy lightness, serious vanity,
Misshapen chaos of well-seeming forms,
Feather of lead, bright smoke, cold fire, sick health,
Still-waking sleep, that is not what it is!
This love feel I, that feel no love in this.
Dost thou not laugh?
Benvolio: No, coz, I rather weep.

Romeo and Juliet, I.1.

And Benvolio finishes the antithesis.

Later in the play, Act II, Scene 3, the Friar presents his philosophy in terms of the balance of nature. This is a useful speech to look at, for it makes you see how the antithetical thought is informing everything, while the precise terms are not immediately apparent. Read the speech through twice, once for sense, and then read it through tapping your hand on something on all the antithetical words — this is an excellent exercise which we will expand on later. Here are some of the antitheses you will pick out:

The *day* to cheer and *night*'s dank dew to dry,

The earth that's nature's *mother* is her *tomb*.
What is her burying *grave*, that is her *womb*;

For naught so *vile* that on the earth doth live
But to the earth some special *good* doth give;
Nor aught so *good* but, strained from that fair use,
Revolts from true birth, stumbling on *abuse*.
Virtue itself *turns vice*, being *misapplied*,
And *vice* sometime's by *action dignified*.

Poison hath *residence*, and *medicine power*.

As he elaborates this theme, so the antitheses get more elaborate: you have to keep more than one in the air at the same time, and some you only discover when you have gone past them. But that does not matter; the important thing is to be aware of the pattern of thought. In the next two lines you have three parts to the antithesis:

For *this*, being *smelt*, with that part *cheers each part*;
Being *tasted*, stays *all senses* with the *heart*.

And then the summing-up:

> *Two* such *opposèd kings* encamp them still
> In *man* as well as *herbs* — *grace* and *rude will.*
> And where the worser is predominant,
> Full soon the canker death eats up that plant.

So the Friar presents his philosophy of the checks and balances of nature: the healing power of herbs and also the poison inherent in them if not used properly: and we see this pragmatism as part of his nature — the very fact that he accepts and does not take sides is the very quality that contributes to the final tragedy.

And this awareness of opposites is part of the life-blood of the writing. For we cannot think or talk of 'good' without having a notion of 'evil'; of 'honour' without 'dishonour'; 'something' and 'nothing'; 'silence' and 'speech'; 'dreams' and 'reality'; 'life' and 'death'; 'truth' and falsehood' and so on. And it enriches our whole perception of the world. It also subconsciously puts us in touch with a whole spectrum of colour and meaning between these opposities. I remember once hearing an Olympic long-distance runner (I am afraid I cannot remember who) talking of how he trained running through the night; and, asked how he felt while he was running, he replied to the effect that he wished there were fifteen words for 'tired', for each stage of tiredness he went through was different. What is important is that it teaches us never to generalize or be descriptive, but that words are always in relation to other words. Our thinking then becomes more defined.

Now, obviously, every page has got examples jumping out at us, but here are four I would like to hook our minds on. The first is *Sonnet 29*:

> When, in disgrace with Fortune and men's eyes,
> I all alone beweep my outcast state,
> And trouble deaf heaven with my bootless cries,
> And look upon myself and curse my fate —
> Wishing me like to one more rich in hope,
> Featur'd like him, like him with friends possess'd,
> Desiring this man's art and that man's scope,
> With what I most enjoy contented least;
> Yet in these thoughts myself almost despising
> Haply I think on thee, and then my state,
> Like to the lark at break of day arising
> From sullen earth, sings hymns at heaven's gate:
>   For thy sweet love remember'd such wealth brings
>   That then I scorn to change my state with kings.

You will notice:

The whole first part of the sonnet is in antithesis to the second.

> The state of disgrace builds through the first nine lines, each image adding to the previous one, until — 'Haply I think on thee, and then my state . . .' and from thereon he describes his reverse state.
>
> The extravagance, and seriousness of the images, lend both perspective and humour — an ability to look at oneself from the outside.
>
> The grace is sweeter because of the intensity of the disgrace.

I wanted to look at this sonnet particularly, because so often within a character the antithesis is laid for a number of lines before you get to the reverse side, yet we must always be aware of the reverse for that is what gives us the thought movement through.

The next example from *Troilus and Cressida* is interesting. The speeches occur near the end of their first meeting — the meeting that Pandarus has arranged — and the images accumulate. However, you will notice:

> That Troilus swears by truth, and Cressida swears by not being false.
>
> That Troilus' images are clear, uncompromising and affirmative.
>
> That Cressida's images have an awareness of destruction.
>
> Therefore the images themselves are indirectly antithetical.
>
> And just in that difference we get an idea of the social forces which inform their thinking — i.e., that a man makes his own destiny, while a woman is at the mercy of outside circumstances. The very choice of the word 'false' is perhaps the worm in the bud.

Troilus: O virtuous fight,
When right with right wars who shall be most right!
True swains in love shall in the world to come
Approve their truths by Troilus; when their rhymes,
Full of protest, of oath, and big compare,
Want similes, truth tired with iteration –
'As true as steel, as plantage to the moon,
As sun to day, as turtle to her mate,
As iron to adamant, as earth to th'centre,'
Yet, after all comparisons of truth,
As truth's authentic author to be cited,
'As true as Troilus' shall crown up the verse,
And sanctify the numbers.
Cressida: Prophet may you be!
If I be false, or swerve a hair from truth,
When time is old and hath forgot itself,

When waterdrops have worn the stones of Troy,
And blind oblivion swallowed cities up,
And mighty states characterless are grated
To dusty nothing; yet let memory,
From false to false among false maids in love,
Upbraid my falsehood! When they've said, 'As false
As air, as water, wind, or sandy earth,
As fox to lamb, as wolf to heifer's calf,
Pard to the hind, or stepdame to her son' —
Yea, let them say, to stick the heart of falsehood,
'As false as Cressid.'

Troilus and Cressida, III.2.

Or, you can look for yourself at Hamlet's speech to Gertrude, Act III, Scene 4, where he forces her to look at the picture of his father and of Claudius, and from there elaborates on their opposite characters. Here the antithesis is straightforward and formal, as indeed it is in the central speech of the play 'To be or not to be . . . '

And fourthly, something more complex between Leontes and Hermione in *The Winter's Tale*, first about dreams and reality:

Hermione: Sir,
You speak a language which I understand not.
My life stands in the level of your dreams,
Which I'll lay down.
Leontes: Your actions are my dreams.

And a few lines later, on being threatened with death:

Hermione: Sir, spare your threats!
The bug with which you fright me with I seek.
To me can life be no commodity:
The crown and comfort of my life, your favour,
I do give lost, for I do feel it gone,
But know not where it went. My second joy,
And first-fruits of my body, from his presence
I am barred, like one infectious. My third comfort,
Starred most unluckily, is from my breast —
The innocent milk in its most innocent mouth —
Haled out to murder. Myself on every post
Proclaimed a strumpet; with immodest hatred
The childbed privilege denied, which 'longs
To women of all fashion; lastly, hurried
Here to this place, i'th'open air, before
I have got strength of limit. Now, my liege,
Tell me what blessings I have here alive
That I should fear to die.

The Winter's Tale, III.2.

The first interchange shows how one character so often responds in terms of the antithesis begun by another. The second passage shows how the building of an antithesis over a number of lines can make the reverse side stronger and more poignant when we get to it.

So, as actors, we have to be ready for the possibility of the opposites all the time, for the argument so often hinges on them, however indirectly. And these opposites have to be given to the audience in such a way that they clarify and balance, and do not confuse.

But also, this awareness of antithesis continually enriches our perception. Look for a moment at the first scene of *King Lear*, from the point where he starts to divide the kingdom, and read from Line 36, 'meantime we shall express our darker purpose', to Line 90, 'Nothing will come of nothing. Speak again.' If you read that through, as we did with an earlier passage, tapping your fingers this time on all the words which deal with property and ownership, you will find that everything he says has to do with quantity — how much — even his notion of love is mixed up with this. But further, because this sense of property has built up through the language of part of a scene, where even the names such as Burgundy and France carry with them the implication of land, when Cordelia finally says 'Nothing', that word carries a whole dimension of meaning: its value is defined in a quite specific way, and its meaning is huge. This is part of the fabric of the language — what is going on underneath the logical meaning.

3 SUBSTANCE OF THE WORD

I mean by this the energy of the word in relation to its meaning. We have already touched on this, both in the passage on muscularity in Chapter One, where we looked at the varying weight of the words in the speech of Cordelia: and also it was very much part of our analysis of metre, where we saw the permutations of long and short vowels in stressed and unstressed positions. So let us look quite specifically at this question of weight.

Technically this is to do with the syllabic length of a word: that is

a) the length of the vowel, in conjunction with
b) the number and length of the consonants, and
c) the number of syllables to the word.

Milton, for instance, built his verse quantitively. Here are two short passages, one from *L'Allegro* and one from *Il Penseroso*. In each case there are four beats to the line, and the syllables in both vary between seven and eight. But notice how short and light the first passage is in comparison with the second.

Haste thee nymph, and bring with thee
Jest and youthful Jollity,
Quips and Cranks, and wanton Wiles,
Nods, and Becks, and wreathed Smiles,
Such as hang on Hebe's cheek,
And love to live in dimple sleek:

L'Allegro

Sweet Bird that shunn'st the noise of folly,
Most musicall, most melancholy!
Thee Chauntress oft the Woods among,
I woo to hear thy eeven Song;
And missing thee, I walk unseen
On the dry smooth-shaven Green,
To behold the wandring Moon,
Riding neer her highest noon,
Like one that had bin led astray
Through the Heav'ns wide pathless way:

Il Penseroso

It is good just to read it and hear the difference. There are wonderful passages in Milton: for instance, in *Samson Agonistes* the Messenger has lines like:

To heave, pull, draw or break, he still perform'd
All with incredible stupendious force . . .

or:

As with the force of winds and waters pent
When Mountains tremble, those two massie Pillars
With horrible convulsion to and fro,
He tugg'd, he shook, till down they came and drew
The whole roof after them, with burst of thunder
Upon the heads of all who sat beneath . . .

The lines are so full of voiced continuant consonants they simply cannot be hurried. Try to speak them quickly and you can't, they don't make sense.

So, VOWELS vary both in length and openness: triphthongs and diphthongs are intrinsically long:

OUR	as in hour
IRE	as in hire
EAR	as in fear
AIR	as in fair
OH	as in cold

OW	as in sound
OI	as in boy
AY	as in safe
I	as in buy

Also intrinsically long are the monothongs:

OO	as in fool
AW	as in bought
AH	as in fast
ER	as in bird or the first syllable of murmur
EE	as in beef

and the following vowels are intrinsically short:

oo	as in cook
o	as in hot
u	as in hut
er	as in the second syllable of murmur
a	as in have
e	as in left
i	as in wish

I say intrinsically long or short because that is part of the quality of the vowel, but within its shape the length can vary considerably.

Consonants. Consonants fall into four groups, the longest being the continuant voiced consonants, which are:

v	as in vain	leave	live
z	as in zeal	raise	has
soft GE	as in leisure		
L	as in leaf	feel	full
N	as in near	line	can
M	as in might	fame	limb
NG	as in		ring
R	as in rich	carry	

and combinations of these are very long.

Slightly shorter are the devoiced continuants:

f	as in fine	laugh	rough
s	as in soul	lease	loss
sh	as in shower	rouche	cash

Shorter still are voiced plosive consonants:

B	as in barn	kerb	rub
D	as in deal	food	hood
G	as in goat	vague	wig

DG	as in jest	large	bridge

And the shortest are the unvoiced plosives:

p	as in pine	heap	tip
t	as in tone	boat	cat
k	as in kick	leak	lick

As you will see, they are always at their shortest at the beginning of a word, and the length at the end can vary a good deal, particularly with a continuant. Combinations of consonants, say two continuants and a plosive can be very long. Also you will notice I have given two examples of final consonants, one with a preceding long vowel, and one with a preceding short vowel, as this also varies the timing.

I have given these sounds in some detail, although I know that a lot of it will be familiar to you, so that we hear afresh the enormous difference in syllable length. For, and this is important, very often the cause of lack of clarity is to do with the actor not allowing for this length — not giving the consonants their room — and this is not to do with speaking slowly, simply of being aware of their timing. That is the practical part; the other part of course is to do with being sensitive to the quality of the thought. I have only briefly gone through the sounds, and if you want a thorough analysis of vowels and consonants, please see Chapter Three of *Voice and the Actor*.

Here are several sequences of vowels with different following consonants. You will notice the variation in vowel length; also that a final 'l' makes it particularly long, and that a word without a final consonant can be as long or as short as you please.

shoot — chew — choose — chewed
caught — store — coarse — call — cause — caused — called
heart — hard — charred — charge — charged
hoot — hoof — whose — hooves
hat — has — had — ham — hand — hands
put — push — pull — pulled
chase — chain — change — changed
back — bag — backed — bang — banged
wit — wish — witch — wished — bridge — swinge
feet — fee — feed — feel — feels
pest — fence — fell — self — ledge — pledged — selves
house — how — mouth — howl — mound — mouths

right — rice — high — rhyme — rind — thrive — thrives

Consonants at the beginning of a word affect its quality, but the length very little.

Number of syllables. The number of syllables in a word also affects the time we take. Lines which have two- and three-syllable words have a totally different feel: the syllables tend to be less full and we speak them more quickly, and the sound becomes more clipped. For us, the interesting thing to note is that after a series of multi-syllabic lines, a line of single syllable words has a particular effect: it takes on a different depth as we move from the sophisticated to the simple.

With all this in mind, let us look again at Cordelia's speech on page 28. If you read it through slowly, attending to each word, here are some of the things you will notice:

Line 1 'Alack' — a short vowel, with a devoiced 'k' at the end, but open so it has possibilities of length.
'he' — long vowel in a stressed position, open-ended, so you can sit on it.
'met' — short. End of line movement quick.

Line 2 'mad' — a short vowel, but open, and with a voiced consonant at the end. Further, it has two 'a' sounds on either side — 'as' — and this oddly gives it emphasis. The openness of the vowel opens its possibilities of meaning, and makes it able to relate to 'sea' in the breadth of its concept.
'sea' — infinitely long, it has no consonant to bound it, and so is open to the possibility of the image.
'vexed' — a short vowel, but the word is full, with three devoiced consonants at the end, 'k', 's' and 't', thus involving movement in the making of it. The combination of consonants takes time to speak, though they are not heavy sounds. Moreover it starts smoothly with 'v'. It is in an unstressed position, yet it is important because it qualifies 'sea', and is an odd word to use, but crucial to our understanding of Lear's state of mind.
A choppy movement before the smoothness of 'singing aloud'.

Line 3 'Crowned' — breaks the metre, and takes the metrical weight of the line, and is long against 'fumiter and furrow-weeds'.
'rank' — a short vowel, but with a nasal continuant and a devoiced consonant at the end, so takes a bit of time. Jarring quality.

Line 4 This line — full of short light syllables, devoiced consonants, broken metre.

Line 5 'Darnel' breaks the metre. But then 'all', 'idle', 'weeds', 'grow' — all long full and open vowels,, with regular metre, carried through to the next line, and leading us to

Line 6 'our sustaining corn' — all long open sounds, at their longest because of the continuant consonants, and somehow it emotionally touches down.

Line 7 'Search' — long open vowel, with the aspirate 'tsh' at the end, peremptory in sound. 'high-grown field' — long sounds.
'field' — substantial with the final 'l' and 'd'. Commanding.

Line 8 'What can man's wisdom' — the two monosyllabic 'a' words both take on weight. The ordinary word 'can' taking on a particular responsibility in the line as it seems the word 'do' is implicit in the meaning. And because it is a simple word taking on so much weight, it has a curious reaching effort contained within it. The two adjacent words with the same vowel seem to hold the line up.

Line 9 A very full line: 'bereavèd' — long vowel with full voiced consonants is very active. 'sense' — short vowel, but because of the final 'n' and quite long 's' you can take quite a bit of time with it.

Line 10 Last line quite simple and straightforward.

What is wonderful about this piece of writing is its sensibility to man in terms of nature, and through the choice and substance of the words, we sense where Cordelia lives, in the realm of healing nature.

Keeping this idea of quantity in our mind, look again at the speech of Brutus from *Coriolanus*, which we looked at on page 39. I will not go through it in detail, but read it carefully through for yourself, and notice:

The predominance of long vowels: e.g. 'all', 'stalls', 'reechy', 'spoil', 'powers', etc.

When the vowels are short, they are given length by the combination of consonants: e.g., 'bulks', 'tongues', 'kisses', 'filled'.

Long combinations of consonants: 'walls', 'horsed', 'ridges', 'dames'.

The large number of two-and three-syllable words.

This fullness in the language combines to give us the sense of extreme frustration which Brutus feels, plus the effort of releasing this into words. And, as I said earlier, it all accumulates until the word 'pother' which undercuts it all, and leads us to the absurdity of the last thought.

I do not want this attention to detail to make our work seem difficult, because it is not. I know some people may be put off by this kind of analysis of text, but this is only because we are reading about it and so it makes it seem studied. The exercises should dispel any such feeling, for it is certainly the physical pleasure in the language we are after, and the resonances of the sounds should be discovered by uttering them and not by reading about them.

And so, later, we will find the special energy which happens when we bring all these verbal components together with the rhythm and the meaning. And this is more than talking about assonance, or alliteration or onomatopoeia, which are intellectual concepts. What I feel to be important is this: it is quite probable that linguistically we made open sounds before we made closed ones; and that therefore the vowel carries our instinctive, primitive meanings, while the consonants break those meanings up into logical sense. If we take this view, then we need to consider afresh how we give ourselves to the vowels, and how we use their movement and length, for this gives us the dynamic of the word.

And this goes right through to our investigation of character. Let us look at five passages, all of very different substance. First, look back at the short passage from Macbeth's soliloquy on page 86, where you will see how the syllabic lengths contribute, not only to the through energy which we were considering then, but to his own self-absorbed contention between his reason and emotion. It is full of short vowels, devoiced consonants, multi-syllabic words until he gets to the word 'time', and then a new movement starts.

Here, from *Coriolanus*, is part of a speech of Aufidius, the leader of the Volsces, to whom Coriolanus defects when he turns his back on Rome. Here the two meet for the first time in peace. Martius Coriolanus has given himself up to Aufidius, not knowing what the reaction will be, and the reply comes:

Aufidius: O Martius, Martius!
Each word thou has spoke has weeded from my heart
A root of ancient envy. If Jupiter
Should from yond cloud speak divine things,
And say 'Tis true', I'd not believe them more
Than thee, all-noble Martius. Let me twine
Mine arms about that body, where against
My grainèd ash an hundred times hath broke
And scarred the moon with splinters. Here I clip
The anvil of my sword, and do contest
As hotly and as nobly with thy love
As ever in ambitious strength I did
Contend against thy valour. Know thou first,
I loved the maid I married; never man
Sighed truer breath. But that I see thee here,
Thou noble thing, more dances my rapt heart

Than when I first my wedded mistress saw
Bestride my threshold. Why, thou Mars, I tell thee . . .

Coriolanus, IV.5.

You will notice the very muscular language.

The thoughts are long and quite intricately formed, and together with the long vowels and quite hard consonants, it is sensual and strong. Not only with the repetition of the name, but in the images themselves, the sense of the body is very present.

Thirdly, a passage from *Richard III*, where the atavistic feeling of the three women is born out by the liturgical rhythm: the open long vowels with hard initial consonants, and the predominance of dark voiced consonants; the regularity of the sense stress with the metre stress. There is no contention here, no argument, but it all bears out the feeling of grief and the hunger for revenge.

Duchess of York:
I had a Richard too, and thou didst kill him;
I had a Rutland too, and thou holp'st to kill him.
Queen Margaret:
Thou hadst a Clarence too, and Richard killed him.
From forth the kennel of thy womb hath crept
A hellhound that doth hunt us all to death.
That dog, that had his teeth before his eyes,
To worry lambs and lap their gentle blood,
That foul defacer of God's handiwork
That reigns in galled eyes and weeping souls
That excellent grand tyrant of the earth
Thy womb let loose to chase us to our graves.
O upright, just, and true-disposing God,
How do I thank Thee that this carnal cur
Preys on the issue of his mother's body
And makes her pew-fellow with others' moan!
Duchess of York:
O Harry's wife, triumph not in my woes!
God witness with me I have wept for thine.
Queen Margaret:
Bear with me! I am hungry for revenge,
And now I cloy me with beholding it.
Thy Edward he is dead, that killed my Edward;
Thy other Edward dead, to quit my Edward. . .

Richard III, IV.4

And so, with the help of various forms of rhetorical patterns, they tell of their woes, and of their combined hatred of Richard: very formal, not subtle — the opposite in fact of Richard's agile political thinking. The stressing is emotional and heavy.

Fourth, something totally different, this speech of Theseus from *A Midsummer-Night's Dream*. It is cool and unstressed and not at all didactic. Theseus and Hippolyta, who have been untouched by the magic of the forest, talk of the night's happenings. Theseus gently mocks the simplicity of the lovers, and, with 'cool reason' philosophizes on the nature of reality and imagination, placing the poet with the lunatic.

Hippolyta: 'Tis strange, my Theseus, that these lovers speak of.
Theseus: More strange than true. I never may believe
These antique fables, nor these fairy toys.
Lovers and madmen have such seething brains,
Such shaping fantasies, that apprehend
More than cool reason ever comprehends.
The lunatic, the lover, and the poet
Are of imagination all compact.
One sees more devils than vast hell can hold.
That is the madman. The lover, all as frantic,
Sees Helen's beauty in a brow of Egypt.
The poet's eye, in a fine frenzy rolling,
Doth glance from heaven to earth, from earth to heaven,
And as imagination bodies forth
The forms of things unknown, the poet's pen
Turns them to shapes, and gives to airy nothing
A local habitation and a name.
Such tricks hath strong imagination
That if it would but apprehend some joy,
It comprehends some bringer of that joy.
Or in the night, imagining some fear,
How easy is a bush supposed a bear?
Hippolyta: But all the story of the night told over,
And all their minds transfigured so together,
More witnesseth than fancy's images,
And grows to something of great constancy;
But howsoever, strange and admirable.

A Midsummer-Night's Dream, V.1.

There is nothing dramatic to notice, but it is just such a wonderful passage. Notice simply:

The light flowing quality.

The sense of feeling your way through the thoughts, and giving them shape.

Light, two-syllable words — 'poet', 'lover', 'beauty'.

Very few initial voiced plosives — 'devil', 'beauty', 'brow', 'bodies' — they therefore become marked.

Feminine endings — 'frantic', 'rolling', 'Egypt', 'heaven', 'nothing', 'imagination'.

Open vowels, many unbounded — 'joy', 'fear', 'bear', and all of Hippolyta's lines. This adds to the sense of inquiry.

Finally, go through this part of a Chorus from *Henry V*, not preconceiving what it means, but hearing what is happening in the sounds, that they are part of the active imagery. Don't be poetic about it, just let the sounds free, and let them be surprising:

Chorus: Now entertain conjecture of a time
When creeping murmur and the poring dark
Fills the wide vessel of the universe.
From camp to camp, through the foul womb of night,
The hum of either army stilly sounds,
That the fixed sentinels almost receive
The secret whispers of each other's watch.
Fire answers fire, and through their paly flames
Each battle sees the other's umbered face.
Steed threatens steed, in high and boastful neighs,
Piercing the night's dull ear; and from the tents
The armourers, accomplishing the knights,
With busy hammers closing rivets up,
Give dreadful note of preparation.
The country cocks do crow, the clocks do toll,
And the third hour of drowsy morning name. . .

Henry V, IV.1.

How the actor works the Chorus depends on the precise relationship he builds with his audience. I think there can be great wit in the notion that he is supplying everything that the play needs in terms of scenery — ships, armies; therefore the words themselves, without being poetic, can take on that size, can be extravagant and true. When you read this attending to each word, not going on until each word is filled with its meaning, you will find so much happening beyond its logical meaning.

So, all these passages are very different, not simply because of the imagery and meaning, but by the very different tactile nature of the sounds, how they feel on the tongue when you are forming them, what effort is required: and this is directly related to how the character thinks, and is every bit as defined as the outward physical characteristics.

4 DISCOVERY AND MOVEMENT OF THOUGHT

I think when we act Shakespeare we always have to confront the question: what comes first, the words or the thought; for it is at its best when the thoughts are discovered at the moment of speaking. And if we take this as the starting point, the words have the capacity to surprise. It is not that the thoughts are necessarily new — they may have been under consideration for some time — but that always this is the first time they have been shaped in this particular way, and we are defining them at the moment of speaking.

I think the parallel with real life is this: when we are living at moments of heightened perception, when we are deciding on an action or talking over our reasons for doing something, there is the process going on inside of finding the right words in order to be accurate, so that in forming the thoughts we are at the same time redefining, changing and leading ourselves to some form of resolution. But I think it is more than this: sometimes words are there before we know it; it is as if the thoughts were there mulling around somewhere, and the words bring them to some sort of consciousness. We often discover and firm up our feelings as we speak. In much the same way, we get the sense of the thoughts clarifying and moving within the characters, so that the thoughts are always in action. This is particularly apparent in the soliloquies, where, in nearly every case, the character argues his position and moves through to some kind of solution.

Now an actor can be aware of the action through a speech, but because of the nature of the writing, the well-shaped and articulate phrases, he is so often trapped into presenting it in literary shapes. Thus, instead of being present in the action of the thoughts, he presents them as a result of having thought, and they become passive. It is a difficult balance, for it is not to do with being naively surprised, but of allowing the words to work on you and lead you — they will be different each time.

Try this for yourself. Here is a speech from the beginning of *Macbeth*: it is an account of a battle which happens before the play begins, in which Macbeth plays a prominent part. Read it through first gently to yourself to get the sense. In reply to the end of Malcolm's speech:

Malcolm: Say to the King the knowledge of the broil
As thou didst leave it.
Captain: Doubtful it stood,
As two spent swimmers that do cling together
And choke their art. The merciless Macdonwald —
Worthy to be a rebel, for to that
The multiplying villainies of nature
Do swarm upon him — from the Western Isles
Of kerns and galloglasses is supplied,
And fortune on his damnèd quarrel smiling
Showed like a rebel's whore. But all's too weak:
For brave Macbeth — well he deserves that name —

Disdaining fortune, with his brandished steel,
Which smoked with bloody execution,
Like valour's minion carvèd out his passage
Till he faced the slave —
Which ne'er shook hands nor bade farewell to him
Till he unseamed him from the nave to the chops,
And fixed his head upon our battlements.

King Duncan:
O valiant cousin! worthy gentleman!

Captain: As whence the sun 'gins his reflection,
Shipwracking storms and direful thunders break,
So from the spring whence comfort seemed to come
Discomfort swells. Mark, King of Scotland, mark.
No sooner justice had, with valour armed,
Compelled these skipping kerns to trust their heels
But the Norwayan lord, surveying vantage,
With furbished arms and new supplies of men,
Began a fresh assault.

King Duncan:
Dismayed not this our captains, Macbeth and Banquo?

Captain: Yes —
As sparrows, eagles, or the hare, the lion.
If I say sooth I must report they were
As cannons overcharged with double cracks;
So they
Doubly redoubled strokes upon the foe.
Except they meant to bathe in reeking wounds
Or memorize another Golgotha,
I cannot tell.
But I am faint; my gashes cry for help.

Macbeth, I.2.

Now, leaving out the interjections of the King, speak it through in this way: mark yourself two places about seven feet apart, then read it speaking one phrase on one mark, walk to the other mark and speak the next phrase, and so on. Walking on each punctuation mark, but stand still to speak. You will have to try it once through to get the hang of the exercise, but then the next time give yourself to the sense of it. You will need to walk quite quickly between the phrases, so you do not hold the sense up too much. What I hope you will notice is this:

His need to be accurate — 'Doubtful it stood'.

His analogy — 'two spent swimmers', a wonderful image for two people locked in battle, in movements that they can hardly control.

That he finds this image out of his own state of dream-like exhaustion.

The detail in the passage, as if he cannot let go for fear he will lose his strength and so will not be able to finish.

Rich images: 'rebel's whore', 'Shipwracking storms', 'carved out his passage' etc.

The triumph of — 'And fixed his head upon our battlements'.

And then the need to start again — 'As whence the sun . . .'

The phrases become disjointed as his strength runs out.

The final image of 'Golgotha' — his image of himself and death.

Now the actor working on this part has to think of many things: his status with the King; the need to get the facts across, the information is very important; the fact that he has lived through this scene himself and has been in battle many hours; and the need to tell the story before he collapses. It is therefore not just a splendid account of a battle, but one man putting the shapes he has seen into the form of words. And by finding out the internal rhythms in this way, this will be made clearer. The speech is rich and full, perhaps it is his last service, yet he can still find dazzling images like 'as sparrows eagles, and the hare the lion!'

Now for the point of the exercise:

The punctuation marks will vary according to the edition you are using; this does not matter. The point is that the punctuation is a very useful guide to how the thoughts are cut up.

Because we are changing position for each phrase, we give ourselves totally to that phrase, therefore its specific quality is more marked: the images become sharper.

The movement in between endorses the movement of the speech, it makes us feel the line through.

When you get single words — e.g., 'Mark, King of Scotland, mark' — they take on a very specific value.

Chiefly, that a speech can be to do with one main thought, but that there are many different qualities and movements within.

Or try it on this speech of Egeus at the very beginning of *The Dream* — the speech that starts off the whole story of the mix-up between the two sets of lovers:

Egeus: Full of vexation come I, with complaint
Against my child, my daughter Hermia.
Stand forth, Demetrius! My noble lord,
This man hath my consent to marry her.
Stand forth, Lysander! — And, my gracious Duke,

This man hath bewitched the bosom of my child.
Thou, thou, Lysander, thou hast given her rhymes,
And interchanged love-tokens with my child.
Thou hast by moonlight at her window sung
With feigning voice verses of feigning love,
And stolen the impression of her fantasy.
With bracelets of her hair, rings, gauds, conceits,
Knacks, trifles, nosegays, sweetmeats — messengers
Of strong prevailment in unhardened youth —
With cunning hast thou filched my daughter's heart,
Turned her obedience which is due to me
To stubborn harshness. And, my gracious Duke,
Be it so she will not here before your grace
Consent to marry with Demetrius,
I beg the ancient privilege of Athens:
As she is mine, I may dispose of her;
Which shall be either to this gentleman
Or to her death, according to our law
Immediately provided in this case.

A Midsummer-Night's Dream, I.1.

Here the movement is quite different. You will notice:

How the speeches begin abruptly.

How, because of his agitation, the thoughts are jumpy, and not strung together smoothly.

'and' takes on particular meaning, as does the repetition of 'thou'.

How he feeds his own anger, and finally comes to the point with 'according to our law' securely behind him.

This movement is part of his character.

This really is an excellent exercise, because it can pinpoint so much: it brings out the intrinsic qualities of the speech, while keeping the thought moving through. I do not want to give any more examples here, because it takes time to absorb one piece of text, and in any case we will look at variations of the exercise later. But I would like to say this: it is an excellent way to begin work on any speech, for it somehow allows you to focus on each part as it happens, while the movement carries you forward and gives you the extra impetus for the next phrase — and it also frees you. It both opens up the internal rhythms and makes you aware of the drive forward.

Perhaps the most important point to make is this: you can almost certainly plot the emotional state of a character by how the thoughts are broken up. With this in mind, here are suggestions of speeches that you may like to look at when you can give them time:

Juliet, III.2: 'Gallop apace . . .'. Her excitement grows as she thinks of Romeo, so that in the middle her breathing becomes orgasmic, along with her imagery, for 'die' was an Elizabethan euphemism for 'come'. After that point the phrases are much longer and calmer.

Leontes, *The Winter's Tale*, I.2, line 179. The whole speech is broken up and splintered; as is his mind, indeed his whole frame, by the extraordinary brain-storm or whatever that has filled him with suspicion of his wife's fidelity.

Aaron, *Titus Andronicus*, II.1: 'Now climbeth Tamora Olympus' top . . .' Quite a different movement, opening out and expansive, high with his own schemes and sense of power.

Tamora, the same play, two scenes later, II.3; 'My lovely Aaron . . .' Sexual, wheedling, convoluted thought.

Burgundy, *Henry V*, V.2. A wonderfully balanced, yet passionate speech. Quite a different kind of movement through.

Henry V himself, meditating before the battle, IV.1: 'Upon the King . . .' Just thoughts, seemingly calm, but with underlying agitation.

And lastly, when you have plenty of time, read Richard II's speech in the Tower, about thought itself. It makes us question where thoughts come from, so often out of left field as it were, and tells us something of the moment of thought — how instant and different.

So those are examples of the way you can think of the rhythms in the central characters. But the exercise is particularly good for the smaller parts, where often the character has to carry a lot of information, such as a messenger speech, where the actor always feels under pressure to get on with it quickly, yet, as with the Captain, the writing is so often dense and rich, and contributes so much to the fabric of the play. Take these two examples from *Antony and Cleopatra*:

Philo: Nay, but this dotage of our general's
O'erflows the measure. Those his goodly eyes,
That o'er the files and musters of the war
Have glowed like plated Mars, now bend, now turn
The office and devotion of their view
Upon a tawny front. His captain's heart,
Which in the scuffles of great fights hath burst
The buckles on his breast, reneges all temper,
And is become the bellows and the fan
To cool a gypsy's lust.

[Flourish. Enter Antony, Cleopatra etc.

Look where they come.
Take but good note, and you shall see in him
The triple pillar of the world transformed
Into a strumpet's fool. Behold and see.

Antony and Cleopatra, I.1.

You will notice:

Compressed rich language.

All the language is to do with excess.

Movement of thought is of one frustrated and angry.

This first speech throws up the dilemma of the play.

Messenger: Caesar, I bring thee word
Menecrates and Menas, famous pirates,
Makes the sea serve them, which they ear and wound
With keels of every kind. Many hot inroads
They make in Italy. The borders maritime
Lack blood to think on't, and flush youth revolt.
No vessel can peep forth but 'tis as soon
Taken as seen; for Pompey's name strikes more
Than could his war resisted.

Antony and Cleopatra, I.4.

It is so full and rich, and the information is so important. It needs to be quick obviously, but the pointing needs to be just right, or we will not get the information.

Finally, whatever piece you work on, notice all the joining words: 'as', 'from', 'for', 'but', 'and', 'with', 'which', 'till', 'nor', and so on. These are the words that change the direction of the thought. And, what is more, they are the words the hearer needs to clock to prepare him for that change. They are important and should never be rushed over: they poise the thought.

5 NATURE OF THE IMAGE, ITS LOGIC, AND ITS INQUIRY INTO NATURE

In working through so far, we have already noticed a good deal about imagery, about the pictures in the language, the metaphor and simile. And I think it is relatively easy to see objectively the reasons for the images used, and certainly an enormous amount has been written on the subject of imagery and recurring image patterns in the plays. Without being literary about it, when you are working on a play, it is always a good thing to look through the whole of it and find out what the recurring images are, for that helps to place the play in our imagination. And this in turn helps the language we have to use ring true, however small the part we have in it.

I work quite regularly with a group in prison; and one time we were looking at *A Winter's Tale*, which is a difficult play, and not all had read Shakespeare before. And, during the first two scenes, I asked those who were not reading to repeat all the words that were to do with the two kingdoms, Sicilia and Bohemia, and their courts. They got very involved with the story, and after a bit one of them said: 'You see, they didn't need scenery in those days: it is all in the words.' I know this is a simplistic thing to say, but I do think we are so intent on making logical sense of everything, we do not allow people to hear all that is there — the undertow.

There is an excellent essay by Maynard Mack called 'The World of Hamlet'*, in which in the opening paragraph, he says that by the world of Hamlet: 'I mean simply the imaginitive environment that the play asks us to enter when we read it or go to see it.' And this exactly expresses the actor's job, and that imaginative environment is different in every play.

What is difficult for the actor, however, is to find the source of the image inside himself: so that it never becomes descriptive or decorative, but is always expressing some kind of need or self-image of the character. This should not be a difficulty for a modern actor, whose way of working is often very much from within; but it very often is, for the images in Shakespeare are big and extravagant, and our naturalism is not enough.

From an actor's point of view the images are of two kinds: those which paint an external picture, and those revealing an inner landscape. But in neither case are the images merely descriptive; they are always an extension of the character, of how he perceives things, and therefore are always a point of recognition. Analogy provides us with the impression that we physically understand the experience.

When Titania describes the plight of the mortals, and blames their condition on Oberon's jealousy and brawls in a speech we all know well, she does it precisely from her own feeling for them, as their protector — their goddess/mother — in these lines:

Titania: The ox hath therefore stretched his yoke in vain,
The ploughman lost his sweat, and the green corn
Hath rotted ere his youth attained a beard.
The fold stands empty in the drownèd field,
And crows are fatted with the murrion flock.

* 'World of Hamlet'. Maynard Mack. *Political Shakespeare.* Essays ed. by Jonathan Dollimore and Alan Sinfield (Manchester U.P.).

The nine men's morris is filled up with mud,
And the quaint mazes in the wanton green
For lack of tread are undistinguishable.
The human mortals want their winter cheer.
No night is now with hymn or carol blessed.
Therefore the moon, the governess of floods,
Pale in her anger, washes all the air,
That rheumatic diseases do abound;. . .

A Midsummer-Night's Dream, II.1.

I won't give it all, but what is amazing is just how packed full of action those lines are. When we read them, or even learn them, we depend too much on the mind. What can be very interesting is to take one line at a time: first speak it, and then mime it – not too literally but filling out the spirit of the picture — and you will begin to realize how detailed each image is, and how filled with three-dimensional pictures, and even whole actions. Each image is a scenario in itself. We will develop this exercise further later.

Not long ago I did a workshop in London with the Kosh Dance Group. It was on *Hamlet*, and we did this exercise: there were four dancers, one woman and three men. The woman was Ophelia, and there were three Hamlets: we improvized round the line of Hamlet 'Lady, shall I lie in your lap?'. We asked the audience to repeat the line at intervals, and we ended with this image: Ophelia sitting, with three Hamlets in her lap, one head below the other. The image was quite shocking, and very powerful, in that it was both sexual and mad. This may seem by the way, but I feel that we so often do not investigate the images freely, and are conventional in our approach.

I was working with a group of schoolchildren on Macbeth, and I stopped on the speech, which we have already looked at on page 86, on the line: 'this bank and shoal of time', and asked each one of them for their precise mental picture of 'bank' and 'shoal', and of course each one was different, yet each contributed in a valid way to the understanding of Macbeth's state of mind at that point.

So, we must take on the images, fill them with our imagination, for it is only this way that we shall get into the skin of the character. Look at these lines of Caesar, which reveal his bitterness at Antony's obsession with Cleopatra, remembering him as he once was:

Caesar: Thou didst drink
The stale of horses and the gilded puddle
Which beasts would cough at. Thy palate then did deign
The roughest berry on the rudest hedge.
Yea, like the stag when snow the pasture sheets,
The barks of trees thou browsèd'st. On the Alps
It is reported thou didst eat strange flesh,

Which some did die to look on. And all this —
It wounds thine honour that I speak it now —
Was borne so like a soldier that thy cheek
So much as lanked not.

Antony and Cleopatra, I.4.

Caesar picks his images of the things that directly make contact with himself. In our own lives, we recognize qualities in other people which fit with an image we would like for ourselves. What is perhaps more interesting is the fact that we very often dislike people because we recognize in them the qualities we dislike in ourselves: it takes one to know one we say. In a sense this is by the way, but it perhaps helps us to find a way of personalizing seemingly objective images. Whatever we say about something, the way we describe it has to be out of our own experience.

When the images are interior, the sense of recognition takes on a different intensity. Let us look at two passages that we have already looked at (I am quite keen on following certain passages through). The first is Othello, page 27. Read it through again, and you will notice:

'Like': takes us into the image; it poises us ready.

'sea': an image always of a force beyond man's control. This is so in all the plays.

'icy current and compulsive course': his unconscious recognition of his own nature.

'my bloody thoughts . . . shall ne'er look back, ne'er ebb': by using the word 'ebb' about his thoughts, he has already identified with his image.

I was working with a group of 'A' Level students, all boys, who knew the play well: but I was determined to get them feeling something beyond what they had already understood of the play. So I made them get in a circle, entwining arms firmly, then got one half to pull one way and one half to pull the other, speaking the words of the speech while they did this. I had to stop them before it got rough, but one student said: I begin to see how he feels, it's like he is drowning.

Now, maybe this is a simplistic exercise for actors, but the point I want to make is this: the image of the sea can never be naturalistic, it is too powerful. It fits exactly with Othello's logic, his own state within the order of things, and it is not a grammatical logic. The actor has to be accurate to his own understanding of that image, not by rendering it poetic, but by knowing its full implications, and therefore its danger. It may come out very quiet. But the physical force of the image is commensurate with the force of his own revenge. We have to release the subversive anarchy of the language.

We have already looked at Cressida's speech on page 93 in terms of antithesis. Let us take another look at the images. Read it through again and you will notice:

'If' is the operative word throughout the whole speech; it connects all the ideas.

Implicit in each image is an action — an action of destruction.

I find it quite helpful to insert 'not only that' or 'even' in between the images for one read through; it endorses the cumulative nature of the speech, and helps to make each image specific.

Sense of destruction is total: 'fox to lamb' etc., and the very hard observation of 'stepdame to her son'.

It grows to — 'stick the *heart* of falsehood' (even).

'*As* false *as* Cressid': The logic of Cressida's imagery is perhaps in the embracing of destruction. But each is making an inquiry into the nature of his being.

To sum all this up:

The characters live where they find their images.

Images are very often extravagant, and we have to find our way in.

The images are never just descriptive, they always arise out of a need within the character: we have to observe the absolute discipline of the image, and not get carried away with it romantically — that only generalizes, and finally makes it sentimental.

There is nearly always a developing logic of the imagery: be ready for the ladders.

Always there is some sort of inquiry on the part of the character into the nature of being.

One last thing, which may seem simple and obvious, but which I think helps us relax into the language and not overload the meaning and therefore overstress: each of the characters in the plays is speaking in imagery and vocabulary with which the others are familiar — the world of the play. So characters are in tune with each other. When Henry, addressing his troops before Agincourt, says:

We few, we happy few, we band of brothers

he is saying precisely what they are ready to hear. That is rather an easy example, and perhaps a little cynical. But of course it goes much deeper than that, in that each character picks up quickly from the other, so that you speak from this point of joint understanding. I mentioned this earlier in connection with the speech of Claudio on page 87, which becomes much more telling when he speaks out of a common family understanding.

It is an acting adjustment, and works for everything. The sense of past experience gives it authority and helps us settle deeper into the words.

6 ARGUMENT AND EMOTION

In all our work — acting — there is a balance that has to be found between thought and feeling and between motive and emotion. And different writing poses very different questions of balance.

When approaching Shakespeare, I think one of two things tends to happen:

1 Because we know it is big, the characters have size and feel larger than normal life, we tend to scale up the emotion accordingly. We go for its emotional size at the expense of accuracy of thought — we have already said something of this in terms of the discipline of the image — and because it is poetry, we go for a poetic quality. Or,

2 We take the opposite course, and because we feel it is difficult to understand, we make it as literal and rational as we can, and so dodge the emotion.

Now everything I have written so far has been to do with this balance in some way. But it is well worth repeating, because it is something we do not easily trust: it is the thinking that gives the feeling its strength; the thought itself is passionate. And when we hover between being 'emotional' and being 'intellectual', it is because we do not trust that the two qualities can exist in the same words. Feeling which is not motivated by thought is sloppy and sentimental and has no view.

It is worth saying here a few generalized things about the differences between our modern way of thinking and Elizabethan modes of thought. I would not presume to write in detail about this. However, if you are interested, there are two excellent essays.* Now I do know that some actors would be inhibited by this approach and prefer to come to the language in a more instinctive way. I also know that we can come to an understanding of the structure in a more physical way. However, the following points are useful to us in terms of making us familiar with the structure:

* 'Shakespeare's Use of Rhetoric'. Brian Vickers; 'Shakespeare and the Thoughts of his Age'. W.R.Elton. From *A New Companion to Shakespeare Studies*, Ed. by Kenneth Muir and S.Schoenbaum (Cambridge University Press).

1 A major change of view between Elizabethan thinking and our own came about with Descartes in the mid-seventeenth century, whose dualism separated mind from matter, soul from body. And so now we tend to think of each part of ourselves as a separate entity. We develop our minds to think logically and factually: we think of our bodies as some sort of a machine. This may seem extreme, but certainly in the US there has been research done to find out how people think of their bodies, and one of the common reactions was they regarded their body as a machine which got you from place to place. And in between, but not connected, are our feelings, to which I suspect we attach the wrong kind of importance by presuming that they dictate our actions.

The Elizabethans, however, did not suppose a disjunction between mind and matter. They perceived each part of their body to have a function, and each part served the whole person — the soul. Thus, the liver was responsible for the vegetal functions, the heart for the vital functions, and the brain for the sensitive functions of thought, imagination, fancy, reason. So;

Mine eye and heart are at a mortal war
How to divide the conquest of thy sight;
Mine eye my heart thy picture's sight would bar, —
Mine heart, mine eye the freedom of that right:
My heart doth plead that thou in him dost lie —
A closet never pierc'd with crystal eyes;
But the defendant doth that plea deny,
And says in him thy fair appearance lies.
To side this title is impanellèd
A quest of thoughts, all tenants to the heart,
And by their verdict is determinèd
The clear eye's moiety and the dear heart's part,
  As thus: mine eye's due is thine outward part,
  And my heart's right thy inward love of heart.

Sonnet 46.

Further, they believed that we were formed by a combination of the four elements — earth, air, water and fire — which, mixed differently for each person, shaped our temperament. And so, all the time we have an awareness of the possibility of change in the disposition of each character. We sense, for instance, that as Othello becomes possessed by jealousy, his whole bodily disposition changes. And in all of the writing we have a strong awareness of the composition of the body and its clearly defined functions. Thus, talk of the heart was not merely romantic, it was to do with a totally specific notion of its function.

2 There was a hierarchy into which everything fitted. The Elizabethans believed that God created the universe out of nothing, and that

there was a scale, or hierarchy, into which everything fitted. So that the order went from God and the angels, down to man, woman, animals, vegetation, and lastly to inanimate things such as stones:

> You blocks, you stones, you worse than senseless things!

The further away from divine perfection, the more inferior in the scale of order. But because man had both soul and body, he was in a unique position in this order; and his actions had implications both outside himself in nature, and within himself in that action could change his own nature and identity.

3 They believed also that within man there was a conflict between his divine soul and his body — his reason and his passion: plenty of grounds for the use of antithesis. And that being a microcosmic model of the universe, if man neglected degree within himself, it would relate to outward political disorder — e.g., the two speeches we have already looked at about Antony. And further, that there was a law of nature by which we recognize right and wrong.

4 Also they believed there was a frame of order, a great chain of being: that God was the ruler of man; the King was ruler of the political world; the eagle was ruler of the birds; the lion was ruler of the animals, etc. The plays frequently act out the opposite: the reality of disorder.

5 Analogy: we have already talked about this in terms of how the actor uses it and its possibilities. However to the Elizabethans it was a habit of thought, a way in which they could perceive themselves in relation to the universe and the great chain of being, and as such it was necessary to their sense of the human position.

6 A great deal of the writing is to do with how you value things — we have already talked about that in terms of the first scene of *Lear*. They put value on things in three ways: the intrinsic value — i.e., qualities of honour, friendship, love, etc.; value in terms of use, how useful in the order of things; and market value — i.e., what they cost. This is a very useful point to hang on to, for the notion of value underpins much of the writing, and is part of the fabric of the plays. The first scene of *Merchant of Venice* for instance is all to do with value, the value of the argosies, the value of friendship and so on.

7 The belief in the influence of the stars on the individual. Their influence was determined by their position at birth or at conception, whichever point of view you favoured. Within that belief there was doubt, and Shakespeare extracted much irony from the notion of what is determined and what is not. So, Edmund, after a scene with his father Gloucester, who is distressed by the bad omens that have been seen — the eclipses of the sun and moon — when left alone says:

> **Edmund:** This is the excellent foppery of the world, that when we are sick in fortune — often the surfeits of our own behaviour — we make guilty of our disasters the sun, the moon, and stars, as if we were villains on necessity, fools by heavenly compulsion, knaves, thieves, and treachers by spherical predominance, drunkards, liars, and adulterers by an enforced obedience of planetary influence; and all that we are evil in by a divine thrusting-on. An admirable evasion of whoremaster man, to lay his goatish disposition to the charge of a star. My father compounded with my mother under the Dragon's tail, and my nativity was under Ursa Major, so that it follows I am rough and lecherous. Fut! I should have been that I am had the maidenliest star in the firmament twinkled at my bastardising . . .
>
> *King Lear*, I.2.

The speech, then was not just making fun of his father, not just humorous, but a serious piece of reasoning about the nature of what was determined and what was not. And it was also about the heat of the conceptual moment, important also in their thinking; and as such it was anarchic in a true sense — both potent and witty.

8 They believed in the Aristotelian idea that 'to know the cause of things was to know their nature'. The idea of causation encompassed both potentiality and the deed itself. In other words, the closer we investigate the cause of things, the better we will know how to act — it would firm up our purpose. And the marvellous thing about this is that it helps us to find the structure of a speech, how the great speeches work things right from the beginning, and from that exploration a path of action is found.

9 In the writing, there are many patterns and schemes of words. They are all forms of rhetoric with which the educated Elizabethan was familiar, much too complex to go into here, but the point is that the patterns draw depth. They are there both to amuse, and to make us aware of the complexity of the thought.

What is important about all this is that we see that there is an inquiry going on all the time into the nature of being, into the cause and end of life, into our position in the universe, and into our own natural function and order. And that inquiry is implicit in the language always; not heavy, but just there. And as actors we obviously do not carry this information round with us all the time, but an underlying awareness of it helps us to find the right balance between the argument and the feeling. This awareness takes the pressure off us to 'do it all', to 'feel' everything. It is there in the fabric.

And so it seems to me it is not possible to act Shakespeare without an awareness of a greater truth and of the nature of poetry. For it is always more than one's own personal statement: the implications are beyond the personal. This of course has much to do with preference, but this is mine.

Now, once you have grasped that the thoughts are part of a whole scheme, it becomes even more exciting to work on. For the images are there as part of the whole. So, for instance, when Juliet hears that Romeo has killed Tybalt, and that he is banished, her wild anguish is expressed through words and ideas that are already part of her.

Juliet: O serpent heart, hid with a flowering face!
Did ever dragon keep so fair a cave?
Beautiful tyrant! fiend angelical!
Dove-feathered raven! Wolfish-ravening lamb!
Despisèd substance of divinest show!
Just opposite to what thou justly seemest —
A damnèd saint, an honourable villain!
O nature, what hadst thou to do in hell
When thou didst bower the spirit of a fiend
In mortal paradise of such sweet flesh?
Was ever book containing such vile matter
So fairly bound? O, that deceit should dwell
In such a gorgeous palace!

Romeo and Juliet, III.2.

To begin with, all she can do is exclaim, and then the thoughts begin to come together, and she starts to question. But the questions are about nature outside herself, and we know that she is aware of grief in a larger context than herself. So with the rest of Juliet, where here feelings are extreme, they are always expressed in terms of argument.

This applies equally to the comedies. See this speech of Lysander:

Lysander: Content with Hermia? No, I do repent
The tedious minutes I with her have spent.
Not Hermia but Helena I love.
Who will not change a raven for a dove?
The will of man is by his reason swayed,
And reason says you are the worthier maid.
Things growing are not ripe until their season;
So I, being young, till now ripe not to reason.
And touching now the point of human skill,
Reason becomes the marshal to my will,
And leads me to your eyes, where I o'erlook
Love's stories written in love's richest book.

A Midsummer-Night's Dream, II.2.

Lysander, under the spell of the magic flower, summons all his reason to persuade Helena that he loves her. The reasoning is ridiculous and impulsive. And this is what is wonderful in all the lovers' scenes in *The Dream* — the impulsiveness of the argument. If you play the lovers' scenes for romance they are not nearly as interesting, for it is in their reasoning that we find all their impulsiveness, and passion and youth. We find the humour through the absurdity of the argument.

Finally, in Edmund's soliloquy, we will see all these points touched on very clearly. The speech precedes the one we have already read — it comes at the beginning of that scene. It is the first meeting with Edmund on his own, and he declares himself, his philosophy and his purpose:

Edmund: Thou, Nature, art my goddess; to thy law
My services are bound. Wherefore should I
Stand in the plague of custom and permit
The curiosity of nations to deprive me,
For that I am some twelve or fourteen moonshines
Lag of a brother? Why bastard? Wherefore base?
When my dimensions are as well-compact,
My mind as generous, and my shape as true
As honest madam's issue? Why brand they us
With 'base'? with 'baseness'? 'bastardy'? 'base, base'?
Who in the lusty stealth of nature take
More composition and fierce quality
Than doth within a dull, stale, tired bed
Go to the creating a whole tribe of fops
Got 'tween asleep and wake? Well then,
Legitimate Edgar, I must have your land.
Our father's love is to the bastard Edmund
As to the legitimate. Fine word 'legitimate'!
Well, my legitimate, if this letter speed
And my intention thrive, Edmund the base
Shall top the legitimate. I grow. I prosper.
Now gods stand up for bastards!

King Lear, I.2.

In terms of the argument you will notice:

His perception of himself in terms of Nature.

His own perception of Nature, that of goddess. This is in itself anarchic, in that it is not a formal god.

The heat of his conception: 'fierce quality' as opposed to 'dull, stale tired bed'.

Sense of right and wrong in nature: 'bastard' versus 'legitimate'.

His perception of his mind and body.

The notion of his own beginning, and of where he is going, his purpose: 'I grow, I prosper, now . . .'

The playing on words: 'bastard', 'base', 'legitimate'.

The image 'brand'. This exactly places him: animals are branded, there is physical hurt attached, something that is always with you.

We have to be specific all the time; for the images give the emotional measure of the text. How else could death be put in its exact place as here:

Hamlet: Had I but time, as this fell sergeant, Death,
Is strict in his arrest, O, I could tell you,
But let it be.

Hamlet, V.2.

7 WORD GAMES AND PATTERNS

I will take this in two parts: first, puns, double meanings, transference of meanings, etc.; and secondly, word patterns to which we always have to be alert. Sometimes they are obvious and sometimes they are not.

First, THE PLAY ON MEANINGS. There is always delight in double meanings. It is the same today as then: comedians build acts on it; much slang is indirectly dependent on it; it is alive and developing. Our only difficulty with Shakespeare is that many meanings have changed or shifted slightly, and so we do not always pick them up. Also, pronunciations have changed, and what once rhymed, does not any more. However, every good annotated text will give all the possible meanings, and you have to choose what you want to play.

There is a constant play on words, and this play on words does not only occur in the comedies, where they are easier to see because they are expected; it is also part of the composition of the whole text, and is used as much, or nearly as much, for darker purposes.

Let us start with a straightforward example, the sonnet which we have already mentioned in terms of antithesis. Here the puns are fairly obvious:

When my love swears that she is made of truth
I do believe her, though I know she lies,
That she might think me some untutor'd youth
Unlearnèd in the world's false subtleties.
Thus vainly thinking that she thinks me young,
Although she knows my days are past the best,
Simply I credit her false-speaking tongue:
On both sides thus is simple truth suppress'd.
But wherefore says she not she is unjust?

And wherefore say not I that I am old?
Oh, love's best habit is in seeming trust,
And age in love loves not to have years told.
  Therefore I lie with her, and she with me,
  And in our faults by lies we flatter'd be.

Sonnet 138.

You will notice:

Four straightforward puns: 'vainly', 'simple', 'habit', 'lies'.

The pun on 'subtleties' — i.e., 'subtle ties', dependent on a change of pronunciation.

'told', meaning both 'spoken' and 'counted', also has a sound association with 'tolled'.

I like the pun on 'made of truth': 'maid' ties up with untutor'd youth'.

We have to wait for 'lies' to be allowed its double meaning until the end; it graduates to that, and transfers to the last line.

The argument is clear: the strength of their relationship is measured in terms of how much they tell the truth to each other, and this is quite ambiguous. Ironically, there is truth in the lies.

Now, read it through out loud for yourself, tapping your hand on every word that is to do with the expression of love, or the belief of love. You will notice:

'swears', 'truth', 'believe', 'lies'
'think', 'knows', 'credit', 'false-speaking tongue'
'says', 'seeming trust', 'told'
'lie', 'flatter'd'.

The intricacy of the word-game played draws the depth of their relationship, and the sense of shared experience.

A lot of the puns carry a secondary meaning, and, because the meaning is not overt, it is powerful in a different way and hits our less conscious selves.

If you read *Sonnet 69* which begins:

Those parts of thee which the world's eye doth view
Want nothing that the thoughts of hearts can mend.

the pun on 'parts' is easy to pick up; it carries the same innuendo today, 'private parts'. But if you read it through you will notice that it is that word which sets the tone of the whole sonnet, leads us to expect something gritty, and prepares us for the unpleasantness of the end:

The soil is this — that thou dost common grow.

'soil' has several meanings — reason, ground, strain, solution — but chiefly its association with earth and dirt.

Now often the secondary meaning has changed, so we rely on notes. I have already mentioned 'die' in Juliet's soliloquy, which has the secondary meaning of 'have an orgasm'. Another one in the same play is the word 'well', which carried then the meaning both of 'healthy' and 'dead'. So there was a terrible irony in the exchange between Romeo and Balthasar. With the audience's knowledge of what had happened, it would have made them gasp:

Romeo: How doth my lady Juliet? That I ask again,
For nothing can be ill if she be well.
Balthasar: Then she is well, and nothing can be ill.
Her body sleeps in Capel's monument,
And her immortal part with angels lives.

Romeo and Juliet, V.1.

And that is a fairly common pun, and dark. It occurs in *Macbeth*, when Ross has to face Macduff with the news of the murder of his wife and children — the real meaning is suspended for quite a long time.

Next are several samples of how words shift in meaning as they are repeated, and often take on a darker emphasis. From *The Winter's Tale*:

Leontes: Go play, boy, play: thy mother plays, and I
Play too.

'Play' shifts from the sense of child's 'play' to love 'play', and then to the sense of 'playing' a part. Something dark happens with that repetition, as he shifts the focus of the word, and withdraws into himself.

And now two pieces of dialogue, both with sinister implications. I think they do not need an explanation:

Richard: We say that Shore's wife hath a pretty foot,
A cherry lip, a bonny eye, a passing pleasing tongue:
And that the Queen's kindred are made gentlefolks.
How say you, sir? Can you deny all this?
Brackenbury: With this, my lord, myself have naught to do.
Richard: Naught to do with Mistress Shore? I tell thee, fellow,
He that doth naught with her, excepting one,
Were best to do it secretly, alone.

Richard III, I.1.

So the play is on the meaning 'Naught to do' which means 'nothing to do with' and 'to do wickedness' — i.e., 'copulate'.

Also from *Richard III*, a short bit from Act III, Scene 2. The whole scene is worth reading for the wonderful ambiguity within it. Hastings, of course, does not know that his number is up; he has been fingered:

Catesby: 'Tis a vile thing to die, my gracious lord,
When men are unprepared and look not for it.
Hastings: O monstrous, monstrous! And so falls it out
With Rivers, Vaughan, Grey; and so 'twill do
With some men else, that think themselves as safe
As thou and I, who as thou know'st are dear
To princely Richard and to Buckingham.
Catesby: The princes both make high account of you —
(*Aside*) For they account his head upon the Bridge.
Hastings: I know they do, and I have well deserved it.

Richard III, III.2.

And the scene continues in this marvellously ambiguous vein.

There are many sound puns of course; simple ones like this in *Richard III* again — 'cousin' and 'cozen':

Queen Elizabeth: Cousins indeed, and by their uncle cozen'd
Of comfort, kingdom, kindred, freedom, life.

and this from *Julius Caesar* — 'soles' and souls:

Marullus: But what trade art thou? Answer me directly?
Cobbler: A trade sir, that I hope I may use with a safe concience: which is, indeed, sir, a mender of bad soles.

These are easy ones, but often they are not so plain, and so we have to keep our ears open for this element of word play which is present all the time, and unexpected and to be discovered if we are alert.

Two things to note though: if the pun is too obscure for a modern audience, do not labour it — so long as you know what it is and play it. People pick up so much by the spirit and the intention. When meaning shifts during dialogue you have to be so ready for it; it has to turn on a sixpence.

And secondly, FORMS AND PATTERNS OF WORDS, that is when a speech is given a certain symmetry by the repetition of certain words, or by putting words in a particular order. This can be very formal, as with passages in *Richard II*, and we have already looked at some of those lines; or at the discovery of Juliet's supposed death, when their lamenting takes on a particular shape of words; or when Richard is giving away his crown:

Richard: I give this heavy weight from off my head,
And this unwieldy sceptre from my hand,
The pride of kingly sway from out my heart.
With mine own tears I wash away my balm,
With mine own hands I give away my crown,
With mine own tongue deny my sacred state,
With mine own breath release all duteous oaths . . .

Richard II, IV.1.

In these cases the patterns it seems are used when only ritual will serve the moment, when plainer speech has lost its purpose. However, patterns are used just as much for comic effect, as with Adriana in *Comedy of Errors*:

Adriana: The time was once when thou unurged wouldst vow
That never words were music to thine ear,
That never object pleasing in thine eye,
That never touch well welcome to thy hand,
That never meat sweet-savoured in thy taste,
Unless I spake, or looked, or touched, or carved to thee.

Comedy of Errors, II.2.

And in the last scene of *Merchant of Venice*, when a large part of the scene revolves round the comedy of the rings that Portia and Nerissa gave to Bassanio and Gratiano, who in turn gave them to the lawyer and his clerk — Portia and Nerissa in disguise. Here is a sequence from the middle of that:

Bassanio: Sweet Portia,
If you did know to whom I gave the ring,
If you did know for whom I gave the ring,
And would conceive for what I gave the ring,
And how unwillingly I left the ring
When naught would be accepted but the ring,
You would abate the strength of your displeasure.
Portia: If you had known the virtue of the ring,
Or half her worthiness that gave the ring,
Or your own honour to contain the ring,
You would not then have parted with the ring.
What man is there so much unreasonable,
If you had pleased to have defended it
With any terms of zeal, wanted the modesty
To urge the thing held as a ceremony?
Nerissa teaches me what to believe,
I'll die for't but some woman had the ring!

Merchant of Venice, V.1.

A speech totally about different values. The humour and delight we get from the games in there is huge — not sophisticated but very real, like the pleasure children get from nursery rhymes, when the rhyme and the rhythm is part of the satisfaction, and the delight in seeing whether the sense can be made to fit into the scheme. Yet it is deadly serious, because it is to do with a passion for both.

These patterns, with many others, are different figures or strophes in rhetoric, which were clearly recognizable to an Elizabethan audience, but which have meaning for only few today. Now, although very interesting, it is probably not relevant for the actor to know each figure by name and for what it is. However, I think it is important for him to know that these were patterns, each used in a specific way and for a recognizable effect. So that we have to be aware that it is there for an effect, as well as to express a truth: and the awareness of the effect will give it a greater truth.

What I am saying is this: that the actor must confront the artifice, you cannot just slip into it and hope for the best — it has to be dealt with and made part of your style in your particular production.

But patterns in varying degrees are there all the time, and we have to let them surface, and a lot we only discover when we are working on a character in depth. We will look at ways of working at this later. There are, for instance, wonderfully light patterns to be found all the way through *The Dream*. Take this passage:

Lysander: How now, my love? Why is your cheek so pale?
How chance the roses there do fade so fast?
Hermia: Belike for want of rain, which I could well
Beteem them from the tempest of my eyes.
Lysander: Ay me! for aught that I could ever read,
Could ever hear by tale or history,
The course of true love never did run smooth;
But either it was different in blood —
Hermia: O cross! — too high to be enthralled to low.
Lysander: Or else misgraffèd in respect of years —
Hermia: O spite! — too old to be engaged to young.
Lysander: Or else it stood upon the choice of friends —
Hermia: O hell! — to choose love by another's eyes.
Lysander: Or if there were a sympathy in choice,
War, death, or sickness did lay siege to it,
Making it momentany as a sound,
Swift as a shadow, short as any dream,
Brief as the lightning in the collied night,
That in a spleen unfolds both heaven and earth,
And — ere a man hath power to say 'Behold!' —
The jaws of darkness do devour it up.
So quick bright things come to confusion.

A Midsummer-Night's Dream, I.1.

You will notice:

Patterns in the form of words relating to the patterns of thought.

Patterns within the syllables, repetition of vowels and consonants.

Their thoughts are so intermixed, it is as if they are breathing together.

With the variation in the sequences, our expectations are quickened, and we are led, almost breathlessly to

So quick bright things come to confusion.

In the same scene there are two more passages of repeated sequences, one with Hermia's vow to Lysander, and one in the exchange between Hermia and Helena.

But not all the patterns are so obvious, and as I said we only find them when working in depth. Just one more example. Read through this speech of Florizel to Perdita, and tap your hand on the verb 'do':

Florizel: What you do
Still betters what is done. When you speak, sweet,
I'd have you do it ever; where you sing,
I'd have you buy and sell so, so give alms,
Pray so, and, for the ord'ring your affairs,
To sing them too; when you do dance, I wish you
A wave o'th'sea, that you might ever do
Nothing but that — move still, still so,
And own no other function. Each your doing,
So singular in each particular,
Crowns what you are doing in the present deeds,
That all your acts are queens.

The Winter's Tale, IV.4.

You will notice:

The delicacy of the speech, with its very gentle repetitions.

The play on the word 'do': the pattern emerges as a ladder in the first half of the speech.

The rhythm breaks on 'when you do dance', and becomes like a wave to fit the thought.

'do' must always be touched so lightly.

The pattern itself deepens the feeling.

So: The actor has to bring together the character's need to express, with the art of expressing.

We have to recognize that there is always delight, release, satisfaction at thoughts expressed accurately and well.

Delight in the skill of expressing thoughts put us in touch with the life-force of the character, even when the purposes are dark. While we are speaking we are still asserting.

8 STRUCTURE OF SPEECHES

What I want to look at now is the structure of speeches. As there are so many speeches of length written, it is important to look at how we deal with them: their energy can so easily get dispersed.

Everything we have talked about so far has been to do with structure in some way, and must be included in our thinking. But it is the inner form which gathers all these properties together, and to which everything else both contributes and fits. And the more precise we can be about the inner structure, the more at ease we will be with the character.

There are three points I want to make:

1 There is a dialogue going on within nearly every speech. Within that dialogue thoughts are moving at different rates, lines are moving with varying emphases, vowels and consonants are adding textures, but the overall argument is happening at a different rate, a different time; and this gives the speech a different movement.

It is as if the character proposes his theme, the argument. He then sets about replying to the initial statement, and continues to argue it through in different blocks of thought until the end. And of course Hamlet's soliloquy 'To be or not to be' is the most perfect example of this, in the sense that you can see the dialogue working quite clearly.

2 The general lay-out of the verse; how the thought structure and the metre structure lie together; whether the thoughts in general run in lines, or stop in the middle of a line. This seems to tell us about the formality of the thinking: how much the mind is motivating the solution, and how much a deeper emotional force is taking over. *Coriolanus*, for instance, is much more rational in the lay-out of the thoughts than is *Romeo and Juliet*.

3 Every speech has to do with pursuing the cause. As I said earlier, they believed in the Aristotelian idea that to know the cause of things was to know their nature. So the following pattern holds — it is plainer to see in the soliloquies because they have a kind of completeness, but it follows for speeches within a scene:

The title, or theme or argument is given at the beginning: it can

> last for anything from half a line to five or six lines — you have to find it.
>
> That thought is pursued, with diversions into metaphor, until the end, which is always some form of resolution. If it does not appear to resolve, it is because for some reason the character cannot resolve.
>
> This resolution ties up with the beginning.
>
> Each individual thought throughout, both refers back to the beginning, and takes us further towards the end.
>
> So in a very real sense the end is in the beginning and the beginning in the end.
>
> The speech covers both potentiality and act, and this is its energy.
>
> I want to repeat that, this is its energy: it is as if the thought is simultaneous — it is suspended for the one moment.

And this surely is what is exciting: that dual sense of time — the fact that it takes time to speak, but at the same time happens in an instant. A view of time not unlike Macbeth's 'bank and shoal of time'; or Eliot's 'the river is within us, the sea is all about us'; but I am being poetic.

I do, however, think this sense of time is important. We always have to confront the fact that the speeches are long — Becket would dispose of the ideas in no time — and I think it is difficult for young people to see why they need to be so wordy. And I think that we tend to drag the speeches and make them heavy because we do not have a sharp enough perspective on time: in practical terms, how the awareness of this energy in the speech lifts the thoughts.

Let us look at a speech or two. First, Brutus's soliloquy in *Julius Caesar*:

Brutus: It must be by his death; and for my part,
I know no personal cause to spurn at him,
But for the general. — He would be crowned.
How that might change his nature, there's the question.
It is the bright day that brings forth the adder,
And that craves wary walking. Crown him! — that!
And then, I grant, we put a sting in him
That at his will he may do danger with.
Th'abuse of greatness is when it disjoins
Remorse from power; and, to speak truth of Caesar,
I have not known when his affections swayed
More than his reason. But 'tis a common proof,
That lowliness is young ambition's ladder,
Whereto the climber-upward turns his face;
But when he once attains the upmost round,

He then unto the ladder turns his back,
Looks in the clouds, scorning the base degrees
By which he did ascend: so Caesar may;
Then, lest he may, prevent. And, since the quarrel
Will bear no colour for the thing he is,
Fashion it thus: that what he is, augmented,
Would run to these and these extremities;
And therefore think him as a serpent's egg
Which, hatched, would, as his kind, grow mischievous,
And kill him in the shell.

Julius Caesar, II.1.

Read this through twice, once for sense only, and the second time moving between points, as we did in an earlier exercise. You can vary it by moving between chairs, and sitting. However, this time we are thinking in terms of a dialogue going on in the speech, so move only on semi-colons, question marks and full-stops. You will notice:

The argument laid in the first half line. Yet this is not a statement, the result of thought, or there would be no need for the rest of the speech.

It is a proposal: it is Brutus awakening to the idea, forming the thought into words.

This is the starting-point from which he genuinely argues his case through the speech, until reaching his conclusion: 'And kill him in the shell'.

Yet, the very fact of uttering the thought at the beginning, weights the argument in favour of the conclusion, so that there is a kind of inevitability to it.

What you find from this focus on the dialogue element is the inevitability of the thought: once on a path it has to keep going. Once you get to the point of speaking the thought, the action becomes inevitable. You also find how the pulse of the character changes within the thought, so:

'He would be crowned' — the thought itself makes him pause, and he investigates his own awareness of nature, and how that can change within a man, and he finds the critical image of the adder from within himself.

You will notice the different lengths of the thoughts: how the middle is coolly reasoned. Thoughts often end in the middle of a line, but the metre is regular.

In each case, when he comes near a decision, the rhythm jumps — 'He would be crowned'; and, 'Crown him! — that!'

In the penultimate line, the sense stress and the metre stress are in contention, and the line suspends a moment before it falls on the long, even sounds of the conclusion, 'And kill him in the shell', back to the beginning of the speech, and to the beginning of an action.

If you think of the images, you will notice:

The sense of the seed of our own actions in our thoughts, which is fed by the image of the serpent's egg.

The finding of the image of the adder, an image which could easily refer to Brutus himself, reflecting his own condition.

I have gone into a good deal of detail on this, because it shows so clearly how the thoughts are structured within a speech. You can do the same exercise with other speeches we have looked at. In Juliet's soliloquy on page 61, which we have already analysed in terms of metre, you will notice:

Her theme is in the first four lines. It could be in the first two, but the thought is not really rounded off until you get to the word 'immediately', where the rhythm comes to rest: and that word sets the tone and tempo of the speech.

She then contemplates night, in easy bursts of thought, from her viewpoint, so the images are 'close curtain', 'love-performing', 'Lovers can see', 'amorous rites', etc.

It starts to jump on 'Come, night' — the pulse is different and the images are very sensuous and active.

After 'And when I shall die' it becomes calm again, contemplative and metaphysical in thought.

The end is impatient, and listless.

It has a very strong structure.

Edmund's short prose soliloquy on page 118. This runs quite quickly:

The initial statement runs right down to 'planetary influence' — seven lines.

The rest just weighs that initial thought up.

Ends with the assertion of his identity.

Edmund's first soliloquy on page 120 is interesting. We have already looked at in terms of its argument. Looking at its inner dialogue makes you notice particularly:

> The different pulse on the lines: 'Why bastard? Wherefore base?', 'wherefore' having perhaps equal stress and so giving it extra weight.
>
> And with 'base'? with 'baseness'? 'bastardy'? 'base, base'?. These words obviously stick — absolutely tied up with 'brand'.
>
> The resolution of 'I grow. I prosper' and the tying up the end in the beginning 'Now gods stand up for bastards'.

I was doing a workshop once in a school on *Lear*, and we worked on this speech. They were low-ability readers, so we were tackling the speech together first to give them confidence. And as we went through it I asked them to substitute words for 'base', 'bastardy', — any words that came to mind. And what came out was interesting — words like 'ignorant', 'stupid', 'black'. Interesting because it teaches us how words stick in our souls.

Again, this has a very clear structure, and so good to work on.

Let us now look at Macbeth's soliloquy, which we have already mentioned briefly twice: look at it for its dialogue, so go only to colons, semi-colons and stops.

Macbeth: If it were done when 'tis done, then 'twere well
It were done quickly. If the assassination
Could trammel up the consequence, and catch
With his surcease success — that but this blow
Might be the be-all and the end-all! — here —
But here, upon this bank and shoal of time,
We'd jump the life to come. But in these cases
We still have judgement here, that we but teach
Bloody instructions, which, being taught, return
To plague the inventor. This even-handed justice
Commends the ingredience of our poisoned chalice
To our own lips. He's here in double trust:
First, as I am his kinsman and his subject,
Strong both against the deed; then, as his host,
Who should against his murderer shut the door,
Not bear the knife myself. Besides, this Duncan
Hath borne his faculties so meek, hath been
So clear in his great office, that his virtues
Will plead like angels, trumpet-tongued against
The deep damnation of his taking-off;
And Pity, like a naked new-born babe
Striding the blast, or heaven's cherubin, horsed

Upon the sightless couriers of the air,
Shall blow the horrid deed in every eye,
That tears shall drown the wind. I have no spur
To prick the sides of my intent but only
Vaulting ambition which o'erleaps itself
And falls on the other.

Macbeth, I.7.

The sense of dialogue brings out:

The Initial proposition, starting with 'If', takes one and a half lines, and ends with 'quickly' — this is the important word.

'If' goes through to 'jump the life to come'.

Contemplation of an action, and the time of an action.

'bank and shoal of time' — time both still and moving.

'It' becomes 'assassination' becomes 'blow'.

'If' always keeps the deed removed from himself, so that 'murderer' is still in the third person.

The weighing up of the outcome of the deed, like the scales of justice.

Images become wilder: coming at him from both sides of his brain.

One feels he has come to no conclusion — no-go: but Lady Macbeth comes in.

Now this shape is much easier to see in any of the soliloquies than it is in a speech within a scene, where the structure of the thought is part of a whole scene. However, it is always worth looking for, for some part of that shape will be present. So here are some speeches within scenes which we will look at briefly.

First look at the two speeches of *Troilus and Cressida* on page 93:

The two speeches take on each other's shape.

Both start with a philosophical comment.

Troilus' initial statement is one and a half lines, down to 'Approve their truths by Troilus'.

He then builds his metaphors cumulatively to the end of the speech, and finishes triumphantly with 'sanctify the numbers'.

Cressida has to answer from an opposite view: there is no further to go along the line of truth.

'If' takes us right down to 'Upbraid my falsehood'. She then starts afresh, and 'When' takes us through to 'As false as Cressid' — not something you can say triumphantly.

Her pace quickens at the end.

In both cases, the main thought is long, with a number of different facets to it, different textures and movements.

The speeches are exactly the same length.

What is wonderful is that they have a like shape, and yet the substance of each, and therefore what you get from their characters, is so totally different.

Now look at this of Lady Macbeth, in the scene following the soliloquy we have just looked at. Her drive in the scene has to be to reinfuse Macbeth with courage and purpose. Each speech in the scene is part of that overall drive, yet look at the shape of this one:

Lady Macbeth What beast was't then
That made you break this enterprise to me?
When you durst do it, then you were a man;
And to be more than what you were, you would
Be so much more the man. Nor time nor place
Did then adhere, and yet you would make both.
They have made themselves, and that their fitness now
Does unmake you. I have given suck, and know
How tender 'tis to love the babe that milks me;
I would while it was smiling in my face
Have plucked my nipple from his boneless gums
And dashed the brains out, had I so sworn
As you have done to this.

Macbeth, I.7.

You will notice:

The subject — 'What beast was't then'.

Then her answer.

Then her philosophical and political arguments: 'they have made themselves'.

Back to herself, her own nature, and her own relationship with beasts: 'the babe that milks me'.

The knowledge of her own potential to act.

Finally, here are five examples, all from one play, *The Winter's Tale*, so the style is consistent, but the movement between each speech is quite different.

They will take time to assimilate, so read them only when you can take the time. Look at them for the inner dialogue, and for their shape and the way the thoughts open up. Move with them, as we have done already, and notice how each movement of the thought shifts the direction of the speech slightly, and takes us further along that path.

You will notice:

1 Camillo: his hesitancy, playing carefully for time, as he begins to apprehend the danger that they are all in from Leontes' sudden and unaccountable jealousy.

'I may be negligent, foolish, and fearful' tying up with 'let me know my trespass'.

All the joining 'if's'.

2 Leontes: the schizophrenic dialogue; the building of the word 'nothing'.

3 Hermione: the clarity and balance of her argument. The sense that she has touched the bottom of misery, and that she has nothing to lose. She has therefore reached a point of truth and peace which is greater than her predicament; she can be articulate.

4 Paulina: her suppressed, righteous anger at the beginning, with the building up of her questions. But her sense and positive thinking prevail as she works through her anger. Her ambivalence at the end of the speech.

5 Perdita: lack of tension, and freedom in the verse — purity of image — innocence.

Camillo: My gracious lord,
I may be negligent, foolish, and fearful:
In every one of these no man is free,
But that his negligence, his folly, fear,
Among the infinite doings of the world,
Sometimes puts forth. In your affairs, my lord,
If ever I were wilful-negligent,
It was my folly; if industriously
I played the fool, it was my negligence,
Not weighing well the end; if ever fearful
To do a thing where I the issue doubted,
Whereof the execution did cry out
Against the non-performance, 'twas a fear
Which oft infects the wisest. These, my lord,
Are such allowed infirmities that honesty
Is never free of. But, beseech your grace,

Be plainer with me, let me know my trespass
By its own visage; if I then deny it,
'Tis none of mine.

The Winter's Tale, I.2.

The thinking is convoluted and clever: that of a politician.

Leontes: Is whispering nothing?
Is leaning cheek to cheek? Is meeting noses?
Kissing with inside lip? Stopping the career
Of laughter with a sigh? — a note infallible
Of breaking honesty. Horsing foot on foot?
Skulking in corners? Wishing clocks more swift?
Hours minutes? Noon midnight? And all eyes
Blind with the pin and web but theirs, theirs only,
That would unseen be wicked — is this nothing?
Why, then the world and all that's in't is nothing;
The covering sky is nothing; Bohemia nothing;
My wife is nothing; nor nothing have these nothings,
If this be nothing.

The Winter's Tale, I.2.

The images become quite unbounded.

Hermione: Since what I am to say must be but that
Which contradicts my accusation, and
The testimony on my part no other
But what comes from myself, it shall scarce boot me
To say 'Not guilty': mine integrity
Being counted falsehood, shall, as I express it,
Be so received. But thus: if powers divine
Behold our human actions — as they do —
I doubt not then but innocence shall make
False accusation blush, and tyranny
Tremble at patience. You, my lord, best know —
Who least will seem to do so — my past life
Hath been as continent, as chaste, as true,
As I am now unhappy; which is more
Than history can pattern, though devised
And played to take spectators. For behold me,
A fellow of the royal bed, which owe
A moiety of the throne, a great king's daughter,
The mother to a hopeful prince, here standing
To prate and talk of life and honour 'fore
Who please to come and hear. For life, I prize it
As I weigh grief, which I would spare; for honour,
'Tis a derivative from me to mine,
And only that I stand for. I appeal
To your own conscience, sir, before Polixenes

Came to your court, how I was in your grace,
How merited to be so; since he came,
With what encounter so uncurrent I
Have strained t'appear thus: if one jot beyond
The bound of honour, or in act or will
That way inclining, hardened be the hearts
Of all that hear me, and my near'st of kin
Cry fie upon my grave!

The Winter's Tale, III.2.

Rhythmically very firm, yet malleable.

Paulina: What studied torments, tyrant, hast for me?
What wheels? Racks? Fires? What flaying? Boiling
In leads or oils? What old or newer torture
Must I receive, whose every word deserves
To taste of thy most worst? Thy tyranny,
Together working with thy jealousies —
Fancies too weak for boys, too green and idle
For girls of nine — O think what they have done,
And then run mad indeed, stark mad! For all
Thy bygone fooleries were but spices of it.
That thou betrayedst Polixenes 'twas nothing:
That did but show thee of a fool inconstant,
And damnable ingrateful. Nor was't much
Thou wouldst have poisoned good Camillo's honour
To have him kill a king — poor trespasses,
More monstrous standing by: whereof I reckon
The casting forth to crows thy baby daughter
To be or none or little, though a devil
Would have shed water out of fire ere done't;
Nor is't directly laid to thee, the death
Of the young Prince, whose honourable thoughts —
Thoughts high for one so tender — cleft the heart
That could conceive a gross and foolish sire
Blemished his gracious dam. This is not, no,
Laid to thy answer. But the last — O lords,
When I have said, cry woe! The Queen, the Queen,
The sweet'st, dear'st creature's dead! And vengeance for't
Not dropped down yet.

The Winter's Tale, III.2.

Tremendous building up of rhetoric.

Perdita: Out, alas!
You'd be so lean that blasts of January
Would blow you through and through. [*To Florizel*]
Now, my fair'st friend,
I would I had some flowers o'th'spring, that might

Become your time of day — [*to the Shepherdesses*] and
    yours, and yours,
That wear upon your virgin branches yet
Your maidenheads growing. O Proserpina,
For the flowers now, that, frighted, thou let'st fall
From Dis's wagon! Daffodils,
That come before the swallow dares, and take
The winds of March with beauty; violets, dim,
But sweeter than the lids of Juno's eyes
Or Cytherea's breath; pale primroses,
That die unmarried ere they can behold
Bright Phoebus in his strength — a malady
Most incident to maids; bold oxlips and
The crown imperial; lilies of all kinds,
The flower-de-luce being one: O, these I lack
To make you garlands of, and my sweet friend
To strew him o'er and o'er. *The Winter's Tale*, IV.4.

Not just romantic about nature — all the flowers have specific meaning.

Now I have given a lot of examples: I do not want this to seem superficial, but I feel it is the only way to make the points clearly; otherwise what I have said would be too generalized. But of course these points will only take on real significance when you are working in depth on a character, when, hopefully, they will endorse your thinking and your instincts.

And I think getting free with the structure in this way is particularly important for actors, and actors in training, in the States, Canada, and to some extent in Australia. I think here there is often a dual attitude to Shakespeare which comes partly a) from a lack of confidence with it — it is not so familiar — after all, every English child does it at school, even if not very well, but it has a familiar ring; and also perhaps there is a feeling that it 'ought' to sound English. And b) partly from a distrust in the sound of the language, arising out of the very strong acting orientation in the Method. I have talked about both these points in Chapter One.

Our discovery has therefore got to be that you need to have a certain awareness and freedom with the language before you can even begin to work on a character: you have to come to terms with speaking it, and with the fact that the music is part of the character. With this in mind, it is really good to get the language on the tongue, to practise it, provided always that you know at what depth you are working.

I suppose what I want to say is this: that if you are tuned to all that is happening in the language it will reinforce all you want to do with the character. It is like finding the resonant pitch of a room, when your voice suddenly takes on an extra richness which takes you by surprise.

And this is what the exercises are about.

Part 3

Shakespeare – the Practical Means

Chapter 5

INTRODUCTION TO THE EXERCISES

Having carefully gone through all that I would call the properties that we need to consider when speaking Shakespeare, we now have to look at ways to work at them so that they become less conscious.

We have to find within ourselves the wish to use them because they feel right and necessary, and life-giving. And we also have to try to co-ordinate them, so that they are not separate points to observe, but rather interact one with the other.

All the exercises I am setting down I have used to good purpose: but they can be adapted and changed as much as you like, according to your needs and the space available, provided you are quite clear about their purpose.

One of the difficulties I have in setting them down is that I try never to do an exercise exactly the same — I do of course, but I always have a sneaking suspicion that I cannot then be discovering anything quite new. Probably this is vain, in more senses than one. But it is quite difficult writing down 'the' exercise. That is why it is important you feel free to adapt, though always go through it several times as set down before you vary it.

The exercises have two purposes:

(1) To make sure you are aware of all the possibilities of the text; and
(2) To release your own strength and subconscious responses, which are nearly always richer than you think.

That is why I would say most of the exercises are to do with putting your concentration on something outside yourself, which then frees your own responses, out of which you discover what you are after. That is a little simplistic of course, because there is always a method behind the exercise.

Some of the exercises have only one specific purpose: but most, in working for one end, will open up other things incidentally, so it is important that you try to notice everything that is happening. All of them will open up the meaning in some way; they will all yield something. Above all — listen.

Here I would like to say that it takes time for the exercises to work for you. Don't hurry them. It takes time for you to feel what the exercise is about, before you can begin to notice what is happening when you are doing it. I have talked a good deal about feeling the language familiar inside you. I feel this to be of the utmost importance: not just that the language feels easy, but that it becomes part of your inner landscape. I feel too much Shakespeare gets acted right up front as it were: everything is pressed out, active in a surface way, with a lot of obvious energy, leaving no place for the actor's inner view — that kind of perspective which can only come when you let your whole life into it. There has to be that sense of inner understanding, which is not just to do with understanding the meaning. And the latter exercises are about allowing just that to happen. In other words they are to do with acting. And this sense of sitting back on the words, this sense of 'cool', is not just to do with Shakespeare.

All the exercises are only a guide to finding the movement of the character: the age, physical prowess, mental agility, wit, emotional resources.

Now for the exercises. But first a word about the text you use:

(i) They can be done on a text you do not know. This is always excellent exercise, for it gets you using language and hearing rhythms that are fresh. Also, because you have no preconceptions about it, you do not judge yourself in quite the same way, and I think you get a freer response. Choose the text that is going to be most useful to you at that moment: allow time to get familiar with it, and, if working in a group, allow time for slow readers.

(ii) Or they can be done on a text that you choose to work on over a period of time. This is useful in that you can then start investigating the language in terms of character and situation. You may even do some of the acting exercises on it.

(iii) Or, of course, you can work them on a text which you are bringing to performance, and this is the most useful of all. However, you have to be selective and sensitive about this, and it has to be done with the total endorsement of the director, or it can be confusing and therefore counter-productive.

I personally believe that a great deal of rehearsal work can be done in this way, but it must be done with everyone's belief in it. The solo work can and should be done at all stages of rehearsal — that can only give confidence — and also scene work in small groups. Needless to say, we have to respect other people's methods of work. Having said all this, I believe the work can only add richness, and should be done all the time.

I hope you will find the group exercises interesting and pleasurable. Obviously it is vital that we practise on our own and acquire as much skill as we can. However, it is when we are working truly with other people that we are at our best and freest. Acting must always be about relating to other people — provoking and responding; and so I hope the exercises will help acting groups as much as the actor working on his own.

I will lay out the exercises in each section for the most part like this:

Purpose of the exercise.
Group work.
Solo work.

If you are working by yourself I think it is important to read through the group exercises as well; it will give you a broader view of them which will add to the solo work. Also it may encourage you to work with another person when possible. We learn so much by hearing other people's responses.

Another reason why I find it difficult to write down the exercises is that so often one mixes them. So feel free to do this, and to jump about in the order you do them, once you have practically found out what is useful about them. Often, the further you get, the more important the simpler exercises become.

Chapter 6

SUBSTANCE OF THE TEXT

1 SOUNDS: VOWELS AND CONSONANTS

Before we get on to the exercises proper, it is good to remind ourselves of all the elements of speech: so

Group and solo

(i) Go through all the lip vowels, putting a light 'h' in front of each:

OO oo OH AW o OW OI

They are mixed monothongs and diphthongs, so notice the lip movement on the diphthongs, and also the different lengths of each sound.

Now the tongue vowels, again noticing movement and length:

AH u ER a e AY i EE I EAR AIR

With each sequence, feel your sound coming to where the movement is.

Now the consonants. First feel the voiced continuants:

Vvv Zzz TH--(voiced) soft GE (as in measure)

They should vibrate and make your head buzz.

Now feel the difference between the voiced and unvoiced plosives:

tetete	dedede
pepepe	bebebe
kekeke	gegege

Use them with vowels, so you feel them impelling the sound out:

TOO	DOO	TOH	DOH
TAH	DAH	TAY	DAY
POO	BOO	POH	BOH
PAH	BAH	PAY	BAY
KOO	GOO	KOH	GOH
KAH	GAH	KAY	GAY

Repeat the sequence with the consonants at the end.

Now to make sure that the nasal consonants, which of course have to be resonated in the nose, are firm and forward, and that their energy is being sent out through the mouth, and not staying with the nose and mask:

POO	BOO	MOO	POH	BOH	MOH
TOO	DOO	NOO	TOH	DOH	NOH
PAH	BAH	MAH	PAY	BAY	MAY
TAH	DAH	NAH	TAY	DAY	NAY

Now feel the final voiced continuants:

OOL	OHL	OOLZ	OHLZ
OOV	OHV	OOVZ	OHVZ
AHL	AYL	AHLZ	AYLZ
AHV	AYV	AHVZ	AYVZ

Use them with any combination of vowels you like. It is good to be free with this.

Then put them in combination of words, so that you do not keep it at isolated sounds: this makes you notice the variable lengths.

It is always good to finish off with a hum, feeling vibration in the head, mask, chest, etc. Move the lips a little as you hum. Settle on a comfortable pitch first, then gradually move it up. Keep the throat really open.

The next exercises are to do with hearing the substance of the vowels. They are quite difficult to do, and it takes time before you settle with them, so have patience.

Group work

(ii) Now try this sequence:

mememe	mememe	mememe	MOO
mememe	mememe	mememe	MOH
mememe	mememe	mememe	MAH
mememe	mememe	mememe	MAY
mememe	mememe	mememe	MI (my)
mememe	mememe	mememe	MEE

When you are used to the sequence, sing it.

Now, the important part: run round the room while you are singing the consonant sequence; stand still for the vowel and open your arms out for it, so that you make a shape with your arms — the shape that the vowel suggests to you.

Be free, and notice the shapes that you find. Of course you have to do the best with the space available.

'm' is the best consonant to use, but you may use any vowel you like.

In the group, it is best to start by singing on the same vowel, but then you can break that and sing vowels of your choice. You will find it difficult to do with short vowels, but try sometimes.

If you have a piano, and can do the sequences on different notes, or perhaps up the scale, that is useful for increasing range.

What is important is that you begin to feel that a vowel has a body and a volume of its own.

(iii) Stand in a circle:

Set up a hum first, feeling the vibrations.

Then, separately, sing a vowel round in the circle: any vowel, but probably best to be a long vowel, and avoid 'yoo' — i.e., making the 'y' sound in front.

Use your breath, and keep the sound open: do not let it be glottal.

Really find the vowel from inside.

What we want to hear is each person's unforced sound. This is not to do with singing, or putting on a sound, or describing sound in any way but to do with hearing a sound that comes from within — listening to an inner response.

I do not want this to seem mysterious: it is simply a matter of getting to the point where you are not trying for an effect, but of spontaneously letting sound spring through a vowel. It happens to be sung, but the singing is not the important part.

It is quite difficult to do at first, because everyone's attention is on you. Once you have found the feeling, it will allow you to sit down on your sound, and will affect the other exercises. It is a good feeling.

The exercise can be varied by the group singing the vowel back to the individual. You must sing it absolutely precisely, so that you repeat the whole timbre of that person, and this makes a good listening exercise.

(iv) This next exercise is valuable, and can be adapted freely. It takes time to get the hang of it, but is worth it because you get a feeling of the dynamic of the vowel, and makes you notice the different impulses in initiating and receiving sound (it does need space though).

Get into two lines, A and B, on opposite sides of the room. Know who you are opposite.

Run the sequence through once, so you know what it is about:

> The end person of line A sings a vowel to his opposite number in line B; who sings the same vowel on the same note.
>
> That person then breathes, and sings a different vowel on any note to the next person up in line A, who then repeats that vowel, and sings a fresh vowel to the next one up in line B.
>
> And so on, up the lines. That is the drill.

Now for the purpose of it:

> Imagine that the vowel is a ball that you are throwing, and then catching.
>
> The movement of swinging your arm to throw the ball allows you to take your breath, and throwing it makes you release the vowel with impetus.
>
> Be careful not to let it be glottal. And the vowel must be on one note only — do not let it slide.
>
> Be precise or it will not work, particularly when catching another's vowel: the note and tone should be as like as possible.

Notice the different impulses between throwing and catching.

When this feels good, the tone free and open, and the listening satisfactory, you can try variations:

Send a feeling on the vowel, and catch that.

Send a message on the vowel, and answer it.

Just keep noticing the changes of texture in the sound, and how you listen to the other person.

(v) Work on a piece of text:

Read it through together — at least once, to get the sense and the feeling of it together, then:

Read it, and sing the last word in each line — you will hear the vowel open out.

Speak it through, but spread your arms on the last word, and make the shape that the vowel suggests.

You can then be clever and vary it by making arm shapes on specific vowels as they crop up, or perhaps on one word per line, but any one that you choose.

I particularly like these exercises which make arm movements and shapes for the vowels. The shapes can vary enormously; go with your impulse, it makes the vowels spread physically through your body and makes you give them full value, and allow meaning to be expressed through them.

In Eurythme, for example, vowels are given a particular shape — for 'EE' the arms are straight up, and for 'AH' they are pointed obliquely up, with the palms forward, as if holding at bay a force from behind. I know very little about it, except that it is a way of training in movement which develops one's own inner rhythm, and which finds a common rhythm between people; and I know that it is used to help people to make sounds when they have lost the ability to speak. For us I think, making these shapes, has a particularly releasing effect.

Solo work

These first exercises are perhaps more difficult to do on one's own than the rest will be, for part of the release that you find comes from doing it with other people and therefore not being able to monitor oneself too much. However:

Work through the vowels and consonants thoroughly as in (**i**). It is so important to place the verbal energy precisely on the lips and tongue, so that it becomes the physical movement of the thought — the thought in action.

If you have room and privacy work on (**ii**). It is perhaps not easy to do it on your own — it works in a group partly because of the volume of sound, and partly because you do not feel self-conscious in any way. However, go through it once so you see the logic of it. Make sure every 'me' is muscularly firm and placed exactly on the lips.

The valuable exercise on your own is to work on a piece of text as in (**v**). Decide what piece of text you are going to do, then work through it spreading your arms first on the last word in each line, then on, say, one word per line. Be precise about the shape you make with your arms. Notice how your imagination starts to fill the word quite differently; also, you will notice the patterns of the open vowels, and which ones perhaps occur frequently.

I remember doing this exercise with Tony Sher, when he was playing Richard III in Stratford, and in the opening soliloquy we suddenly noticed how in the first part of the speech the sound 'OW' becomes important, and in the second half the sound 'I' takes over: even when in an unstressed position it seemed to take on a certain significance.

What the exercise does is to stop you being over-concerned with the meaning, with serving up a conclusion, because it makes you aware of the fullness of the words which contribute to the thought.

Suggestions for text work

Henry V: Chorus to Act IV. 'Now entertain conjecture . . .'
The Dream, II..1: Titania. 'These are the forgeries of jealousy . . .'

Both these are very rich in open vowels.

2 HEARING THE LANGUAGE: SUBSTANCE OF TEXT

This work is to do with hearing what is happening in the language, both in terms of rhythm and in terms of word quantity, apart from its grammatical sense. It is important, therefore, that you know the meaning of the text you work on well, or these connections will not be made. Choose any piece of text that will be useful: any one passage that we have already used would be good, and I will refer particularly to the Cordelia speech (page 28), and to the Troilus and Cressida speeches (page 93).

What these next exercises will hopefully do is allow us to hear and feel how, within one whole thought, there is contained many different movements and textures, all of which contribute to the complexity of the whole. They are the layers of the thought.

Group work

(i) Get in a circle. Speak the passage round, one person at a time, from punctuation mark to punctuation mark. Someone may only have one word — that is part of what we will mark.

Within an awareness of what the whole passage is about, each person must receive what he has been given from the last person, allow his own phrase to open out, and hand it on to the next. So there is an individual contribution which is part of the whole, and the language is always moving. (If this sounds a little pretentious, all I mean is — be totally behind what you are saying, but also be aware of passing it on.)

You will notice:

The lengths of thoughts and their movement.

You will mark the rhythm that single words give.

The quantity of the words — i.e., whether the vowels are long or short, whether single consonants or combinations, and the substance that this gives.

How the rhythm itself leads us to the meaning.

(ii) Repeat this, but instead of speaking, sing the words round.

Be brave with this — respond to what you are hearing in the words, and just sing them. It should not sound like a recognizable tune, and try not to let it get into the area of hymns or chants.

When it works well, the sound and the meaning will reinforce each other.

Also, when it is working well, and people are sensitive to each other, quite glorious sequences of sound emerge, of different volume and intensity.

What happens is this: because it is a slightly absurd thing to do, and you cannot make sense in a conventional way, you allow the sounds to make their own sense. It often points up humour which one had not noticed before — a humour which comes out of the total commitment to the sound.

(iii) The same exercise again, but this time whisper it round. Make sure it is a pure whisper, and no voiced sound comes in — some people find this difficult.

Again, because you have taken away the element of voice which is trying to make good sense, and 'behave' properly, you will be free to notice the energy of the words — their particular dynamic.

Specifically you will notice:

The time it takes to speak certain combinations of consonants; and this is particularly useful when thinking about the energy needed to fill different spaces, as we shall see later — so often clarity is lost because we do not give the consonants their room.

The differing lengths of the vowels.

In all the exercises it is important to feel that you can be individual without being individualistic — i.e., you can be extravagant and inventive yet still keep sensitive to each other. It is quite healthy to feel irritated when someone breaks the chain in some way!

At this point I would like to say a circle is quite the best configuration in which to begin exercises. This is nothing new I know, and the reasons are plain: it does get everyone concentrated, and it also is good from a practical point of view. However, when everyone is secure in what they are doing, it is good to start moving, otherwise one tends to get a little formal and serious in the wrong way. But keep returning to the circle when it is helpful.

However, when you are ready, start walking and running, and even jumping. This is both exhilarating and releasing, and words immediately take on different energies and start to surprise.

So, organize it like this:

Let each person settle on the phrase they are going to say — i.e., let each person take a phrase in sequence and stay with it. Try to work it so that the whole passage is used, and so you may not want to stick solely with punctuation marks.

Speak the passage while moving round the room, walking, running, etc. Keep the flow going.

Try it as far away from each other as possible. If it is possible, you can also do it hiding from each other. This is very good because of being uncertain where people are; so, hide first, and then try to get to the other side of the room without being seen. Obviously this can only work if you have space.

It is good once also, when moving round, to shout the passage. It removes any sound of the 'poetry voice', and it makes you realize that you can be tough with poetry without necessarily losing its sensitivity. Also, quite another energy comes into play — which is maybe to do with childhood — and it gives it a different urgency. Always be careful not to hurt your voice.

(iv) It is good to finish up this sequence of exercises by standing quite still, in any part of the space, and either:

Whisper the passage through.

Or speak it through very quietly.

Make sure that every syllable can be heard.

This is also quite excellent done in the dark, if that is possible. It both changes the quality of the listening, and it also makes one drop in the words that much more clearly.

These exercises are good for changing your relative spaces, and this affects the way you talk to each other; yet you relate just as positively.

(v) This exercise is to make us aware of the caesura within a line.

So in the circle:

Take a piece of text and speak it round a half line at a time. This means that the person speaking the first half of the line has to judge when the break comes — sometimes you will not do it right, but that does not matter.

The valuable thing is that you will hear where that poise in the line comes, and occasionally you will find there are two. You will also hear when the line has to run smoothly without a break, and so you will find all those extra rhythmical possibilities.

I do want to stress how important it is to allow the listener to hold a word for a split moment and take it in, particularly so when a speech is quick, and where there is a lot of information to be picked up, as in a Messenger speech. The quicker text is spoken, the more important that pointing becomes.

(vi) This next exercise I rate very important, for it is to do both with defining the vowels and hearing their particular dynamic, and with defining the meaning: it is extraordinary how the meaning comes into focus when we complete the vowel.

So come together in a group or a circle, whichever you prefer.

Now you know the passage well, speak it through, fully comprehending its sense, but with this difference:

Verbalize the vowels only. This is quite difficult to do to start with, but it will soon work.

Take care that the vowels are supported, and open and not glottal, so feel the breath behind them.

Really give yourself to the sense which is behind the vowel.

When you speak the passage through normally again, you will notice:

How much fuller the vowels are.

The meaning has become more defined, and more fully understood.

You will hear when vowels take on a pattern — they do not necessarily repeat, but their particular cadence and rhythm will emerge.

(vii) The same exercise can be done with consonants, but a shorter passage will serve, for it is much more difficult to keep the sense intact.

It does not open up the meaning in the same way, but it does help us to gauge how forceful the language is, its muscular strength, and how full it is in terms of numbers of consonants and whether devoiced or voiced.

The consonants I suppose indicate to us the mood of the character: for instance, a passage with a predominance of unvoiced continuants — 's', 'sh' — immediately feels conspiratorial. More than that, it often indicates to us a character living in the baser part of his nature — e.g., Leontes, page 136, or Macbeth, page 132. A passage with a predominance of voiced plosives is perhaps more positively forceful; whereas long combinations of continuant voiced consonants indicate fulness of thought and feeling.

These are very general indications, but the point is the quality of the consonants should be noticed, and should be used positively, for they are also part of the thought.

Try both the Macbeth and the Brutus speeches for this, and also one of Henry V, which on the whole is forceful but light.

The exercise is also good for getting the thought on to the word.

Text work

If you do the exercises on the Cordelia speech, and even take it through to her following one, which I will give you below, you will find all the points and the patterns that we have already talked about on page 28.

You will notice:

The odd rhythms of the first part, plus the open vowels.

The shortness and lightness of the middle, plus the patterns of the short vowels: 'hardokes, hemlock, nettles, cuckoo-flowers. . . '

Particularly the pattern of the long vowels on 'all the idle weeds that grow In our sustaining corn'; how they root the sense and take us to the core of her personal imagery.

The imperative quality of 'Search every acre . . .', with its long open vowels.

The more withdrawn, searching quality of the last two lines.

The different style of the second speech, if you go through to it, like a prayer:

All blest secrets,
All you unpublished virtues of the earth,
Spring with my tears! Be aidant and remediate
In the good man's distress. Seek, seek for him,
Lest his ungoverned rage dissolve the life
That wants the means to lead it.

I think these two speeches contain the most rich and wonderful sense of sound substance and meaning bearing on each other — unforced, light, but so profound. The vowel exercise is particularly rich.

On the Troilus and Cressida speeches, when you sing them round you will notice:

How different the two sound: Troilus is much more affirmative in sound than Cressida, even though the phrases are cut up in similar ways.

It is quite interesting to vary the singing of the phrases round on the Troilus speech.

Let each phrase be sung back to the individual by the group, as exactly as possible, so that each phrase gets sung twice. It points up its heroic nature and its extravagance.

It is difficult to pinpoint why the speeches sound so different, but they do. It is, by the way, interesting to look at the two or three preceeding speeches — particularly the one of Troilus beginning: 'O that I thought it could be in a woman . . .' which sets the other two up, and is a good deal more tentative in sound.

With Cressida you will find:

Very delicate cadences when you sing it.

When you whisper, the words will be light and open-ended.

When you shout, it will bring out her quite violent awareness of what it is to be destroyed.

The vowels are fuller than in Troilus' speech, and make more satisfying patterns, particularly:

'swerve a hair from truth';

'when waterdrops have worn the stones of Troy';

'Yea, let them say, to stick the heart of falsehood . . .' The whole thought seems to gather on that word 'heart' — it is the ultimate.

Cressida's words become progressively more simple — i.e., more monothongs, whereas Troilus' language becomes more complicated and rhetorical.

In both speeches the accumulation of images is apparent.

You must judge how long you want to go on with the exercises at any one time. If you go on too long, the words become meaningless: and worse, the joy goes. You must always be sensitive to what is right for the group; and this of course will depend on how regularly you can work.

If you are working regularly, then go through the exercises quite lightly, varying the texts a good deal. The awareness will grow each time, and the result will be cumulative and unpressured. If you are together seldom, then you need to take longer on them to feel their benefit and explore them fully. So then it is good to focus on one text for several sessions.

I have referred back to these speeches, because it is useful to carry all the ideas through on one or two specific passages — and these happen to make the points clearly. If you are focusing on one play, start with the simpler passages that flow easily and are more lyrical. Then you will see the difference between them and the more emotional and jagged passages; tackle them later.

What happens when we do these exercises is this:

> Because the exercises are slightly absurd — i.e., not logical, they release us from the need to make sense, and our imaginations can then be released through the sound. The meaning is still there in the back of our minds, but we are able to give ourselves to the sound.
>
> We then have some different perception of the words and their textures.
>
> Some part of this perception will remain when we speak it in its normal context.
>
> And that perception will be conveyed to the audience: for we have to place the language — to hear and mean at the same time.

The benefit of course is that everyone is taking part, and feeling the energy going through. So notice what is happening, and particularly notice when it is working well. When it does not work well, it is usually because someone is trying too hard with their individual word or phrase, wanting to make it different for its own sake, and not receiving the impulse from the last person. It is interesting too to notice when you are disappointed with how it is being carried on, when it does not fit with what you want to hear. What is important is that as the group becomes more focused, the more individual each member can be, and yet keep within the framework that has evolved and is acceptable. You will also notice a lot of humour coming through. Also, when the group is really listening to each other, very sensitive and delicate cadences emerge, not to do with any received idea of singing, but to do with each person expressing through sound.

Suggestions for other text work

> *The Tempest*: Ariel, I.2, from line 189. String together his first three speeches.
>
> *Love's Labour's Lost*: Berowne, IV.3, from line 303 to the end.
>
> *Merchant of Venice*: Lorenzo, V.1, from line 154 to the end, also his next speech.
>
> *The Winter's Tale*: Any Perdita or Florizel in IV.4.
>
> *The Dream*: Theseus, V.1. His first speech there. But there is so much in *The Dream* you could use, and it could be interesting to use some of Pyramus and Thisbe — to hear poetry at its most primitive.
>
> *King Lear*: There is so much here you can use: particularly Lear at the beginning of the storm scene, III.2, and Edgar, II.3

Solo work

The only thing you miss when working on your own is the sense of passing on the text, and hearing other's responses. All the other exercises can be done quite as successfully.

(i) Try singing it through this way:

Get in a good position, and prop your text up in front of you so that it is easy to see.

Prepare yourself, so that your breath is rooted. It is useful to go through a few lines of text with your arms moving windmill fashion. This is excellent as it gets more air into the body (you need it to oxygenate the blood), and the arm movements stop you being tense, or holding on to the breath — so you will use plenty of breath.

When this feels right, cup your hands round your mouth, under your nose, and speak a few lines to feel the sound forward in the mouth.

Now go back to the beginning of the piece and sing it through like a passage of opera recitative. Do not be coarse with it, but allow the nature of the language to influence the sounds you find. You want to find the quality of sound that fits the thought, so that you are open to the texture of the passage.

When you have done this, speak it through again normally, getting the sense you want, and notice how the sounds will have opened up.

How, for instance, you can linger and poise on a word that you had not specially noticed before; also, how the end words of the line take on an extra meaning.

This is an excellent bridge into finding the balance between speaking for sense and motive, yet allowing for the music and extravagance of the language.

(ii) Whisper it through. As with the group exercise, you will hear what the words are doing: the length of the vowels, and the combinations of the consonants, and how the type of consonant affects the nature of the thought. If, for instance, there is a predominance of unvoiced consonants as 's', 'sh', 'p', 'f' etc., the language has a different texture. You feel particularly how long it takes to say some words and give them their full energy. We can never fully hear this when we are relying on the voice to carry the meaning.

(iii) Speak the vowels only, again as for the group exercise, and taking care that the vowels are open and never glottal:

Really fill the vowels with the meaning of the whole word.

Notice how, as the vowels become more defined, the meaning becomes more precise.

(iv) Speak only the consonants. Feel their energy and how they are disposed through the text. Use this also to feel the sound forward in the mouth, so that when you come to speak the text normally you get the feeling that the thought is absolutely placed where the language is being formed.

Finish always by speaking the piece through as you want it, for sense and feeling, but noticing how that is being fed by the extra freedom and music you have found.

3 LANGUAGE FABRIC

By this I mean the choice of language, which we have talked about a good deal, and which of course is connected with the sound components we have just been working on. It is specifically to do with honouring the meaning to the full; not by thinking but by feeling the language in action.

The following work is to make us aware of the underlying choices which contribute to the nature of the thought: how thought patterns are built up, not only through the emotive words and the strong images, but also through the connections of words which surround them; and how we cannot afford to take any word for granted, for everything contributes to the texture of the thought and is part of the whole fabric, through which we find the patterns and ladders in the writing.

Because the exercises are complex I am giving them in four sections, with group work and solo work for each section as it comes.

The first exercise I feel to be perhaps the most important of all for it makes us attend to each word fully. In effect it is not really an exercise, rather an attitude to text which should always be part of our work. However, we need to start it as an exercise, so that it can lead us to that attitude.

It comes of course from Peter Brook: and the first time I saw him working in this particular way I think I did not fully understand its importance. He was working with a group of actors rehearsing *Antony and Cleopatra*, and he took specifically the Messenger speeches in I.4. to work on. Now I had watched him doing many exercises over that period, and over the period of *The Dream* rehearsals. All of the exercises were to do with acting and response, and all have influenced my work, but I would not pretend to write about them. But in this case it was the particular sense of 'attending to the word' that grabbed me, and which has led me to find many of the voice exercises I have since used.

(a) **Attending to the word**. With this exercise you have to resist thinking in terms of clumps of sense, of giving the result of a thought phrase. Rather you have to fill each word completely before you allow yourself to take the next word — i.e., do not let yourself think the next word until you have completed the word you are on, even if it is 'and', 'it', 'the' or 'but'. We have to see how each word actively leads us to the next. To begin with it is slow: and you have to be sensible and keep the meaning of the whole passage clearly in your mind, so that you must work it on a passage that you are well familiar with, so the individual words are not in any sense isolated or staccato. But really feel the energy and texture of each word complete and fulfilled before you allow yourself to go on to the next. To start with, it is difficult not to let yourself be controlled by the sense — just resist it.

Group work

Set it up like this:

> Get together in a group, settle on a passage — the Macbeth soliloquy on page 132 would be excellent, but it really can be anything so long as everyone knows the sense well. Read it together, taking each word as it comes, and not going on to the next until the thought of each has been fully honoured.
>
> You will need someone listening — different members of the group can take this in turns — making sure that you are fulfilling the words and not mentally jumping to the next before each is completed, and gently questioning the words which are not satisfactory. You will find you will hear it so clearly.
>
> It would be difficult to pin-point exactly what you will notice, because different words will come to the surface, and new resonances of meaning will strike each person differently.
>
> Sufficient to say that you will hear a lot of words afresh, and that you will notice particularly the linking words, and how they shift the direction of the thought and drive it through.
>
> Also, how stress becomes irrelevant, for it is the interplay between the words that is important: so that the language can be much lighter at the same time as being fully explored.
>
> Also the energy of one word is always poising towards the next.

In *Macbeth*, for example you will notice:

In the first sentence how 'when', 'then', moves the thought through to 'quickly':

And then: 'if, 'and', 'that', 'but', drive through to 'jump the life to come':

Also the changing tense of the verbs, indicating the transitive nature of this thought.

All this stresses the lightning quality of the thought: how the issues are worked out, but at speed.

So the exercise is important a) to allow yourself time to investigate the words fully and settle in them, so that your inner responses come into play — very often implicit in the image is an idea much bigger than we had allowed ourselves to notice. While we are busy making sense, we often do not let this inner texture through. And b) to sense that each word is always on the move, taking us through to the next and contributing to the restlessness of the thought on its movement of discovery: and that therefore there are two time-scales in operation — time is needed to speak the words and point them, yet the thought itself is instantaneous.

Look now at these lines of the First Lord in *As You Like It.* At first sight it seems lyrical and unprovocative, until you investigate it, and then you will find words of such extremity of feeling that will be surprising, and give another dimension to the speech:

First, it is quite easy, unstressed language, and the sense is quite clear.

The First Lord is simply giving an account to the Duke and the other Lords of having seen Jacques sitting by a brook, talking to a wounded deer. We start with the Duke suggesting they go kill venison:

Duke: Come, shall we go and kill us venison?
And yet it irks me the poor dappled fools,
Being native burghers of this desert city,
Should in their own confines with forkèd heads
Have their round haunches gored.
First Lord: Indeed, my lord,
The melancholy Jacques grieves at that
And, in that kind, swears you do more usurp
Than doth your brother that hath banished you.
Today my lord of Amiens and myself
Did steal behind him as he lay along
Under an oak whose antick root peeps out
Upon the brook that brawls along this wood,

To the which place a poor sequestered stag
That from the hunter's aim had ta'en a hurt
Did come to languish; and indeed, my lord,
The wretched animal heaved forth such groans
That their discharge did stretch his leathern coat
Almost to bursting, and the big round tears
Coursed one another down his innocent nose
In piteous chase; and thus the hairy fool,
Much markèd of the melancholy Jacques,
Stood on th'extremest verge of the swift brook
Augmenting it with tears.

As You Like It, II.1.

You can take just the descriptive part of the speech. What I want you to notice is just how long it takes to fully investigate words like:

'wretched', 'heaved', 'discharge', 'stretch', 'innocent', 'piteous'.

It takes time for them to be fully realized, and for the images to be physically imagined; for them to have depth and contain your inner view.

Unless they have that depth, and unless the discomfort and cruelty implicit in the words is fully found, then the argument about the rights of the natural inhabitants of the forest and the fact that those rights are being usurped by the Lords, will be tame and will not let us into the philosophical indignation which the speech is about. We have always to look for what is cruel, or uncomfortable or disturbing because it is always there, the realism in the poetry.

So what I am really on about is that it takes time for words to be realized as well as understood grammatically; and we have to set aside time to do that.

You do not have to take too long over the exercise at any one time, but it is important that you do it often, for it informs how you look at text, and therefore how you can live through the words. What you will find will not necessarily be heavy or serious — the humour comes through in this way too — you will find all sorts of extravagances and patterns which will be funny. When you have finished with the exercise, let it go, because obviously in the end swiftness is all-important. However, the resonances will remain.

You will want to work this on passages you know to begin with, but here are suggestions for further work:

Coriolanus: Brutus, II.1. This we have looked at already.

> This is good to work on because the imagery is packed full, the adjectives rich, and the verbs compressed in meaning.
>
> It is also interesting in that there is an absence of joining words, and this makes us feel that we are precipitated into the middle of each thought. This feeds the sense of exasperation that is there.
>
> The word 'him' is important, and is played around with, though not necessarily stressed.
>
> The sounds are very full — it takes time to get your mouth round them. They make you aware of the difficulty of expressing thoughts. The word 'tongues' is very active, implies movement.

As You Like It: Rosalind, IV.1, from line 85. Both the First Lord's speech and this are wonderful to work on, as indeed is so much from the play. I have not brought it in before, as a good deal is written in prose, and so far we have been concerned with verse. But, as we shall see later, prose has rhythms and structures which have to be filled similarly, so it is good gradually to move into that area.

Again, the language is unstressed and lucid, deceptively so, for the concepts are large.

Notice:

> 'The poor world is almost six thousand years old'; 'Patterns of love'; 'Hero had turned nun'; and of course 'men have died and worms have eaten them, but not for love'.

The ideas open and accumulate in the same way as for verse.

Coriolanus: Aufidius IV.7, from line 28 to the end.

> This is a difficult speech, so it would need preparation before working it in a group — the sense would have to be quite clear.
>
> The language is exotic and muscular and full of pride: that of the superior animal — merciless.
>
> Aufidius is weighing up Coriolanus' strengths and virtues. This weighing up is apparent in the structure. As he does so, he feeds his own deep resolve to break with Coriolanus.
>
> The last lines are passionate.

Now of course you would want to know this play well to tackle it properly. However, it is glorious language to speak, so see what you get out of it by fulfilling the words and allowing the muscularity to inform the thought.

Solo work

This is precisely the same as for group work. It should be done quite big, so that you can hear what happens. Do not feel that you have to make it sound good or do anything with it; just allow the words to contain all that is in your imagination.

I believe it is quite essential to work this on a section of the part you are studying, for it helps you to get inside the specific vocabulary, and also to be more accurate to the thought.

(b) Awareness of choices. The principle of this next exercise is very simple: we have touched on it earlier when talking of antithesis, ladders or imagery, etc. It can be adapted freely to fit in with what you are doing. You can combine it with other exercises, and what is more, it is useful at any stage of work, particularly in rehearsal.

Its purpose is simply to increase our awareness of the language choices — the sub-text — which are always tied up with the objective of the character.

As a first example, let us take the first three speeches of *A Midsummer-Night's Dream*. Opening scenes always yield a great deal on this exercise, and as we have already noted, we are taken into the vocabulary of the play.

Theseus: Now, fair Hippolyta, our nuptial hour
Draws on apace. Four happy days bring in
Another moon — but O, methinks how slow
This old moon wanes! She lingers my desires,
Like to a stepdame or a dowager
Long withering out a young man's revenue.

Hippolyta: Four days will quickly steep themselves in night;
Four nights will quickly dream away the time:
And then the moon — like to a silver bow
New-bent in heaven — shall behold the night
Of our solemnities.

Theseus: Go, Philostrate,
Stir up the Athenian youth to merriments.
Awake the pert and nimble spirit of mirth.
Turn melancholy forth to funerals:
The pale companion is not for our pomp. [*Exit Philostrate.*
Hippolyta, I wooed thee with my sword,
And won thy love doing thee injuries;
But I will wed thee in another key:
With pomp, with triumph, and with revelling.

A Midsummer-Night's Dream, I.1.

Now we will go through the different stages of the exercise.

Group work

(a) Sit all together on the floor, and speak the words through firmly but gently, and while doing so tap your hands on all the words connected with time.

These will not only be the obvious words such as 'hour', 'day', 'night', but other words will also seem relevant, such as 'quickly', 'apace', etc.

There are no actual references to time in the third speech, yet implicit in the verbs is the sense of past and present.

Do not worry if words have passed before you realize that you wanted to tap on them — you will have noticed them, which is the important thing.

(b) Let two people sit back to back in the middle of the floor, and speak the text through.

> The rest, sitting round, this time repeat all the words to do with love and sexuality as they are spoken. Speak the words firmly, but not too loudly or you will drown the speaker and so will not be able to hear the text.
>
> It is crucial that you do not look at your text, but do it all by listening.
>
> This you will find a lot more complex, and the choices sometimes ambivalent. Phrases such as 'Long withering out a young man's revenue' and 'Stir up the Athenian youth', though not directly connected with love, are feeding the underlying sense of desire which is part of the motivation of both characters.

(c) Now the group can stand up, and one half attach themselves to Hippolyta, and one half to Theseus — stand slightly behind them. Now let two speak the text through again, with Hippolyta and Theseus moving round the room, the others being drawn behind:

> This time the group should repeat all the words to do with drawing or pulling, anything to do with an outside force — you will find plenty. As you move round you will feel how the movement reinforces the sense that these two are being pulled by their desires, but are also dependent on outside forces.

It is a quite wonderful piece of writing, and the words supply everything and lay the vocabulary for the play. If, for example, you did a similar exercise on the following part of the scene, it would highlight Egeus' sense of outrage at his daughter being enticed away by Lysander — by some other power.

(d) You can vary it in this way:

Let the two characters be apart, and let the body of the group get between them.

The objective of Hippolyta and Theseus is to get together, and the aim of the rest is to keep them apart, not by pushing or touching, but simply by moving in between. Maybe they get together triumphantly at the end — just see how it works.

While you do this, keep repeating one of the sets of words, whichever you choose.

This is a very useful series of exercises. I have given a simple passage to illustrate it, but it can be used for any scene. Three words about it:

First, it is not always easy to find a set of words which releases the undercurrent of the scene. However, if the first set you choose is not particularly helpful, it does not matter, and it will always throw up an idea for another.

Always useful concepts to start you off are in those words to do with

time
honour
worth
power
love
nature
reality and fiction
(being and seeming)

Sometimes it is useful simply to work on the antitheses, as we have already noted; sometimes on verbs.

Opening scenes are always useful to work on, as the vocabulary is laid there.

It is not always necessary to have a particular concept to repeat: often just repeating words that grab you, that are interesting, set you off.

Second, you can vary the tapping exercise: for instance, you could put several upturned waste bins round the room, and the group can then move round the room tapping the bins on the appropriate words.

This would be particularly useful for a speech that has to do with honour, or belief or worth. It would be particularly good for instance on the Troilus speech on page 93, and would highlight his heroic thinking.

It would not be so useful for these three *Dream* speeches, which are essentially dignified, but excellent for something which is rougher.

Third, the movement I outlined for the group, though clearly not to do with staging in any way, is invaluable in helping us to find the physical response to the words.

Any kind of physical obstacle will release the physical urge within the words. In this passage you will have felt it on 'lingers my desires' and 'Stir up the Athenian youth', etc.; what is important is that it allows the words to be both rough and poetic.

As you will see, the exercises are good not only for general group work but they can be geared to rehearsals at any stage, where the words chosen will be to do with the objectives of the character, and the movement and obstacles invented will be to do with the objective of the scene. This is also excellent for involving those characters with less to say, and to let them feel part of the whole thinking.

Suggestions for other group work, from passages we have already looked at:

A Winter's Tale: Florizel, page 127. We have already been through this tapping on the word 'do'. Extend this now, and tap on all the words which refer to actions; so as well as verbs, it will include nouns such as 'function', 'deeds', 'acts'.

Merchant of Venice: Bassanio and Portia, page 125. Work the words which are to do with value, both material value, and the worth of a person — their virtue:

A Midsummer-Night's Dream: Lysander and Hermia, page 126. Perhaps here words to do with time: both to do with youth and age, and with time of the moment, and how brief life is.

Julius Caesar: Brutus, page 129. Words to do with height — also connected with power.

Macbeth: page 132. This we have already talked about at length, but certainly it would be interesting to tap on the verbs — not only at the beginning where they change tense, but all the way through. The verb 'catch' progresses to 'jump', then to 'striding', then to 'o'erleaps', and finishes with 'falls'.

Coriolanus: Aufidius, page 101. Here, words to do with domination — who is the master — for this is what the play is about, both on a personal level between Coriolanus and Volumnia, and between Coriolanus and Aufidius: and on a political level between the tribunes and the senators, or the Volscis and the Romans.

These are probably enough examples: I have not touched on the Histories, but they would be rich in words to do with honour, national pride, religious duty, etc.

Work on the duologues is useful in this way:

(e) Sit back to back on the floor, leaning against each other. Speak the dialogue through, and the one who is not speaking the text, voices the words that the other is saying — any that may seem useful to that piece of text.

For instance:

Measure for Measure: The Isabella and Claudio dialogue in III.1. Here you might choose to verbalize the words to do with family relationship — words which imply their long knowledge to each other:

Romeo and Juliet: III.5 to line 64. Here where you might choose to repeat all the words to do with day and night — the images lead us to the darkness of their thoughts.

Merchant of Venice: Lorenzo and Jessica, V.1. Here words to do with the old myths: it is interesting that Lorenzo starts the game they play — 'On such a night . . .' with the image of Troilus. He casts himself in that heroic role, and this gives a humour to the rest of the scene, in that they both see themselves in terms of the old stories.

This exercise can be adapted to scenes with two or three people. You do not necessarily have to set a theme of words; sometimes it is very good to repeat the words that grab you — but always about one word a line.

It is quite simple, but what it does do is allow each character to get inside the other's thoughts and to be ready for them — not to pre-empt them, but to be there. After all, in everyday life, when you are talking with people you know well, you are ready for their vocabulary, it is familiar. They may be putting fresh ideas, but the background knowledge is there. And that is exactly what these exercises help the actor to achieve: the common background of the characters out of which the ideas spring. It furthers the sense of inner landscape.

It also prepares us for the darkness which is so often there in the thoughts: the depth of experience and the knowledge of the harshness of nature. There is so often cruelty implicit in the image, even in the lightest comedy passage. That cruelty was a recognized part of life, and we must never short-change it.

We will explore this exercise in other ways later, but I want to sow the seed now, so that you can see how practical it is in terms of acting.

Solo work

It is important that you read through the group exercises, so that you know the thinking behind them. I think this helps in rehearsals, even when group work is not being done.

> First, you need to get really relaxed. It is good, therefore, to sit on the floor, and rock gently feeling your weight. Make sure the breath is working well.
>
> Then go through the speech, and tap on the floor on the words you want to explore. You can vary this by singing the words instead of tapping.
>
> Repeat the words that are connected with the concept you choose.
>
> You will find it interesting because it will never be straightforward; always ambiguities will emerge and you will discover just how much ideas are played with.
>
> It will always help to place the imagery of the character for you — in a sense, how a character casts himself.
>
> You could choose to work the exercises simply on opposites: for instance, the Juliet speech on page 119 'O serpent heart . . .' where each thought is antithetical. This would be difficult, but we only reach the extremity of her feelings by being in touch with the opposites, and the cruelty implicit in them. It is her view of Romeo at that moment, and therefore of the nature possible in one person, and this should make us uncomfortable.
>
> It is interesting to contrast this speech with Romeo's speech about love in I.1 — pre-Juliet love that is — which we looked at on page 91. This is also built on opposites, but the concepts are much more general, for he has not yet been touched to the soul, to the quick.

Other suggestions for work

Measure for Measure: Isabella, II.4, from line 171. Use all the words to do with shame and honour — right and wrong. Implicit here is the sense of her own body, and therefore also the physical response to shame.

A Winter's Tale: Hermione, 1.2., her speech beginning line 90. Use all the sexual words. Notice just how sensual her language is here in contrast to her later text.

A Winter's Tale: Paulina. We have already looked at it on page 137. 'What studied torments . . .' Perhaps here repeat the words connected with tyranny.

King Lear: Edmund, page 120 'Thou, Nature . . .' Words to do with law would be interesting: the balance of man's law with nature's laws.

Othello: Emilia, IV.3, from line 83. A simple one — husbands and wives. This is a marvellous speech about her view of the relationship between the sexes, about who is the master. To work it in this way helps to make it very precise — it has such a very special awareness and music.

(c) **Miming the image.** I have talked about this briefly before in relation to Titania's speech, 'These are the forgeries of jealousy . . .' on page 111. It is extremely useful in that it makes you think accurately through the images, realize them fully, and find just how packed with action they so often are. It is not an exercise you need to do for long at any one time, but it is worth coming back to often.

It is simply this:

Take a speech that you know, and mime it, as if to someone who is deaf or who does not understand the language.

Take care not to be too literal — i.e., do not make it into a version of deaf and dumb language, but try to capture the essence of the images: you will be surprised how complex they are.

For a group you can set it up in this way:

One person speak the text, one thought phrase at a time, then wait and allow time for the group to mime it. The group can either repeat the words as they mime or not, whichever works best.

Solo work:

Speak the thought phrase aloud first, so that the thought is firmly in your mind, and then mime it. Take your time, and be as imaginative as you can.

This is useful to do on at least one speech of the part you are working on.

This is a liberating exercise, best done on a lyrical passage, as it would be difficult to communicate detailed information through it. But nearly any soliloquy would yield a lot, or indeed any speech which is exploring inner feelings, an inner life.

For instance, Juliet's 'Gallop apace . . .' would be very rich. The action within the images at the beginning are clear, but what you would find which I think would be surprising, is the range of images — they are coming at her from all sides, so her choices are remarkable.

Also I think the imagery near the end of the speech is interest ing —

'O I have bought the mansion of a love,
But not possessed it . . .'.

So often in Shakespeare the image of a body or person is that of a house or temple, or building of some sort. Here you get the image of an empty house which has not been filled. It is important in that it makes us see the body or person with a different perspective, in terms of its relationship with the universe.

(d) Substituting words. It is quite useful sometimes to do an exercise which substitutes words — it jolts you into an awareness of the original choices, and often helps you to find the spontaneity of an image.

For group work, set it up like this:

Take, say, the Prologue from *Romeo and Juliet*. Speak it round in the group, a line at a time, and substitute one word in each line — i.e., a verb for a verb, or a noun for a noun.

Do not try to make logical sense, so do not try to find a word that necessarily means the same, but keep the grammar intact: so you allow it to be absurd.

Useful also is the substituting of names: for instance, English place names for Greek or Roman ones. Or, in passages which are about old mythological heroes, such as the Jessica–Lorenzo dialogue which I have mentioned, substitute names of modern heroes or film stars.

> The important thing is to react as spontaneously as possible. What is good about it is that it helps you to get a freedom with the language, and get a slightly different perspective on it — this particularly with names, which always must conjure up images without being pointed too heavily.
>
> Solo work is exactly the same: substitute one word per line, and be as free with it as you can. It will always make you notice words in a different way.

What I want you to feel from these exercises is this: because you are becoming familiar with the language in ways that are not to do with thinking harder, but to do with receiving it in more instinctive ways, you will then not press the meaning out through stress, and words will then have much more life and colour.

CHAPTER 7

METRE AND ENERGY

1 METRE

I have covered quite carefully all the technical points of the iambic pentametre and its variations. All that matters now is that we start to feel that beat in our bones, as it were, so we feel the pulse and the variations instinctively — so that we know, for instance, when it needs to be used formally and when it breaks into a much more prosaic style. Also we have to find out how we want to use it, and this will vary with each production, as each production takes on its particular style.

What I want you to feel is that there is something very subtle which happens when you get to the point of knowing sense, knowing sound, but also knowing the underlying beat. It gives a lightness to the language without diminishing its strength. It is there underneath buoying you up, and this should be exhilarating and not restricting.

I have purposely given exercises for the sound and fabric of the language first, because it seems to me important that you find that freedom before you come back to the discipline of metre. And always, when working on a part, find what your motive and drive is within the character, and then come back and test out the metre — the pulse will always add to the meaning.

Because the style of any writing is always integral to the meaning, it follows that once you are in tune with the style, you will not need to press out the meaning.

Basically of course, there is little more you can do than tap the metre out gently, to hear when it goes with the sense stress and when it does not. But here is a sequence of three exercises, the first for both group and solo work, and the other two for group work.

I thought initially it would be good to use a sonnet, as it is uncomplicated by considerations of character, and so the pulse can be felt very clearly. So let us take the following, which is metrically very straightforward, and see just how much play you can get within the stress of the sense.

When I do count the clock that tells the time,
And see the brave day sunk in hideous night;
When I behold the violet past prime,
And sable curls o'er-silver'd all with white;
When lofty trees I see barren of leaves,
Which erst from heat did canopy the herd,
And summer's green all girded up in sheaves
Borne on the bier with white and bristly beard:
Then of thy beauty do I question make
That thou among the wastes of time must go,
Since sweets and beauties do themselves forsake,
And die as fast as they see others grow;
  And nothing 'gainst Time's scythe can make defence
  Save breed to brave him when he takes thee hence.

Sonnet 12.

(i) Read it through first for sense, and then again gently tapping out the metre, hearing when the sense does not coincide.

You will notice:

Line 1 Very regular, one-syllable words, endorsing the regularity of the movement of a clock: no caesura. However 'when' has to take some stress, as it places the thought of the sonnet in time.

Line 2 Though the stress is on 'brave' and 'sunk', 'day' has to have stress as it carries the sense. Also both 'brave' and 'day' have long open vowels, so the weight of the line there can be very variable, and you have to compensate by making the first part of the line light.
'hideous' is a jarring word, with a very full second syllable.

Line 3 'When' has a certain weight, because it is carrying through from the first 'When' and taking the thought on.
'violet' has three syllables and is given two pulse beats. However, you would not stress the last one fully, and so it makes you able to spend time on the word and make it remarkable.
It also allows you to stress both 'past' and 'prime'.

Line 4 This is a regular line. 'curls' is particularly long.

Line 5 'When' again has to link with the first 'When' and take the thought on; it therefore needs a certain stress. And this jumps against 'lofty trees' which are both heavy words. 'barren' breaks the metre as the stress must be on the first syllable. This makes the word rough.

Line 6 Very regular, except that you would not use the full two stresses on 'canopy', and this gives a different movement at the end of the line, allowing a poise before 'the herd', giving it a lightness.

Line 7 The lightness carries through to this line, which is also very regular.

Line 8 'Borne' has to take a lot of stress, both because of the weight of its meaning, and the length of the vowel, but this is balanced by the next two short words. The alliteration of 'borne' and 'bier' also gives a certain emphasis.
The end of the line is regular.

Line 9 'Then' is very strong because it links with the beginning 'when', and is moving the argument towards some conclusion.
'make' has stress, and this gives it an active meaning.

Line 10 Very regular — the stressed words being long and so backing up the seriousness of the thought.

Line 11 Again regular stress, though not so rhythmically settled as the previous line.

Line 12 Again regular, the antithetical words 'die' and 'grow' being open-ended long vowels, so taking a lot of weight.

Line 13 ''gainst Time's scythe' all three words must be stressed, and so the line is hard and jagged, made more so by the hardness of the consonants on ''gainst'.

Line 14 A regular line, but holding up a little on the word breed, where the caesura is, and which contains the point of the sonnet. Everything else has been driving through to that one word.

Now speak it through again, keeping the sense firmly in your mind, but specifically trying not to be emphatic, and therefore allowing the words to knock against each other lightly. Allow the variable lengths of the words to affect the speaking.

What I want you to feel is something quite subtle: that you do not have to press out the emotive words, or the words that carry the meaning, but that all the words are negotiating with each other, and the meaning that is thrown up is more interesting.

Now this does not stop you stressing heavily on something which you particularly want to stress — for instance, you may want to stress 'sunk' heavily, and certainly 'breed' requires all its value. But the point is that the language can be much lighter and more buoyant than we often allow it to be when we are over-concerned with pressing out the meaning.

(ii) This next exercise is very useful, you do not have to take a long time over it, but it should be done often, for it makes us so aware of the movement of the language.

Two people in the group take it — sitting opposite each other — and speak one word each. Try to keep the sense complete.

It may take two or three goes before you hear the purpose of it, but you will notice:

How each word has a particular place: for instance, 'count' would not be so precise without the word 'do'.

None of the important words would be so telling without the unimportant ones.

How multi-syllable words alter the structure of a line.

How sequences of single syllable words give quite a different texture to the thought.

You will hear a different music, which I hope is to do with the inter-relation of words, and how each acts on the sense of the other. Too much stress will destroy this.

(iii) Get in a circle, and speak one word round, trying to keep the sense intact. Ideally it should sound like one person speaking.

This is an excellent exercise, not only for sensing the metre and sense stress, but also for picking rhythms up from each other, while keeping the individual response to the words.

It is good for hearing the cadence of a line.

Now you can do this sequence of exercises on any speech, and of those we have already looked at I would suggest:

Ophelia on page 83. The language here is so tangible, and expressive of her state of mind. Some lines are very full of possible stresses, others very liquid and easy, and several times there are two stressed words next to each other. Too much emphasis would destroy the quality of her thoughts.

Brutus: 'All tongues speak of him . . .' on page 39. This is excellent because it is so packed. Just the first word 'All' has its weight — it is not 'some' or 'many' but 'all'.

Leontes on page 136. Because it is so jagged and irregular, and it builds so relentlessly.

If you have time, it would be very useful to take say three speeches from the same play, and work the exercises on all of them, and see how the rhythms change within one play. Each time choose a different play, and select from as wide a range as possible. Here is a list of what you could try:

Richard III: Richard's opening soliloquy — Lady Anne — Queen Margaret.

Here you would hear the different between the fairly prosaic, talking rhythms of Richard, with the slightly more formally poetic rhythm of Lady Anne, and the total rhetoric of Margaret, formal and metrically stressed.

Love's Labour's Lost: Berowne — Boyet — and the last speeches of Rosaline.

You will hear the lightness and gaiety of Berowne, the slightly more poetic structure of Boyet, and the much more serious and poetic sound of Rosaline at the end.

Richard II: Bolingbroke: 'Go to the rude ribs of that ancient castle';
Richard II: 'What must the king do now, must he submit?'
and one of the Gardener's speeches.

The balances here are very different — Bolingbroke's speech is full of action, not particularly poetic.

Richard's speech is highly formal, using specific forms of rhetoric;

and the Gardener is just wonderfully alive, the speech free, and quite naturalistic in comparison, yet absolutely regular in terms of metre.

Romeo and Juliet:

Any of the Nurse in I.3.
Juliet: 'Thou know'st the mask of night is on my face . . .'
Capulet: III.5. 'God's bread, it makes me mad . . .'

You will hear the Nurse's very naturalistic speech rhythms; Juliet's heightened poetic style; and Capulet — very formal poetic structure, quite jagged because of his own disturbance.

A Midsummer-Night's Dream:

Egeus' first speech.
Oberon: Any one of his speeches in II.2.
Theseus: V.1.

Egeus — very broken up but colloquial in sound; Oberon's language is highly poetic and exotic: and Theseus, poetic but rational.

Julius Caesar:

Marullus: I.1.
Cassius: to Casca in I.3.
Antony: III.1. 'O pardon me thou bleeding piece of earth'.

Marullus is quite fiery and jagged; Cassius, passionate, formal and rhetorical; and Antony again quite formal — but inwardly passionate. The writing throughout the play is formal and public in sound, never quite touching us.

Henry V:

Any of Henry's speeches.
Chorus to Act IV.
Burgundy: V.2.

They are long speeches, and you would not necessarily want to do them right through, but they are wonderful in that they use the pulse of the iambic beat so simply and forcefully, yet the language is always direct and personal.

Henry's rhythms vary from being very firm and rousing as with the soldiers before battle, quite rational and conversational in the more political moments, and thoughtful and indrawn as in the soliloquy before battle in IV.1.

The Chorus to Act IV is one of the richest descriptive passages in Shakespeare: the beat is very regular, but the language so full and muscular, and the interplay of sense and metre relaxed and easy, which makes it an excellent speech to work on.

Burgundy: This is a wonderfully reasoned passage; the thoughts are long, but within them there is tremendous variety of movement, and again it is an excellent speech to work on for finding rhythmical changes.

The Winter's Tale:

Leontes: I.2. 'To your own bents dispose you . . .'

Paulina: III.2. Any of her speeches.
Perdita and Florizel: Any of the speeches in IV.4.

In this play, the intensity of the feeling is always in conflict with the metre, but it is the fact that the beat is there underneath making a resistance to the flow of the language which gives it its passionate and disturbing strength. Even the lyrical passages of Perdita and Florizel are not smooth.

It is good to balance the tension of the language in this play with that of Henry V.

Hamlet:

Hamlet: III.1. 'To be, or not to be . . .'
Ophelia in the same scene — her soliloquy.
Player King: III.2.
Claudius' soliloquy in III.3.

There is something very complete about Ophelia's speech, like a poem on its own. I think the language in *Hamlet* is very unpressured — it is always lucid and articulate, and does not have the tension that you find in the other plays. Even Claudius' speech working out his guilt is well-reasoned and smooth — it is never rough — and it is good to look at the unsophisticated rhythms of the Player King in contrast.

Because Hamlet's speech is so familiar, and because it flows so easily, it is particularly good to look at it in terms of the discipline of the metre, and see how much that adds to it, and gives it its inner tension. Maybe you will hear something new.

Now these are just suggestions, and of course any of the plays will yield a lot.

Solo work

As in the first exercise, take any of the passages I have suggested and tap out the metre noticing how the sense stress lies with the metre stress, and explore how light you can be with it.

When you are well into rehearsal with a part, and have discovered a lot about the thinking and the motivation within it, it always pays to come back to the discipline of the metre, and test it out lightly on some of the speeches. You will find this always adds to the subtlety of the meaning, and helps you to feel the changes of tempo more precisely.

This is particularly true of speeches which have wit and irony. If you are lucky enough to be working on Iago, or Edmund, or Adriana in *Comedy of Errors*, this process would be particularly valuable.

I have stressed lightness because I want you to feel that the metre is always buoyant, but of course there are times when the metre asks to be used more directly, when a liturgical rhythm needs to dominate.

We just have to be open to all the changes, and realize that there are no rules, only structures which have to be recognized. I feel quite strongly that no-one should ever be given a stress — this will always confuse and restrict. Stress must always be found by the speaker through greater clarity of thought.

I believe that generally there is not enough work done to find a common attitude to rhythm within a particular production, and actors are left to find their own way. Of course it is the individual voice that an actor brings to a part which is vital, but a common sharing of energy within the text must be found, and that awareness must be rooted in a knowledge of the structure. We must make it sound as alive and direct as everyday speech; we must also honour the rhythm and size of the text.

2 ENERGY THROUGH THE TEXT

These next exercises are to do with feeling how energy moves from

a) line to line,
b) thought to thought,
c) sense structure to sense structure.

Again, I think it would be useful to take a sonnet first to see how the exercises can progress.

The expense of spirit in a waste of shame
Is lust in action; and till action, lust
Is perjur'd, murderous, bloody, full of blame,
Savage, extreme, rude, cruel, not to trust;
Enjoy'd no sooner but despisèd straight;
Past reason hunted; and no sooner had,
Past reason hated, as a swallow'd bait
On purpose laid to make the taker mad, —
Mad in pursuit, and in possession so;
Had, having, and in quest to have, extreme;
A bliss in proof; and prov'd, a very woe;
Before, a joy propos'd; behind, a dream.
All this the world well knows; yet none knows well
To shun the heaven that leads men to this hell.

Sonnet 129.

Group work

(i) Speak it through together as many times as you wish to get the sense. Now speak it, walking briskly around the room, changing direction on every punctuation mark, commas and all.

You will notice how the thought is cut up.

You will probably feel quite giddy at the end, which is exactly the purpose of it, for I want you to feel how volatile the thought is, even frenetic: this takes us precisely into the emotional state of the thought. It becomes even more telling when you do it on a speech, when you are feeling the movement in terms of character.

Now obviously punctuation varies with the edition of the text, and this is so in all the plays. Some academics will argue that the punctuation was added at a later date; this is not important for our purpose. What matters is that the punctuation, being integral with the syntax of a sentence, is always a good guide to the movement of the thoughts.

(ii) Speak the sonnet through again as a group.

This time put something on the floor that you can kick — nothing that you can damage — and kick that object on the last word of each line. This will make you move round the room a bit, which is good.

Make sure you kick on the word, and not just after it, for I want you to notice just how active those last words are, and how they lift you into the next line. Your voice will respond without you consciously lifting it.

Notice:

shame — lust
blame — trust
straight — had
bait — mad
so — extreme
woe — dream
well — hell

With the exception of 'so' and 'well', the emotional story of the sonnet is almost told in those final words.

And this is so in the structure of the plays: the final words in a line so often lead the story through, and are always active.

(iii) Now use the same principle of kicking on a word, but do it on the last word of the whole thought structure — i.e., on semi-colons and full-stops (in speeches do it on question marks also).

What I want you to notice with this is a dialogue going on within the sonnet — one thought being debated and leading us on to the next.

You can vary this by doing it standing still, but splitting the group into two, one group speaking one thought structure and the second group speaking the next thought structure, and so on. This furthers the idea of a debate going on within the sonnet.

Notice that within the larger thought structure there are still the different textures of the individual parts of the thought.

This is a good sequence of exercises, and it is good to work through on a sonnet first to see where it takes you. But of course a sonnet is a complete piece of writing in itself, and so is unlike a speech which is part of the larger movement of a play, and which will never fit quite so neatly into the framework I have set down. This of course is good, because what you will find will be much more complex and surprising. So now, let us look at how it works on a speech.

Let us look first at Helena's soliloquy in the first scene of *A Midsummer-Night's Dream*:

Helena: How happy some o'er other some can be!
Through Athens I am thought as fair as she.
But what of that? Demetrius thinks not so;
He will not know what all but he do know.
And as he errs, doting on Hermia's eyes,
So I, admiring of his qualities.
Things base and vile, holding no quantity,
Love can transpose to form and dignity.
Love looks not with the eyes, but with the mind,
And therefore is winged Cupid painted blind.
Nor hath love's mind of any judgement taste;
Wings and no eyes figure unheedy haste.
And therefore is love said to be a child
Because in choice he is so oft beguiled.
As waggish boys in game themselves forswear,
So the boy love is perjured everywhere;
For ere Demetrius looked on Hermia's eyne
He hailed down oaths that he was only mine,
And when this hail some heat from Hermia felt,
So he dissolved, and showers of oaths did melt.
I will go tell him of fair Hermia's flight.
Then to the wood will he tomorrow night

Pursue her; and for this intelligence
If I have thanks it is a dear expense.
But herein mean I to enrich my pain,
To have his sight thither, and back again.

A Midsummer-Night's Dream, I.1.

This is a thoughtful speech, not agitated like the sonnet, so it is a good one to start on.

First do it moving on all punctuation marks. You will find the movement of the individual thoughts, and several places where the thoughts run over one line, into one and a half or two lines.

Now kick on the last word of each line. You will notice how these words lift you into the next line, impel the energy. If the thought runs on over the end of the line — i.e., enjambs, then that word will have particular energy. If one thought has come to rest in the middle of the line, then you have two sets of energy moving you on.

Finally, find the dialogue within the speech, so do the third part of the sequence: kick or move on the last word of the whole thought structure — i.e., on the semi-colons, full-stops and question marks, or speak it in two groups, so you get a sense of the debate taking place.

It is really interesting to notice how she states her theme in the first line, then develops it in personal terms first, and then in philosophical terms, aware of herself in the situation. She finally comes round to the practical solution, and resolves her predicament.

You can do this sequence on any of the speeches listed on pages 175 to 177 — they would all prove rewarding. The third part of the exercise particularly points up the debating nature of the soliloquies — Hamlet's 'To be, or not to be . . .' is of course perfect — but all of the soliloquies are like a dialogue through which the character argues himself towards some sort of resolution, or at least towards a clearer knowledge of his dilemma. Angelo, for instance, in *Measure for Measure*, at the end of Act II, Scene 2, discovers feelings within himself that he had not previously recognized, and which lead him to pursue his desire for Isabella. This would be an excellent speech to work through the exercises on.

However, the structures in a soliloquy are more clearly defined, and so the exercises will throw up more surprising things in terms of rhythm in speeches which are part of dialogue. With this in mind, here are other suggestions for work:

Look first at this speech of Hermia from *The Dream*:

Hermia: Puppet? Why so? — Ay, that way goes the game.
Now I perceive that she hath made compare
Between our statures. She hath urged her height,
And with her personage, her tall personage,
Her height, forsooth, she hath prevailed with him.
And are you grown so high in his esteem
Because I am so dwarfish and so low?
How low am I, thou painted maypole? Speak!
How low am I? — I am not yet so low
But that my nails can reach unto thine eyes.

A Midsummer-Night's Dream, III.2.

This is wonderful to do — the changes within it are so sudden, and the rhythms so different in that you get three smooth pieces mixed in with the broken lines.

Also notice the final words and the story they tell:

game — compare
height — personage
him — esteem
low — speak — low — eyes

Other suggestions to look at

Also look again at Egeus from *The Dream*, page 107. Here, even more pronounced than with Hermia, are the swings between the very broken passages, and those which carry on smoothly for two or more lines, giving a very strong impression of someone quite unbalanced by anger — indeed his anger is so strong that he can contemplate the putting to death of his daughter.

Also again look at Leontes, on page 136. 'Is whispering nothing . . .'

Particularly here you get the sense of a dialogue within his mind, of thoughts coming from both sides of his brain, feeding each other.

Notice also the repetition of the word 'nothing' in the strong positions at the end of the lines.

(iv) As a variation of the last exercise, try this:

Instead of the whole group speaking the text, let two people stand opposite each other (best if they stand on the outside of the group) and only those two speak it through in the long thought structures — i.e., to full-stops, semi-colons or question marks.

In this way the whole group can hear the thought structures, and the dialogue going on within the speech, and this is very useful.

You can of course vary this, either by getting the two speakers to walk quite rapidly round the edge of the group as they speak, and also by getting the rest of the group to speak the thematic words — not too loudly or you will miss hearing the text and so start to preempt the words.

(v) This next exercise is I think quite splendid, in that it gets a group to be aware of each other, yet brings out each person's individual energy — i.e., you get a common group awareness within which individual voices can spring. At first it seems impossible and too chaotic, but when you get the hang of it you will find it soon comes together.

It is simply this: First get familiar with the sense of the speech you are going to use; then get into quite a close group.

The aim is to speak the speech through, one person only speaking at a time, but in any order, and in any length of phrase, though best not too long a phrase and it can be only one word. This the group has to sense.

Now to begin with you may get several people speaking at a time, but as it comes together, you will find you get a shared sense within the group, and you will be able to achieve it.

You may find it helpful to begin with if you put your hand up when you want to speak. As you get better I think this becomes unnecessary.

What you get from it is this:

Because of a certain competition involved in taking over your phrase, new energies keep taking the text forward.

Because different voices are speaking, you hear how different the texture of the language is within one speech — something that is smoothed over when you are concerned with making sense of it.

It points up just how thoughts and images are being thrown up all the time, extravagant and extraordinary, out of left field as it were. You start to be alive to where all the images come from, and because your mind is taken by keeping the speech going, you find you are being that much more extravagant and bold.

And also it points up how subversive the language is so often: it is not well-behaved.

Any of the speeches on the list are good to use. You will find with speeches which are predominantly thoughtful, the different nature of the thoughts will emerge; and with those which are active or stirring, the energy will start to erupt and become more physical.

Other suggestions: Bolingbroke and Northumberland in *Richard II*.

Solo work

The exercises I am going to give you for working on your own are slightly different, though the principal is the same. But I think they are some of the most valuable exercises you can do when you are working on a part, for they help you to break down a text physically and find its energy; and also they help you to find your way into a character.

As you will have seen, often when you put your attention into a physical activity, however simple, insights into the character are thrown up, simply because you are not over-concentrating on the words and making sense, and you give your subconscious responses a chance.

So, take a speech from the character you are working on, and work through the following sequence. I have already described this briefly, but here it is in detail:

Put two markers, chairs are best, about six feet apart.

The aim is to stand still at the marker when you speak, and move to the other marker on punctuation marks.

(i) First walk on every punctuation mark so that you get the movement of the individual thoughts.

(ii) Then walk only on the end of the whole thought structure — i.e., on full-stops, semi-colons and question marks, so you will feel the structure of the whole thought, plus the sense of dialogue, but of course noticing the movement of the individual parts of the thought.

It is important that you walk swiftly between the markers so that you keep the sense of continuum in the speech, but be quite still and settled when you speak.

That is all there is to the exercise, but what is excellent about it is this: your mind stays with the phrase you are saying. Somehow you do not move mentally to the next part of the speech until you move physically, with the result that you give yourself totally to the phrase you are speaking; so you find its specific value and its specific dynamic. It therefore increases the variety and gives it a different life.

(iii) This is a variation of the above, but not quite so strict. It is important to do if you have a soliloquy, or a long thoughtful speech.

Put say three chairs in different parts of the room.

This time there is no definite plan as to where you should move within a speech, but simply move to a different chair when a new mood takes over the speech, a new strand of thought.

If it is a thoughtful speech it is useful to sit on the chairs. It is an excellent way of clarifying the different attitudes in one piece of text — the different tacks that the mind takes to come round to the central point or resolution.

Often you will find it pin-points the changes between the practical or personal elements of a speech, and the philosophical or cosmic ideas which are also there.

This works particularly well for any soliloquy — e.g., Juliet's 'Gallop apace . . .' or Isabella in *Measure for Measure* — where thoughts range over several areas of consciousness. It helps to identify those different areas and give shape to the whole speech. However, it also works well for any speech of some length.

Adapt the exercise how you like. Sometimes it is good to sit on the floor for instance, but keep the positions very precise.

As I have said these are quite simple methods, but they are really most valuable, not only in finding the variety and movement in a speech, but also the structure which gives it its particular dynamic.

3 SUBVERSION — OR MAKING LANGUAGE YOUR OWN

I can think of nothing else to call it. What I really mean is ways of making words sit at a deeper level.

What seems to me important is that we do all we can to allow the language to erupt. So often it contains violence and discomfort; always it is direct and straight and has the capacity to disturb, but in our need to make it make sense we explain it into blandness. And what I suggest we need to do is jostle people into awareness.

Now I do not want to seem to be saying that we should concentrate only on the aggressive part of the language, but until we fully accept that part, the humour will not erupt either and so much irony will be missed. When we narrow it down we narrow the joy out as well.

It seems to me that our aim is to be both rough and poetic.

So here are a few exercises which help us to find that physical voice that we all have, straight and uncompromising: and also ones, slightly absurd, which help us to release the joy in the language. They need not be done for long, but long enough and often enough to make the point.

Group work

(i) Decide on the text, know it for sense, then get into a fairly tight group.

Simply it is this: you speak it through together, jostling each other as you do it. Someone perhaps needs to keep a watch on it, so it does not get over rough; otherwise keep it going.

What happens is this: although you know it is set up as an exercise and therefore not serious, it is still irritating to have someone jostle you — and so something else happens vocally, the voice sits down as it were, and you find it coming from a different place. Always a different note comes into the voice, a more direct note.

Do not do it for long, but just long enough to feel that voice working for you.

It is excellent to do on a soliloquy, like one of Hamlet's which outwardly seem to be philosophical, but it soon makes you realize how disturbing some of the images are. Or maybe on Angelo in *Measure for Measure* — you find how dark his thoughts are — the words just come from a different area within yourself.

(ii) Get into a circle and link arms quite firmly.

Speak the text through, and this time pull — one half of the circle pull one way, and the other half the other way.

In this way you will find the physical weight of the words.

For this it would be excellent to use some of Lear in the storm scene, or Othello when his feelings are becoming out of control.

Again, make sure that noone gets rough, and nobody is hurt. But it is so good to feel the strength of the words, and how vowels open out when you make that effort, and you feel the undertow of the words.

(iii) Take a piece of text and work it through a couple of times; then let each person choose one phrase that they like, and repeat it several times so they are sure of it.

Then let the group get round the edge of the room.

Then, one at a time, but in any order, let each person run as fast as they can to the other side of the room, letting out their phrase quite loudly.

You have to feel that the middle of the room is a no-go area, and get across it as quickly as you can. But what you will feel is a sense of elation at releasing the words as you run.

(iv) Then this exercise, slightly absurd, and for which you need space and a certain amount of imagination!

With the speech you are using, make each person in the group responsible for a part of the text so that it can run in order.

Then hide at the edge of the space, so that each person is out of sight of anyone else. Now keep the text going, at the same time try to move to the other side of the room without anyone else seeing.

This obviously only works if you have a fair amount of space, but it is good in that the movement of the speech shifts with the different relative spaces and with a certain sense of conspiracy which comes from the exercise.

(v) Each member of the group lies full-length on the floor — you will have to get as much room round you as you can.

Feeling the weight of your body on the floor, simply speak the text through, rolling over at the changes of thought.

Again this is a slightly absurd exercise, and should not be done for long, certainly not long enough to get giddy; but it is just so good to feel your whole body become part of the words you speak — they just begin to take on a different texture. And because it is slightly ridiculous, you are free to enjoy the language.

It is also always good to speak text rocking on the floor, feeling your weight. It always helps the voice to sit down inside.

These next exercises can be done equally well in a rehearsal situation. They all involve setting up a resistance to the speaker, some sort of barrier which has to be got through; and though only one person will be speaking the text and feeling a response to it, what the rest of the group will hear will be just as valuable. So here they are:

(vi) One person only to speak the text.

The aim is for that person to start at one end of the room and get to the other side. However, three or four members of the group will try to stop him: you have to commit yourself totally to the objective.

You will hear what happens to the words when a physical barrier has to be got through, and when the ingenuity of the speaker has to be used.

Of course never let it get too rough. But done in the right spirit it is very releasing.

(vii) Again only one person to speak the text, and for this a soliloquy is excellent to use.

The rest of the group talk quite loudly so that the speaker finds it difficult to be heard. At a given moment the group stop talking and allow the speaker to finish, but hear the urgency and commitment in the words.

As an acting exercise you can set it up slightly differently, in that the rest of the group just talk among themselves and pay no attention to the speaker.

Either way, it must highlight the need to communicate, and perhaps the loneliness of solitary thoughts.

(viii) Again only one person to speak the text, but the rest of the group to heckle him.

You can either heckle through the precise words of the text, or by reacting in your own words to the thoughts expressed.

Again this adds to the sense and the need to communicate, and makes the speaker find different ways of reacting to the text.

(ix) Another excellent exercise is to set up a game, like tig or football, or pig-in-the-middle, while you are speaking the text.

Be as imaginative as you can about how you use them: for instance, sometimes it is good to find an absurd thing to do, like making a very large gesture when you are speaking lines, or mimicking the person who is speaking. Their purpose is always to stop us being over-literal.

Chapter 8

ACTING, TEXT AND STYLE

I think we must always be interested in trying to integrate the inner way, and by that I mean those methods which an actor uses to prepare him for his character, with a way of presenting language.

We need the language to be informed by what I call the inner landscape — the way in which an actor makes the words his own and inhabits them. But we also need the language to be presented in a way that the audience hears not only what the actor is feeling, but something beyond that, beyond the naturalistic, which makes what is spoken remarkable. And this goes every bit as much for modern text, as for that which is more formal and poetic.

We can be too present, too ready: and what we have to realize is that a perspective is always there. We need to 'present' and 'be' at the same time. And the speaking can only be shallow if time is not given at the beginning to the nature of the task.

Now all the exercises I have so far set down have been about getting familiar with the language and being free. And nearly all of them can take you into rehearsal, and can be adapted and used freely, either by the actor to prepare in parallel to rehearsal, or as part of rehearsal itself. But the exercises I want to look at now are specifically for text which you are bringing to performance, to help integrate the motive and the speech, and get that extra sense of placing the word. There are not many, and they are all quite simple, and always they are to do with putting one's focus on something else, and so allowing less thought-motivated responses through — so we do not predetermine what it means. And all of them you can use as a springboard to other work.

Here I will give exercises for solo work, followed by scene work.

Solo work

(i) It is always good to go through a good proportion of your part sitting on the floor, rocking forward and back quite firmly, feeling your weight.

Take time over this because the more steadily you rock, feeling that rhythm, and the weight of your whole body going down into the floor, the more your voice will sit down inside you as it were, and so the more authentic it will become.

It is often difficult to make yourself take enough time — one half feels that you don't have the right to take it, that it is a self-indulgence, but it does pay off to take the time.

As a variation to this, it is also good to lie full-length on the floor. Feel your whole body in touch with the floor, and speak a part of the text like that. You can roll over when the thought changes.

Feel the vibrations in the chest and back, and notice how the feel of the words changes.

(ii) Set up an activity. This will depend on the room you have available, but here are suggestions:

If you have some shelves of books in the room, spread the books on the floor as far apart as possible, and speak the text while arranging them back on the shelves in order — the more you spread them the more work you will have to do to put them back, which is good.

Notice how the activity allows the language to take care of itself, and how you find new stresses and new intonations and how much more fluid it is.

Or, if there is furniture to move in the room, set yourself a particular task, such as stacking the chairs on one side.

The important thing is to be precise about the task in hand; make that the important thing in your mind, and let the text take care of itself.

(iii) Now for one which I feel is particularly valuable in finding the inner response, in finding a way to allow the words to hold and be cool even when the feeling behind them is strong so that the intention is not blurred by fussy demonstration.

It is simply this: draw a picture while speaking.

If the text is meditative, then draw the first house you lived in that you remember, or the first school you went to.

If the text is fussy and precise then draw the pattern on the carpet, or anything around you that has a pattern.

If the text is active, and of now, then draw what you can see out of the window, or simply draw what is on the other side of the room.

These are all possibilities and will give a different texture to the speaking. Try them out and see which helps the most.

The picture that evolves is unimportant. What matters is that your concentration has been focused on something very precise, and that will make you precise with the words.

There is also something sensuous about drawing a picture — this also informs the text. I think it would be good to model something with modelling clay while speaking. I have never tried that but I am sure it would prove useful — it would be tactile.

If you draw something which is in your memory, however roughly — and a house is always a good thing to draw because it is simple but evocative — it informs the words in a very special way and one's inner self comes to the surface.

When you read about this exercise you will possibly think that the emotive strength will be weakened. In practice I think you will find the opposite happens, and that the feeling will be distilled and will be communicated more strongly.

(iv) Another helpful exercise is this: imagine you are writing the speech down as in a letter; not slowly, but needing to find the exact word for what you have to say.

This achieves a sense of coining the words as you speak them, and also of the pleasure you get from finding the exact words to frame your thoughts. Perhaps pleasure is the wrong word — perhaps it is a sense of their value.

It enables you to both live through the words, but evaluate them at the same time.

When working on a part, you will of course investigate thoroughly the emotions involved. You will find the relevant feelings within yourself which you can compare with those of the character. This is the central part of an actor's work. However, we do not always integrate that awareness with the words that have to be spoken. So try this:

(v) Think of a particular feeling that you have had recently that is vivid in your mind; it can be a feeling of momentary anger or hurt or, better still, it can be a specific feeling about conditions of life

— i.e., a reaction which is perhaps a political one to some item of news. It is not heart-searching that is important — that you do in rehearsal — what I want is that you remember accurately a specific reaction that you have had in the recent past.

With that uppermost in your mind speak part of your text.

I want you to feel that there are many things happening when you speak: while we are speaking about one thing our minds are often coloured by other events. This will add a whole different texture to the words.

These last three exercises have been to do with this sense of perspective: by removing oneself slightly from the words, or perhaps by letting them come from a slightly different part of ourselves, they gain power and clarity, and become more completely filled.

They also help to further that feeling of being able to value or assess what you are talking about. When, for instance, Enobarbus describes Cleopatra in her barge, we know that he knows her worth — both the value of her spirit and her value in terms of worldly goods.

I think this sense of knowing the value of what you are saying is deeply important. When Troilus swears:

> When right with right wars who shall be most right!
> True swains in love shall in the world to come
> Approve their truths by Troilus.

We know precisely how he assesses himself, as with Cressida in her answer. When Lorenzo says to Jessica in the last scene of *Merchant of Venice*:

> . . . in such a night
> Troilus methinks mounted the Troyan walls,
> And sighed his soul toward the Grecian tents
> Where Cressid lay that night.

he is valuing his and Jessica's love with that of Troilus and Cressida — with humour yes, but it is still there with that sense of what the value of their love is. With this following dialogue from *As You Like It*:

> **Rosalind:** Nay, an you be so tardy come no more in my sight: I had as lief be wooed of a snail.
> **Orlando:** Of a snail?
> **Rosalind:** Ay, of a snail: for though he comes slowly, he carries his house on his head — a better jointure, I think, than you can make a woman. Besides, he brings his destiny with him.

Rosalind knows precisely the weight, the size, the feel of a snail, and its value in the order of things.

I had to digress, because I think this is such an important point: knowing the value at the same time as feeling the emotion.

(vi) Also a good exercise for this, and for clarifying one's thoughts, is the following:

Speak a part of your text through, a thought phrase at a time, first in your own words, and then in the words of the text.

Take time over this, so you find the motive that makes you finally express the thought.

Now for two exercises to free you physically:

(vii) Speak some of your text through feeling a different weight and size. This is often quite helpful in finding an attitude to the text.

For instance, if you are relatively small and thin, it is helpful to think of yourself being quite large and heavy. Take your time, sit on the floor and imagine that weight.

This is a really helpful exercise if you are playing perhaps a character like Charmian in *Antony and Cleopatra*, where, because you are not driving scenes, because you are waiting for someone else's motives to take charge, it is easy to become self-effacing. In fact, what we need from Charmian is a very strong sense of her right to be there, that she is earthed as it were, for she gives a balance to the scenes.

This also makes one take one's time, something which is often difficult to do when playing someone subservient.

If you are large, it is then good to think of the reverse — that you are light and move quickly. This actually makes you speak quicker, and this often informs what the text is giving you.

I think one's own physical size affects the way we work often more closely than we realize, and holds us within certain limits. It is good therefore consciously to try to break the patterns that may result.

(viii) Also good is to do some physical routine while speaking a part of your text.

For instance, set yourself a particular sequence of physical exercises, and carry them through while speaking;

or, jog lightly round the room on your toes, as if sparring with a boxer;

or imagine that you are playing tennis, or riding a horse or motor bike, something which gives you physical enjoyment, and speak while either imagining or miming the action — even a dance like a tango. You will find that the sense memory transfers to the speaking, and a physical buoyancy will show in the words.

All these exercises are only suggestions to start you off, and they will no doubt make you think of others: the important thing is to use what is useful to you, and leave those which are not — everyone works from a slightly different basis, but do try them all thoroughly first.

Scene work

Now for work in scenes with two, or perhaps three, characters.

(i) Excellent as a starting-point is this:

Sit back to back on the floor, leaning your weight fully against each other; or if in a three, with your weight as equally placed as possible.

Speak the dialogue through in this position.

This is excellent, partly because you feel each other's vibrations, and so pick up a certain communication through that; and partly because, by not looking at each other, you listen more acutely.

This exercise can be developed, as we have seen earlier, in this way:

The character or characters not speaking repeat roughly one word per line that is being spoken. You will always hear something fresh — ladders of thought and word games will emerge very clearly.

(ii) This exercise can be done sitting back to back, or facing each other, or standing.

It is quite simple, and can be done in two ways:

(a) Speak the text through, and the character(s) who are listening, comment, either through their own words or the words of the text, on what is being said to them as you speak.

This clarifies your relationship to the other character in terms of the precise words used, and therefore makes one more accurate.

(b) Wait until the other character has finished speaking: then speak your next thoughts, in your own words, before you speak the text. This clarifies your own choices in terms of that relationship, and again makes the words you finally choose that much more precise. You realize your relationship, and what you want out of it, in terms of the text.

Both these exercises are very useful in making us clarify the language for ourselves, and the choices we make in it. The first particularly focuses on answering accurately, something which we often do not do in our anxiety to get ready for what we have to say next. Therefore, we often do not fully explore the wonderful sense of language being bandied to and fro, and the life that springs from that, from truly answering what has been said.

(iii) Because we are so busy making an impact with the dialogue, again we often do not allow ourselves the time and the room to live through it. This next exercise, the same as the one given for solo work, just lets you feel that sense of space within the words.

Lie full-length on the floor, as far apart as possible.

Speak the text through, rolling over — half a turn — on each change of thought, either towards or away from each other, depending on what the thought is giving you.

It is important to feel your weight fully on the floor.

The distance between you makes you reach through with the dialogue; always good, particularly in an intimate scene. The sense of reaching over a space links with the need to reach into the other character, and so you lift the words more.

(iv) This next exercise is to do with setting up occupations.

These activities must arise either out of the space you are in, and using it in a specific way, or by finding a particular activity related to the needs of the two characters to communicate. They should not be to do with any idea of blocking the play: this would simply make you start acting, and any discovery through words would be blocked! What you do in the exercise, however, may of course finally influence the blocking, and you may discover more precisely where you want to be in relation to each other.

Again the exercise comes in two parts:

(a) Using the space, quite simply set up activities in which you are both involved, like moving furniture.

> Always be quite precise about what you want to achieve. Make that important, and speak the dialogue as you do it. Notice how it frees the language and rhythms.

Then work it so that the activities are related in some way to the characters' needs from each other:

> For instance if x wants a reaction from y, then only y does the activity, and x moves round trying to attract his attention.
>
> The activity may simply be sitting down at a table copying something from a book.

It is often quite useful to do the exercises both ways round: Shakespeare is always so ambivalent, that different needs and therefore different tones will open up. Nothing is ever black and white — it keeps us from making up our minds too early as to what the scene is about.

The activities can be either physically active, or quite still; it does not matter. It is the concentration of them that pays off.

> (**b**) Activities involving a particular action between the characters.
>
> For instance, x tries to make y comfortable.
>
> To do this he makes a bed somewhere in the space, using coats or cushions, whatever may be available. He then gets y to lie down, covering him with a coat, maybe taking off his shoes, making him as comfortable as possible.
>
> y can either resist or go with it, whichever seems appropriate.
>
> There could then be an adult-child relationship develop, which could end with x cradling y's head in his lap.

I remember working this as an exercise with Lear and Goneril in I.4. Here Goneril, in a very callous and hard way, is beginning to strip Lear of his followers, and therefore of his authority; but because she was touching him and being physically gentle with him, and treating him almost like a child, it opened up all sorts of things about that relationship and about their past, and this made the words she spoke even more terrible. It also made one feel how Lear was palpably losing his authority, his identity.

This exercise has many possibilities, and is very valuable: the touching gently and cradling gives a whole different texture to the tone and how you use the words.

(v) Setting up resistances. I suppose all the exercises have been to do with this in some way, but here are two suggestions:

> The first to do with keeping distance between you.
>
> x wants to get face to face with y. y does all he can to prevent this by running round the room, putting any obstacle in the way, hiding, etc.
>
> x hides an object from y, who then tries to find it. x watching all the time and moving round.

These are both quite simple, but useful in breaking up the thought patterns.

(vi) Drawing a picture. I explained this fully in (iii) for solo work.

Get quite a bit of space between you. Preferably look out of different windows, and draw what you see, but equally you can draw what you see on the opposite wall of the room.

It is important to have space between you, and to be looking in different directions.

> Keep the dialogue going. Notice how different it becomes, yet how unforced: it seems to come from a different part of one's consciousness.
>
> Again you can choose to draw what is in your memory, and this will give a different quality. Be quite specific in your choice: if the picture is of your home, say, then it will have pleasure; it it is of a school or college, it will have another kind of memory, not so personal, and that will also give a different texture.
>
> You may choose to draw each other. Just use what seems appropriate to the scene.

I really like this exercise, for you find both personal involvement and a sense of presenting it very particularly. It works wonderfully on a scene such as the one between Cordelia, Regan and Goneril at the end of Act I, Scene I of *King Lear*: each is so full of their own thoughts, yet making some sort of communication with each other.

Also it is good to do this exercise without drawing a picture, simply each character looking out of a different window and concentrating on what you see.

> Also good is to play noughts and crosses with each other: it is specific, and involves competition.

Now two exercises which help clarify thought changes.

(vii) Sit at a table, as large a one as possible, with many more chairs than characters.

Work it like this:

> Sit at the table as far apart as you can. Speak the dialogue and change your seat at each change of thought.
>
> Only move one chair at a time, but move either towards or away from the other character(s) as you feel right. Move near who you want to be near to.
>
> You can move whoever is speaking.

This is excellent in that it pin-points the change of thoughts, and how you feel in relation to each character and each thought.

(viii) With very much the same end in view, but slightly more complicated, try this:

> Put two rows of six chairs facing each other, the rows about three feet apart, and put one chair at the head of the rows.
>
> Each character sits at the end of the row, one on each side.
>
> At each change of thought, you can move up one chair, and cross to the opposite row if you wish. You can move back or up, but only one chair at a time.
>
> Either x or y, to be decided on beforehand, needs to get to the top chair. This is their drive, and therefore makes them drive the scene.
>
> You can alternate who has that drive.

This is particularly interesting if there are three characters in the scene.

You notice who controls the scene, and perhaps who is standing back, who is in the role of an observer.

I am thinking particularly of the two main scenes between Rosalind and Orlando and Celia (*As You Like It*, Act III, Scene 2, and Act IV, Scene 1) where Rosalind drives, Orlando follows and Celia observes.

This exercise helps to throw up Celia's precise attitude to what she is witnessing. We notice how little Celia speaks, yet how positive when she does — she is not passive.

It also works for more complex political scenes, such as the one with Willoughby, Northumberland and Ross (*Richard II*, Act II, Scene 1).

It would also work for Hamlet, Rosencrantz and Guildenstern, at the end of III.2., when they are trying to work information out of Hamlet: the thoughts become so clearly defined.

It is excellent for finding out where changes of thought occur, and what effect they have on the other characters, even those who are not speaking. In particular, how it feels not to be driving the thought — perhaps this is the most interesting part of it.

All these exercises make you notice how active the silence of a character is.

(ix) An exercise which is very good to highlight the suspense within a scene, and which feeds the words in a new way, is this:

> Make your space in the middle of the floor, for two or three characters. You need two other people to make the exercise work.
>
> Mark out the square in which the scene happens. The other two place themselves on the outside of the square, one on each side.
>
> These two walk from front to back of the square, like sentries, and vice versa, at random when the scene is playing; but whenever they get between the markers of the square, the actors must stop speaking and wait until they have passed.
>
> It is excellent in that it highlights the need to communicate, and it gives a sense of urgency to the scene, and of finding the exact word to alight on.
>
> It seems complicated; it is in fact quite simple — just test it through once before doing it properly.

As you will see, I have given the exercises mainly for scenes with two people, but they can be adapted quite easily for three or four, or even five. It is also helpful with the larger number to play a simple physical game:

(x) Either play tig while doing the scene; or set up a rough kind of football, with a goal at each end of the room, and a ball.

This is excellent to do when you have been working hard on breaking down a scene — it breaks patterns and releases the physical vigour of the language.

There are of course many other exercises that can be done, involving putting a scene into a different context, for instance making it modern and giving it a modern accent — the conspirators in Julius Caesar could be Mafia — but these are more to do with acting than with language exercises; they do not necessarily make us feel the vitality of the language as it is; it is a little on a par with paraphrasing. However, they can be useful sometimes, and they can help to break patterns. But I think they are easy to invent, and one should just be free with them.

Group work

Now of course all the group exercises I have given so far can be used as preparation for rehearsal, and I think they speed the rehearsal process. Most of them can be adapted to the needs of specific scenes, and I think I have indicated how they may be used. But I want now to focus on a few which I think are particularly useful in rehearsal. They all need a good space so you can move freely: all are to do with setting up some kind of resistance.

First I want to say that I do believe it to be useful for the whole company to take part in some of the work done on certain of the central scenes of a play, even though they may not be part of it. This not only helps the company to become part of the central thought of the play, and the predicaments posed so that their contribution is richer; it is also tremendously useful for the actors playing those scenes to have resistance set up for them by the rest of the company, and to feel their involvement.

With this in mind, here are the exercises:

First for soliloquies:

(i) The actor to speak the text, either standing still or moving round.

The rest of the company to heckle in some way, either by challenging him through the words of the text — repeating them; or by questioning what he speaks in their own words — i.e., questioning his motives.

This is excellent in that it helps the actor to get a sense of the thoughts being provoked — each one by the one before.

Soliloquies, because they are to do with private thoughts and are in essence ruminative, often become merely passive. We have to find the challenge within them which makes the character need to define his thoughts: the active need to talk.

While heckling, the company can move about the room, jostle him, do whatever may be helpful.

(ii) Also useful is to set up the situation where the actor wants to tell the rest; but they refuse to listen, talk to each other or turn away.

> Again this pin-points the need to communicate, and also, I think, the sense of the loneliness of thoughts.

Again, this can be done moving, sitting down or however you like.

(iii) Set the actor a particular distance to travel within the space: a target he has to reach before the end of the speech.

Let two or three of the rest hold him back, prevent him from reaching the point set. Hopefully he will be inventive, and find some way to reach the target.

> You will hear how the words respond to the movement.
>
> You will hear something of the physical effort required to compass the thoughts. In other words you will hear the relationship between the physical and the emotional involvement — something of the energy involved within extreme feelings.

Be as inventive as you can about using the space. Sometimes, in a church hall for instance, you may have a gallery to use — that is marvellous, as you have much more space in which to be inventive. Also you can get out of sight and so the possibilities increase, such as hiding, and more varied exercises can be set up.

I am thinking particularly of Hamlet's soliloquies, where there is a very strong feeling of a structure, a castle, full of people all oblivious to his dilemma, his questions. So exercises can be set up where people are talking everywhere, and where his loneliness is central.

Or with Edgar, when he is escaping from Lear's Court disguised, exercises could be set up where people are calling him from all sides, even mocking.

The good thing about the exercises is that they stimulate both the inward drive of the thought, and the need to communicate it to an outside world.

All these exercises can be adapted for work on speeches within a scene — Lear in the storm for instance; or Richard II in his public scenes.

What seems to me important about all this work is that it helps the actor to give the language a larger context. It does not diminish the individual input of the actor, but it helps him to find a style which is open, which makes him more easily share his thoughts, in a sense by expecting them to be shared — to let them drop into each person's consciousness without effort, and allow the hearer to feel he is part of them.

For a scene between two characters, where the emotions are heightened, set up the following:

(iv) Set the two actors apart — their aim is to come together, to touch. The rest keep them apart, not by touching them physically, simply by continual movement between them.

Again you will get a sense of the need to communicate — more than just words, but a deep sense of longing.

I am thinking particularly of Hamlet and the Ghost, where you feel that each needs to reach the other and touch, but that the gulf is impossible to bridge.

This would work equally well for Romeo and for Juliet. Other possibilities would emerge.

For scenes with a large number of people:

Interesting to work on is a scene with a large number of people, such as one of the Court scenes in *The Dream*, where the essence of the scene is public, but where two people want to make private contact within it.

(v) The latter exercise can therefore be adapted, and set up like this:

Each member of the scene to become partisan to one or other of the main characters, and by diversions, by watching and forestalling their movements, keep them drawn back and away from each other. The two main characters can freely move around the space, maybe set a particular circle to be covered.

The important thing is to get a sense of drawing them away from each other.

This can also work if perhaps only one of the main characters wants to get close to the other: Hamlet and Ophelia for instance.

Again, for a scene where there are a large number of people on stage, and where one person is in authority and the rest perhaps vying for attention, you can set an exercise up in this way:

(vi) The ruling character moves quite fast round in a prescribed circle. The rest get as close as possible, and the one who is speaking has to be right at his ear.

This can get quite rough, but it is exactly that which will release us from being polite, and help find that absolute urge to speak — the necessity to do so.

(vii) Also good, within a large scene, is to speak it quite normally through for sense, but for each character to move near to the person he wants to be near to at any given moment. This can change while someone else is speaking; but is an excellent way of finding exactly where you are within the thought of the scene.

And lastly, here are two exercises to do with style: specifically to help us find a way of feeling and presenting the language at the same time, so we do not bombard the audience with our feelings, but allow them to hear the thoughts and hold them — and this without diminishing their emotional weight.

(viii) This requires two actors to one character, the second to place himself just slightly to the side and behind the first.

The scene should be played through normally, but with the second actor repeating everything the first does and says, a split second behind, for it must be done through listening.

This is difficult, and you may have to do it a couple of times to get the hang of it.

It is excellent in that you hear the space of the words. I am thinking particularly of *The Dream*, IV.1, where Theseus and Hippolyta are out hunting early, with the sound of their hounds baying in the distance giving a feeling of space to the whole scene.

They discover the lovers sleeping, and when they wake they exchange the memory of the night's events — the sense of whether it was a reality or a dream.

The scene ends with Bottom waking up alone and recounting his own dream. The echoes and associations in the text are particularly rich.

Firstly, the exercise is excellent for concentration, for those who are repeating the text. But also, what it allows you to hear is the space that the words hold, the echoes and associations in the language, something beyond the immediate. And those echoes and associations are present in all the plays.

Finally this last exercise is a company one, and is to do with presenting a poem. The idea came out of work being done in rehearsal with Howard Davies, on *Henry VIII*. Howard's emphasis, I would say, is always on the clarity and directness with which an actor contacts his audience, and allows them into his thoughts, and he finds many ways of making this happen. And I think exercises which I use which involve the speaking of thoughts and then the text have been sparked off by some of his work in rehearsal. I think this one is particularly useful.

(ix) Divide up into twos, and each pair take a poem — you will find a few to start you off on page 266 — and find a way of presenting that poem to the rest of the group. This will take ten or fifteen minutes.

It is absolutely open as to how you do it, but try not to be too literal about it — try to use its sound as creatively as possible.

Sometimes the results are quite funny, which is good ; but you will also see just how imaginative you can be with the sound, without taking away from the honesty of purpose. It makes us free to present sound, and perhaps understand a little more how creative this can be.

As I say, all these exercises can be adapted and used in any way that is appropriate. Hopefully they will all help to integrate the finding of one's inner truth with the need to communicate that to an audience.

Chapter 9

FURTHER POINTS OF TEXT

1 PROSE

Shakespeare's prose is wonderful to work on because you find out so much about how speeches are built: perhaps because there is no metre to deal with, you see very clearly their structure, how the premise is laid at the beginning and then elaborated on, how one thought builds to the next, and this in fact feeds back into the work on verse.

Now because it is prose, our instincts often are to deal with it in a modern way, which is to do with undercutting and throwaway inflections, and this particularly in the comedy writing, but in fact the speeches do not work like that: they have a cadence — a poising and a pointing — which is in its way as precise and demanding as verse. And when you throw a line away, it must be through choice.

Now obviously the texture of prose is quite different to that of verse: it is never heroic. I was going to say that it never has the same emotional ring, but then something like Mistress Quickly's description of Falstaff's death has tremendous emotional resonance — or even Bottom's dream. But I suppose in terms of feeling, it is always just a bit more accessible to our own experience. When you are doing a part which switches between the two, it is important that you mark the changes, and find why the reasoning of the character demands the switch.

So I would say this: with prose you need to pay particular attention to the syntax of the thought, for this will give you the cadence of the lines — i.e., the way the inflection needs to move and lift. Within each whole thought structure, that is to semi-colons, full-stops, question marks as before, you will find small phrases which lift and turn the thought, and have to be kept in the air. So in fact all the exercises which I have given, except those dealing with the beat only, will tell you how the rhythm works and give you the structure.

But also, extremely important is an awareness of note, the pitch of a word. Because there is not a poetic shift of sound — places where the poetry palpably needs a lifting or dropping of the pitch — it is essential that each new thought is started on a slightly different note, otherwise the speaking will be flat and will not engage the ear and it will not take us anywhere. Now the exercises I have given for walking between phrases to find the impetus to begin the new phrase should make you find that note naturally, for it is always to do with finding a renewal of energy. However, it is something that you need eventually within yourself musically — you need to train your ear to hear it, for we have to satisfy the listener with what the music of the piece demands. We have to make that musical awareness real in terms of acting.

Let us look now at five prose pieces:

First, Orlando at the beginning of *As You Like It*. It needs no introduction for it is at the beginning of the play, and sets the story up. I shall write it out twice, first as it is written, and then in separate thought structures, with marks to separate the small phrases, so it resembles something akin to the pointing in a psalm.

Orlando: As I remember, Adam, it was upon this fashion bequeathed me by will, but poor a thousand crowns, and, as thou sayest, charged my brother on his blessing to breed me well; and there begins my sadness. My brother Jacques he keeps at school, and report speaks goldenly of his profit: for my part, he keeps me rustically at home, or, to speak more properly, stays me at home unkept — for call you that 'keeping' for a gentleman of my birth, that differs not from the stalling of an ox? His horses are bred better, for, besides that they are fair with their feeding, they are taught their manage, and to that end riders dearly hired; but I, his brother, gain nothing under him but growth, for the which his animals on his dunghills are as much bound to him as I. Besides this nothing that he so plentifully gives me, the something that nature gave me his countenance seems to take from me: he lets me feed with his hinds, bars me the place of a brother, and, as much as in him lies, mines my gentility with my education. This is it, Adam, that grieves me, and the spirit of my father, which I think is within me, begins to mutiny against this servitude. I will no longer endure it, though yet I know no wise remedy how to avoid it.

As You Like It, I.1.

1 As I remember, / Adam, / it was upon this fashion bequeathed me by will, / but poor a thousand crowns, / and, / as thou sayest, / charged my brother on his blessing to breed me well; /

2 and there begins my sadness. /

3 My brother Jacques he keeps at school, / and report speaks goldenly of his profit: /

4 for my part, / he keeps me rustically at home, / or, / to speak more properly, / stays me at home unkept — / for call you that 'keeping' for a gentleman of my birth, / that differs not from the stalling of an ox? /

5 His horses are bred better, / for, / besides that they are fair with their feeding, / they are taught their manage, / and to that end riders dearly hired; /

6 but I, / his brother, / gain nothing under him but growth, / for the which his animals on his dunghills are as much bound as I. /

7 Besides this nothing that he so plentifully gives me, / the something that nature gave me his countenance takes from me: / he lets me feed with his hinds, / bars me the place of a brother, / and, / as much as in him lies, / mines my gentility with my education. /

8 This is it, / Adam, / that grieves me, / and the spirit of my father, / which I think is within me, / begins to mutiny against his servitude. /

9 I will no longer endure it, / though I yet know no wise remedy how to avoid it. /

You will notice:

1 The crux of the problem set out in quite a complex sentence. The listener needs the end words of each phrase lifted (i.e., those before the mark), not necessarily paused on, in order to get the main points of the argument.

2 A simple statement, which spreads.

3 This sets up the antithesis between his brother and himself: I have broken it on a colon to point that up.

4 Quite involved syntax: it hinges on the word 'keep'; but it has to drive right through to 'stalling of an ox' for us to get the complete sense.

5 This next thought is again involved, but must come in one drive so we feel the measure of his frustration. Yet each phrase has its place.

6 'but I' — the antithesis of horses.

7 A complicated sentence, hinging on the antithetical words 'something' and 'nothing'. Again it drives right through to education, because that is a twist of the beginning of the thought, and we must hear it as one. It is the most complex phrase so far.

8 Back to the simplicity of the beginning, back to Adam, and beginning to wind down.

9 The final statement and resolve to take action, though as yet the precise action is in question.

As you will see there is a lot of information in the speech, both about the hard facts of the situation, and about Orlando's feelings and his relationship with his brother and his dead father.

Moreover, there is a good deal of pressure on the actor to bring on the energy needed to start the play. It also needs to be quick, so good pointing is particularly vital for the facts to be understood.

One final point: it is always important that the beginning of a scene is started fractionally slower, so the audience can get in tune with your voice. Therefore you can use the phrase 'As I remember, Adam . . .' to draw in your audience.

The more you perform the play the more readily you will be able to judge the exact amount of energy required to start the play off, so that you can place it right with as little tension as possible and judge the right note to start on.

Particularly useful for finding the structure are those exercises:

(a) To do with walking between markers, first on each punctuation mark, and then at the end of the whole thought structure. This helps you to feel how quickly the thoughts turn, and with Orlando, how his frustration bursts out.
(b) Singing the phrases through lightly, which will clarify just which words need to be spread on and lifted.

Now look at this speech of Benedick from *Much Ado About Nothing*, which switches between long involved thought structures, and very short ones, and a question thrown in. We laugh with the rhythms, which are comedic, as much as with the reasoning. I shall write it out with the pointing, as with Orlando:

Benedick: I do much wonder that one man, / seeing how much another man is a fool when he dedicates his behaviour to love, / will, / after he hath laughed at such shallow follies in others, / become the argument of his own scorn by falling in love; /

and such a man is Claudio. /

I have known when there was no music with him but the drum and the fife, / and now had he rather hear the tabor and the pipe. /

I have known when he would have walked ten mile afoot to see a good armour, / and now will he lie ten nights awake carving the fashion of a new doublet. /

He was wont to speak plain and to the purpose, / like an honest man and a soldier, / and now is he turned orthography; /

his words are a very fantastical banquet, / just so many strange dishes. /

May I be so converted and see with these eyes? /

I cannot tell; /

I think not. /

I will not be sworn but love may transform me to an oyster; /

but I'll take my oath on it, / till he have made an oyster of me, / he shall never make me such a fool. /

One woman is fair, / yet I am well; /

another is wise, / yet I am well; /

another virtuous, / yet I am well; /

but till all graces be in one woman, / one woman shall not come in my grace. /

Rich she shall be, / that's certain; /

wise, / or I'll none; /

virtuous, / or I'll never cheapen her; /

fair, / or I'll never look on her; /

mild, / or come not near me; /

noble, / or not I for an angel; /

of good discourse, / an excellent musician, / and her hair shall be of what colour it please God.

Much Ado About Nothing, II.3.

This is wonderful to work on: you see how the rhetoric is used in the repetition of form of words; how the lists quicken and build, and how all this is undercut by the last thought phrase. The comedy is in the rhythm. The first phrase should be done on one breath.

And this sense of cadence and structure has to be observed in the serious speeches as well, for it will give us their measure too. Look now at Mistress Quickly:

Bardolph: Would I were with him, / wheresome'er he is, / either in heaven or hell! /

Hostess: Nay, / sure, / he's not in hell: / he's in Arthur's bosom, / if ever man went to Arthur's bosom. /

'A made a finer end / and went away an it had been any christom child; /

'a parted e'en just between twelve and one, / e'en at the turning o'th'tide; /

for after I saw him fumble with the sheets, / and play with flowers, / and smile upon his fingers' ends, / I knew there was but one way; /

for his nose was as sharp as a pen, / and 'a babbled of green fields. /

'How now, Sir John?' / quoth I, / 'What, / man, / be o'good cheer!' /

So 'a cried out, / 'God, / God, / God!' / three or four times. /

Now I, / to comfort him, / bid him 'a should not think of God — / I hoped there was no need to trouble himself with any such thoughts yet. /

So 'a bade me lay more clothes on his feet; /

I put my hand into the bed, / and felt them, / and they were as cold as any stone; /

then I felt to his knees, / and so up'ard and up'ard, / and all was as cold as any stone.'

Henry V, II.3.

The cadences within those phrases are so clear, and the rhythm so powerful, and the pictures painted so vivid. And of course the actor playing that would fill it with all the emotional truth within them, but that emotion has to be disciplined through the particular phrasing and pointing which is there. That is what will transmit the feeling.

And now Casca, in *Julius Caesar*. This is interesting because of its mixture of rye humour, very laid back, yet he ends the scene with something quite chilling. This speech of Casca comes at the end of a long scene, during which we have seen Cassius win Brutus over to his plot of killing Caesar; we have seen Caesar process to the Capitol and heard the noise from the crowd. Casca arrives from the Capitol, and we pick the scene up a little way through:

Brutus: Was the crown offered him thrice?

Casca: Ay, / marry, / was't, / and he put it by thrice, / every time gentler than the other; /
and at every putting-by mine honest neighbours shouted.

Cassius: Who offered him the crown?

Casca: Why, / Antony.

Brutus: Tell us the manner of it, / gentle Casca.

Casca: I can as well be hanged as tell the manner of it; /

it was mere foolery; /

I did not mark it. /

I saw Mark Antony offer him a crown; /

yet 'twas not a crown neither, 'twas one of these coronets; /

and, / as I told you, / he put it by once; /

but for all that, / to my thinking, / he would fain have had it. /

Then he offered it to him again; /

then he put it by again; /

but to my thinking, / he was very loath to lay his fingers off it. /

And then he offered it the third time; /

he put it the third time by; /

and still as he refused it, / the rabblement hooted, / and clapped their chopped hands, / and threw up their sweaty night-caps, / and uttered such a deal of stinking breath because Caesar refused the crown, / that it had, / almost, / choked Caesar; /

for he swooned, / and fell down at it. /

And for mine own part, / I durst not laugh, / for fear of opening my lips and receiving the bad air. /

Julius Caesar, I.2, from line 226.

As you can see this is wonderful undercutting humour, and it goes on in this vein for a little longer.

You will notice how the short feeding lines of Cassius and Brutus need to be part of the rhythmic structure.

Casca goes on further to describe how the crowd got angry because he had refused the crown; and several speeches on, on line 281, he says this:

> I could tell you more news too: / Marullus and Flavius, / for pulling scarfs off Caesar's images, / are put to silence. /
>
> Fare ye well. /
>
> There was more foolery yet, / if I could remember it. /

The repetition of the word 'foolery' ties it up with added irony.

What is interesting about Casca's text is that in the very next scene, having witnessed the extraordinary violent storm, and other strange happenings which he interprets as omens, he returns and describes all he has seen to Cicero — in verse? The whole tenor of his speech has changed:

Cicero: Good even, Casca: brought you Caesar home?
Why are you breathless? and why stare you so?
Casca: Are not you moved, when all the sway of earth
Shakes like a thing unfirm? O Cicero,
I have seen tempests, when the scolding winds
Have rived the knotty oaks, and I have seen
Th'ambitious ocean swell and rage and foam,
To be exalted with the threatening clouds;
But never till tonight, never till now,
Did I go through a tempest dropping fire.
Either there is a civil strife in heaven,
Or else the world, too saucy with the gods,
Incenses them to send destruction.

Julius Caesar, I.3.

It is useful to notice these changes from prose to verse, and to hear how the phrasing of the one style feeds into the other. One further thing about Casca's text: there is a quite chilling music in those last few lines of his earlier prose scene, about Marullus and Flavius being put to silence; and this is something I want you to notice, and which we will talk about in the next section.

Just one more quite short prose passage, from *Hamlet*:

Horatio: If your mind dislike anything, / obey it. /
I will forestall their repair hither and say you are not fit. /
Hamlet: Not a whit. /
We defy augury. /
There is special providence in the fall of a sparrow. /
If it be now, / 'tis not to come. /
If it be not to come, / it will be now. /
If it be not now, / yet it will come. /
The readiness is all. /
Since no man knows of aught he leaves, / what is't to leave betimes? /
Let be. /

Hamlet, V.2.

In each example I have purposely left in some of the shorter feeding lines — they need as careful pointing. For instance, Bardolph has to serve up 'heaven and hell' for Mistress Quickly to answer: 'Nay, sure, he's not in hell: he's in Arthur's bosom . . .' And the point I want to make is that short lines need to be just as carefully poised as any longer speech, and this can be quite difficult as so often one feels under pressure to serve them up quickly.

Also very clear in these prose speeches is the sense of characters setting up the ideas, and then answering them, or debating them: this is very much the case in Benedick's speech, and also with Hamlet.

I wanted to set the pointing out like this on speeches of different emotional weight and colour, to stress how each phrase has its own music, and its own space and time whether the content is practical and informative, or emotional and descriptive. The music of the phrasing must be observed. And this ties up with all I have said to do with the audience needing to hear the language as well as understand its meaning — needing to hear the space between the words.

2 HEIGHTENED MUSIC

What I want to look at here quite briefly are those moments which are to do with what I call a heightened music. I do not mean here the very poetic lyrical verse of say *Romeo and Juliet* in the first balcony scene, or Richard II's high poetic utterances, or the intensity of Ophelia. I am talking about the moments in a play when the whole timbre changes for a moment, and we are put in touch with a different sound. They are moments which occur in just about every play; they sometimes come from the least poetic character, and they are unexpected, so we have to be ready for them. I have already mentioned the last short speech of Casca in *Julius Caesar*:

> I could tell you more news too: Marullus and Flavius, for pulling scarfs off Caesar's images, are put to silence. Fare you well. There was more foolery yet, if I could remember it.

What I am talking about has to do with a sense of other music, of an understanding beyond ourselves, where something pauses and we have to listen. Perhaps it is best put in Lorenzo's words in the last scene of *The Merchant of Venice*:

Lorenzo: How sweet the moonlight sleeps upon this bank!
Here will we sit and let the sounds of music
Creep in our ears; soft stillness and the night
Become the touches of sweet harmony.
Sit, Jessica. Look how the floor of heaven
Is thick inlaid with patens of bright gold.
There's not the smallest orb which thou beholdest
But in his motion like an angel sings,
Still quiring to the young-eyed cherubins;
Such harmony is in immortal souls,
But whilst this muddy vesture of decay

Doth grossly close it in, we cannot hear it.

[*Enter Musicians.*

Come ho, and wake Diana with a hymn,
With sweetest touches pierce your mistress' ear
And draw her home with music.

[*Music.*

Jessica: I am never merry when I hear sweet music.
Lorenzo: The reason is your spirits are attentive.
For do but note a wild and wanton herd
Or race of youthful and unhandled colts
Fetching mad bounds, bellowing and neighing loud,
Which is the hot condition of their blood,
If they but hear perchance a trumpet sound,
Or any air of music touch their ears,
You shall perceive them make a mutual stand,
Their savage eyes turned to a modest gaze
By the sweet power of music. Therefore the poet
Did feign that Orpheus drew trees, stones, and floods,
Since naught so stockish, hard, and full of rage
But music for the time doth change his nature.
The man that hath no music in himself,
Nor is not moved with concord of sweet sounds,
Is fit for treasons, stratagems, and spoils,
The motions of his spirit are dull as night,
And his affections dark as Erebus.
Let no such man be trusted. Mark the music.

The Merchant of Venice, V.1.

That is clearly a highly lyrical passage, and the other examples I am going to give are not necessarily so. However, what the passage does do is make us listen differently for the moment: it makes us attentive in a different way. And I think the very next passage, a short scene between Nerissa and Portia, has the same quality, and to my mind contains Portia's most poetic language:

Portia: That light we see is burning in my hall;
How far that little candle throws his beams!
So shines a good deed in a naughty world.
Nerissa: When the moon shone we did not see the candle.
Portia: So doth the greater glory dim the less.
A substitute shines brightly as a king
Until a king be by, and then his state
Empties itself, as doth an inland brook
Into the main of waters. Music! hark!
Nerissa: It is your music, madam, of the house.
Portia: Nothing is good, I see, without respect;
Methinks it sounds much sweeter than by day.

Nerissa: Silence bestows that virtue on it, madam.
Portia: The crow doth sing as sweetly as the lark
When neither is attended, and I think
The nightingale, if she should sing by day
When every goose is cackling, would be thought
No better a musician than the wren.
How many things by season seasoned are
To their right praise and true perfection!
Peace!

[*Music ceases.*

How the moon sleeps with Endymion,
And would not be awaked.

The Merchant of Venice, V.1.

That central bit about listening is perhaps at the core of what we have to perceive:

It is your music, madam, of the house.
Nothing is good, I see, without respect:
Methinks it sounds much sweeter than by day.
Silence bestows that virtue on it, madam.

I cannot analyse these moments, but I will give you one or two other examples that have struck me. Sometimes, as here, they are accompanied by actual music, sometimes by a sound which may be real or imaginary, and sometimes they happen purely through the text. Always they make us hear something which is beyond the moment, and they always give us a sense of another reality: and we have to be alert to them.

Hear this from Antony and Cleopatra:

[*Enter a company of soldiers.*

First Soldier: Brother, good night. Tomorrow is the day.
Second Soldier: It will determine one way. Fare you well.
Heard you of nothing strange about the streets?
First Soldier: Nothing. What news?
Second Soldier: Belike 'tis but a rumour. Good night to you.
First Soldier: Well, sir, good night.

[*They meet other soldiers.*

Second Soldier: Soldiers, have careful watch.
Third Soldier: And you. Good night, good night.

[*They place themselves in every corner of the stage.*

Second Soldier: Here we. An if tomorrow
Our navy thrive, I have an absolute hope
Our landmen will stand up.

First Soldier: 'Tis a brave army
And full of purpose.

[*Music of hautboys under the stage.*

Second Soldier: Peace! What noise?
First Soldier: List, list!
Second Soldier: Hark!
First Soldier: Music i'th'air.
Third Soldier: Under the earth.
Fourth Soldier: It signs well, does it not?
Third Soldier: No.
First Soldier: Peace, I say!
First Soldier: What should this mean?
Second Soldier: 'Tis the god Hercules, whom Antony loved,
Now leaves him.
First Soldier: Walk; let's see if other watchmen
Do hear what we do.
Second Soldier: How now, masters?
All: [*speaking together*] How now? How now? Do you hear this?
First Soldier: Ay. Is't not strange?
Third Soldier: Do you hear, masters? Do you hear?
First Soldier: Follow the noise so far as we have quarter.
Let's see how it will give off.
All: Content. 'Tis strange. [*Exeunt.*

Antony and Cleopatra, IV.3.

Notice how the verse and prose are mixed. Now the passage is obviously to do with a pagan belief in gods, and is dramatically set up, but here are other perhaps more ordinary moments which give a sense of listening for something other than what is directly present.

(i) 'the isle is full of noises . . .': which I have already talked about on page 36, and which gives us a very strong sense of place, and of how he belongs to what Hopkins would call its 'inscape'. That is to say we get a sense of not only what it may look like, but a feeling of its very essence.

(ii) The Nurse at the end of the supper scene at Capulet's house in *Romeo and Juliet*, I.5: all the Capulets have been there and Romeo and his friends, and Romeo and Juliet have met, and there has been dancing and masks, and finally, when everyone has gone, there is this dialogue between the Nurse and Juliet:

Juliet: Come hither, Nurse. What is yond gentleman?
Nurse: The son and heir of old Tiberio.
Juliet: What's he that now is going out of door?
Nurse: Marry, that, I think, be young Petruchio.
Juliet: What's he that follows here, that would not dance?

Nurse: I know not.
Juliet: Go ask his name. — If he be marrièd,
My grave is like to be my wedding bed.
Nurse: His name is Romeo, and a Montague,
The only son of your great enemy.
Juliet: My only love, sprung from my only hate!
Too early seen unknown, and known too late!
Prodigious birth of love it is to me
That I must love a loathèd enemy.
Nurse: What's this, what's this?
Juliet: A rhyme I learnt even now
Of one I danced withal.

[*One calls within*: 'Juliet'.

Nurse: Anon, anon!
Come, let's away. The strangers all are gone.

Romeo and Juliet, I.5.

In just that one phrase 'The strangers all are gone' we get a whole picture of a half-empty, echoing house, and an image of those moments when we are left alone in a place where many people have been assembled.

(iii) Theseus and Hippolyta, when they enter in to Act IV, Scene 1 of *The Dream* as they are out hunting. They are accompanied by the sound of horns and dogs baying:

[*Horns sound*.

Theseus: Go, one of you; find out the forester;
For now our observation is performed.
And since we have the vaward of the day,
My love shall hear the music of my hounds.
Uncouple in the western valley; let them go.
Dispatch, I say, and find the forester. [*Exit an Attendant*.
We will, fair Queen, up to the mountain's top,
And mark the musical confusion
Of hounds and echo in conjunction.
Hippolyta: I was with Hercules and Cadmus once,
When in a wood of Crete they bayed the bear
With hounds of Sparta. Never did I hear
Such gallant chiding, for besides the groves,
The skies, the fountains, every region near
Seemed all one mutual cry. I never heard
So musical a discord, such sweet thunder.
Theseus: My hounds are bred out of the Spartan kind;
So flewed, so sanded; and their heads are hung
With ears that sweep away the morning dew;

Crook-kneed; and dewlapped like Thessalian bulls;
Slow in pursuit, but matched in mouth like bells,
Each under each. A cry more tuneable
Was never hallooed to nor cheered with horn
In Crete, in Sparta, nor in Thessaly.
Judge when you hear.

A Midsummer-Night's Dream, IV.1.

I have already mentioned this passage as being good to do with two people to one character. And certainly, when I have worked it through that way you get the most amazing sense of their space, and of the way the words open this up quite beyond their logical meaning. It has a quite wonderful music.

(iv) Also in *The Dream*, the final speeches of both Pyramus and Thisbe in the Mechanicals' play have resonances of sound which take us beyond their absurd logic. Just take the final one:

Flute (as Thisbe):
Asleep, my love?
What, dead, my dove?
O Pyramus, arise.
Speak, speak. Quite dumb?
Dead, dead? A tomb
Must cover thy sweet eyes.
These lily lips,
This cherry nose,
These yellow cowslip cheeks
Are gone, are gone.
Lovers, make moan —
His eyes were green as leeks.
O sisters three,
Come, come to me
With hands as pale as milk;
Lay them in gore,
Since you have shore
With shears his thread of silk.
Tongue, not a word!
Come, trusty sword,
Come blade, my breast imbrue.

[*She stabs herself.*

And farewell friends.
Thus Thisbe ends.
Adieu, adieu, adieu!

[*She dies.*

A Midsummer-Night's Dream, V.1.

(v) In *Love's Labour's Lost* an extraordinary change of sound comes at the very end of the play. It happens when Marcade brings the news of the death of the Princess's father:

Marcade: God save you, madam.
Princess: Welcome, Marcade.
But that thou interruptest our merriment.
Marcade: I am sorry, madam, for the news I bring
Is heavy in my tongue. The King your father —
Princess: Dead, for my life!
Marcade: Even so; my tale is told.

Love's Labour's Lost, V.2.

And from this point the jesting stops and the language is quite different. The story is resolved, and the play ends with the wonderful song of Spring and Winter, the last verse being:

When all aloud the wind doth blow,
  And coughing drowns the parson's saw,
And birds sit brooding in the snow,
  And Marian's nose looks red and raw,
When roasted crabs hiss in the bowl,
Then nightly sings the staring owl:
    'Tu-whit
Tu-who!' — a merry note,
While greasy Joan doth keel the pot.
Armado: The words of Mercury are harsh after the songs of Apollo.
You that way; we this way.. [*Exeunt.*

Love's Labour's Lost, V.2.

(vi) I think, in a slightly different way, there is this kind of music in much of Rosalind, interspersed with her wit: for instance, in this most wonderful prose speech, which has its very specific prose pointing and cadence, there is a melancholy music at the end:

Rosalind: No, faith, die by attorney. The poor world is almost six thousand years old, and in all this time there was not any man died in his own person, videlicet, in a love-cause. Troilus had his brains dashed out with a Grecian club, yet he did what he could to die before, and he is one of the patterns of love. Leander, he would have lived many a fair year though Hero had turned nun, if it had not been for a hot midsummer night: for, good youth, he went but forth to wash him in the Hellespont and being taken with a cramp was drowned, and the foolish chroniclers of that age found it was 'Hero of Sestos'. But these are all lies; men have died from time to time and worms have eaten them, but not for love.

As You Like It, IV.1.

(vii) I think in *Othello*, in the last scene between Desdemona and Emilia, there is also this kind of music. It may be something to do with the wistfulness of the Willow song which Desdemona sings, but also the dialogue between the two has a listening quality, which is quite different from the rest of the play. There is something quite extraordinary about Emilia's speech on husbands, and that scene (Act IV, Scene 3) is worth reading quietly over.

(viii) And finally, the last speeches both of Antony and of Cleopatra have this sense of another reality which we have to listen for, to apprehend. Here is Antony's last speech, followed by Cleopatra:

Antony: The miserable change now at my end
Lament nor sorrow at, but please your thoughts
In feeding them with those my former fortunes,
Wherein I lived; the greatest prince o'th'world,
The noblest; and do now not basely die,
Not cowardly put off my helmet to
My countryman; a Roman, by a Roman
Valiantly vanquished. Now my spirit is going;
I can no more.
Cleopatra: Noblest of men, woo't die?
Hast thou no care of me? Shall I abide
In this dull world, which in thy absence is
No better than a sty? O, see, my women,

[*Antony dies.*

The crown o'the'earth doth melt. My lord!
O, withered is the garland of the war,
The soldier's pole is fall'n; young boys and girls
Are level now with men. The odds is gone,
And there is nothing left remarkable
Beneath the visiting moon.

Antony and Cleopatra, IV.15.

You will find many other places where this quality of music takes over; just keep listening for it. It always takes us beyond the logical, and gives us a way into the essence of the character.

3 SCENE STRUCTURES

I have talked a good deal about through energy, and how one line impels to the next, one thought to the next, one speech to the next and so on, and I particularly went into detail on the short scene from *Richard II* between Bushy, Bagot and Green, on page 88. All this has to do with the rhythm of a scene. But there are several further things to be said about scene structures, some of which I have said before in other ways, but I think they are useful.

Just as every speech has a definable pattern, so each scene has a rhythm and structure of its own, which in simple terms works like this:

(i) The statement of the predicament at the beginning. The predicament either of the plot or the emotional state.
(ii) The subsequent development and/or debate.
(iii) The resolution.

In this way all scenes, as speeches do, open up and flower.

Now obviously I have put this in very simplified terms, and how the pattern unfolds depends on the texture and complexity of the scene. In the big central scenes the structures will emerge through the interplay of the characters and the choices made, and often the primary statement is not overtly apparent. We cannot usefully break them down here except to say that when you have been through a rehearsal process and found the complexity and motive, always come back to look at the structure of the whole scene, for that will give you the shaft through, and keep you buoyed up.

For instance *Macbeth* (Act I, Scene 7) starts with the soliloquy: 'If it were done . . .' which in fact ends unsolved. Lady Macbeth then takes on the debate, and during the scene each speech knits in with the last, with broken lines; and their thoughts are so close that they are breathing and thinking together, and the scene ends with:

Macbeth: I am settled; and bend up
Each corporal agent to this terrible feat.
Away, and mock the time with fairest show:
False face must hide what the false heart doth know.

This directly ties up with the opening premise, or could it be riddle. The power of that rhythm is tremendous, but of course only when the work has been done in depth.

In the huge and complex central scene of *Othello*, the central theme of jealousy is set up at the beginning by the discovery of Desdemona and Cassio together, which in turn has been set up by Iago. The two main dialogues between Othello and Iago depend on the rhythmic closeness between the two, and the fact that Iago is as it were speaking from the other side of Othello's mind. The scene moves inexorably forward from Othello seeing his disgraced Lieutenant Cassio talking to Desdemona coupled with Iago's 'I like not that', to the final words of the scene:

Othello: . . . Now art thou my Lieutenant.
Iago: I am your own for ever.

What happens between those two points is massive, but the audience must be made aware of those two points because it is that unity which begs the question of how much Iago is in control, and how much is predetermined.

Again, in the magnificent scene between Hamlet and Gertrude in *Hamlet* (Act III, Scene 4), it is the debate between them that is important. In story terms the scene starts with Polonius hiding behind the arras, and ends with his dead body being lugged off by Hamlet with customary wit:

Hamlet: Indeed, this counsellor
Is now most still, most secret, and most grave,
Who was in life a foolish prating knave.
Come, sir, to draw toward an end with you.
Good night, mother.

But it is the debate between Hamlet and Gertrude which is as momentous as the killing of Polonius and the appearance of the Ghost, and that debate is set up by their opening lines:

Hamlet: Now, mother what's the matter?
Queen: Hamlet, thou hast thy father much offended.
Hamlet: Mother, you have my father much offended.

And so the play of words goes on, setting up the ambivalence of their relationship.

And so, in *As You Like It*, in the second forest scene between Rosalind and Orlando (Act IV, Scene 1), the premise is set up in the first words between them:

Rosalind: . . . Why, how now, Orlando, where have you been all this while? You a lover! And you serve me such another trick, never come in my sight more.
Orlando: My fair Rosalind, I come within an hour of my promise.
Rosalind: Break an hour's promise in love? He that will divide a minute into a thousand parts, and break but a part of the thousandth part of a minute in the affairs of love, it may be said of him that Cupid hath clapp'd him o'th'shoulder, but I'll warrant him heart-whole.

The scene then is about Rosalind's particularly rigorous definition of what love is. She is both humorous and deadly serious — and thus sets us up ready for the lengths she will go to in order to be satisfied as to the truth of Orlando's love.

Now what I have said is of course simply about the structure of those scenes, and not about the development of the characters within them —

a book could be written on each! What I want to look at now is some structures of short scenes.

I think there is something very exciting about the music of some of the short scenes: they are sometimes like a poem. What is interesting about them is that each actor has to bring his own rhythm dictated by the character, and yet be part of another whole rhythm. Look at this short scene from *Titus Andronicus*, just twenty-six lines:

[Enter Titus, his three sons, and Marcus.

Titus: The hunt is up, the morn is bright and grey,
The fields are fragrant and the woods are green.
Uncouple here and let us make a bay,
And wake the emperor and his lovely bride,
And rouse the prince, and ring a hunter's peal,
That all the court may echo with the noise.
Sons, let it be your charge, as it is ours,
To attend the emperor's person carefully:
I have been troubled in my sleep this night,
But dawning day new comfort hath inspir'd.

[Here a cry of hounds, and wind horns in a peal, then enter Saturninus, Tamora, Bassianus, Lavinia, Chiron, Demetrius and their Attendants.

Many good morrows to your majesty;
Madam, to you as many and as good:
I promised your grace a hunter's peal.
Saturninus: And you have rung it lustily, my lords;
Somewhat too early for new-married ladies.
Bassianus: Lavinia, how say you?
Lavinia: I say, no;
I have been broad awake two hours and more.
Saturninus: Come on then; horse and chariots let us have,
And to our sport. Madam, now shall ye see
Our Roman hunting.
Marcus: I have dogs, my lord,
Will rouse the proudest panther in the chase,
And climb the highest promontory top.
Titus: And I have horse will follow where the game
Makes way, and run like swallows o'er the plain.
Demetrius: Chiron, we hunt not, we, with horse nor hound,
But hope to pluck a dainty doe to ground. *[Exeunt.*

Titus Andronicus, II.2.

There is a wonderful shape to Titus' speech, with its description of the freshness of the morning: the more you go with the description at the beginning, and with the sense of him rousing not only Marcus and his sons, but also his own spirits, the more it points up his anxiety of the night. The beginning of the speech is in antithesis to that. With the entrance of Saturninus and the Court the scene is full of bustle and noise, and Titus and Marcus are still trying to rouse the spirits and be pleasing. Each speech must have its special placing for the final chilling couplet of Demetrius to have effect, with its implications of another and darker kind of hunt. The scene moves swiftly, yet nothing must be rushed, and everything must be kept in the air until that end.

Scenes very often break down into two or more parts — i.e., you have the main beat(s) of the scene between the protagonists, where big issues are at stake; and then you have the coda, where perhaps two or three people are left on stage either as a comment to what has gone before, or to play a scene in antithesis to the main one. It often acts rather as a chorus. This happens in *Antony and Cleopatra*, Act II, Scene 2, when, after Antony, Caesar and Lepidus have had their great power meeting, Maecenas, Agrippa and Enobarbus are left. Maecenas and Agrippa question Enobarbus about Egypt and from that comes that wonderfully ironic and rich description of Cleopatra: Enobarbus is at once an accurate observer and also deeply involved in his own description.

Two more examples:

(i) the last beat of Act II, Scene 4 in *King Lear*. The main part of the scene contains Lear's rage with Regan and Goneril, and his final break with them, and they let him go out into the storm. This end beat has a music of its own. Cornwall, Regan and Goneril are left:

Cornwall: Let us withdraw; 'twill be a storm.
Regan: This house is little; the old man and's people
Cannot be well bestowed.
Goneril: 'Tis his own blame; hath put himself from rest
And must needs taste his folly.
Regan: For his particular, I'll receive him gladly,
But not one follower.
Goneril: So am I purposed.
Where is my lord of Gloucester?
Cornwall: Followed the old man forth. He is returned.

[*Enter Gloucester.*

Gloucester: The King is in high rage.
Cornwall: Whither is he going?
Gloucester: He calls to horse; but will I know not whither.
Cornwall: 'Tis best to give him way. He leads himself.
Goneril: My lord, entreat him by no means to stay.
Gloucester: Alack, the night comes on and the bleak winds
Do sorely ruffle. For many miles about
There's scarce a bush.

Regan: O sir, to wilful men
The injuries that they themselves procure
Must be their schoolmasters. Shut up your doors.
He is attended with a desperate train,
And what they may incense him to, being apt
To have his ear abused, wisdom bids fear.
Cornwall: Shut up your doors, my lord; 'tis a wild night.
My Regan counsels well. Come out o'the storm. [*Exeunt.*

King Lear, II.4.

The dialogue is so spare and still, coming as it does out of the previous rage: no-one is giving anything away, and each is filled with their own thoughts, half with what has gone before and half with the storm outside. There is a sense of waiting to see what will happen — the scene is suspended in time, and this is heightened by the repeated references to the storm, and the twice-spoken 'Shut up your doors'.

(ii) Read for yourselves the last beat of Act II, Scene 1 in *Richard II* between Willoughby, Ross and Northumberland. It comes at the end of the big scene between Gaunt and Richard, when the Gaunt makes his dying plea for good government of the land. We subsequently learn of his death and of Richard's immediate confiscation of his lands. This scene between the three lords begins:

Northumberland: Well, lords, the Duke of Lancaster is dead.
Ross: And living too; for now his son is duke.
Willoughby: Barely in title not in revenues.
Northumberland: Richly in both if justice had her right.

And there the predicament is stated. Then the debate starts, and gradually, encouraged and fed by Northumberland, Willoughby and Ross express their dismay at the economic state of the country and their own fear of being dragged under. Gradually, as Northumberland picks up on their feelings, he becomes politically more open until we get to his final speech, a triumph of rhetoric, where he whips them up into committing to join forces with Bolingbroke:

Northumberland: Then thus: I have from Le Port Blanc,
A bay in Brittaine, received intelligence
That Harry Duke of Hereford, Rainold Lord Cobham,
The son of Richard Earl of Arundel
That late broke from the Duke of Exeter,
His brother, Archbishop late of Canterbury,
Sir Thomas Erpingham, Sir John Ramston,
Sir John Norbery, Sir Robert Waterton, and Francis
Coint,
All these well-furnished by the Duke of Brittaine

With eight tall ships, three thousand men of war,
Are making hither with all due expedience,
And shortly mean to touch our northern shore.
Perhaps they had ere this, but that they stay
The first departing of the King for Ireland.
If then we shall shake off our slavish yoke,
Imp out our drooping country's broken wing,
Redeem from broking pawn the blemished crown,
Wipe off the dust that hides our sceptre's gilt,
And make high majesty look like itself,
Away with me in post to Ravenspurgh.
But if you faint, as fearing to do so,
Stay, and be secret; and myself will go.

Ross: To horse, to horse. Urge doubts to them that fear.
Willoughby: Hold out my horse, and I will first be there. [*Exeunt.*

Richard II, II.1.

The shape of the whole scene is quite wonderful. Each speech has to answer the last precisely, and take the thought on: they are perfectly phrased and pointed. Both Ross and Willoughby hold back to begin with, but gradually become more forthright, until Northumberland feels the time is ripe and with a firm 'Then thus . . .' he names those who have joined with Bolingbroke, each of whom represent power. It is a formidable list. He then gives himself two lines to pull the pressure off: 'Perhaps they had ere this . . .', before he starts the final thrust with 'If then we shall shake off our slavish yoke . . .', and here he includes himself and feeds them with the ideals of majesty. And he ends with the scornful 'But if you faint, as fearing to do so . . .', and he just gives away by that 'you' how much he has manipulated them. By the final couplet we know that they have both been hooked totally.

In all the Histories you will find scenes like this which have a similar cumulative energy, as indeed in all the plays which are predominantly to do with power — *Julius Caesar*, *Troilus and Cressida*.

And finally, and I have kept it till last I suppose because it is so very rich, let us look at the opening scene of *Hamlet*. I would say it can be done, and often is, quite naturalistically, making absolute sense, but with no regard for its particular pointing. Or it can be done with a sense of listening for something else, paying attention to the poise of each line, and this way it contains that sense of heightened music I was talking about earlier.

[*Enter Francisco and Barnardo, two sentinels.*

Barnardo: Who's there?
Francisco: Nay, answer me. Stand and unfold yourself.
Barnardo: Long live the King!
Francisco: Barnardo?

Barnardo: He.
Francisco: You come most carefully upon your hour.
Barnardo: 'Tis now struck twelve. Get thee to bed, Francisco.
Francisco: For this relief much thanks. 'Tis bitter cold,
And I am sick at heart.
Barnardo: Have you had quiet guard?
Francisco: Not a mouse stirring.
Barnardo: Well, good night.
If you do meet Horatio and Marcellus,
The rivals of my watch, bid them make haste.

[*Enter Horatio and Marcellus.*

Francisco: I think I hear them. Stand ho! Who is there?
Horatio: Friends to this ground.
Marcellus: And liegemen to the Dane.
Francisco: Give you good night.
Marcellus: O, farewell, honest soldier.
Who hath relieved you?
Francisco: Barnardo hath my place.
Give you good night. [*Exit.*
Marcellus: Holla, Barnardo!
Barnardo: Say —
What, is Horatio there?
Horatio: A piece of him.
Barnardo: Welcome, Horatio. Welcome, good Marcellus.
Marcellus: What, has this thing appeared again tonight?
Barnardo: I have seen nothing.
Marcellus: Horatio says 'tis but our fantasy,
And will not let belief take hold of him
Touching this dreaded sight twice seen of us.
Therefore I have entreated him along
With us to watch the minutes of this night,
That, if again this apparition come,
He may approve our eyes and speak to it.
Horatio: Tush, tush, 'twill not appear.
Barnardo: Sit down awhile,
And let us once again assail your ears,
That are so fortified against our story,
What we have two nights seen.
Horatio: Well, sit we down,
And let us hear Barnardo speak of this.
Barnardo: Last night of all,
When yond same star that's westward from the pole
Had made his course t'illume that part of heaven
Where now it burns, Marcellus and myself,
The bell then beating one —

[*Enter the Ghost.*

Marcellus: Peace, break thee off. Look where it comes again.
Barnardo: In the same figure like the King that's dead.

Marcellus: Thou art a scholar. Speak to it, Horatio.
Barnardo: Looks 'a not like the King? Mark it, Horatio.
Horatio: Most like. It harrows me with fear and wonder.
Barnardo: It would be spoke to.
Marcellus: Speak to it, Horatio.
Horatio: What art thou that usurpest this time of night,
Together with that fair and warlike form
In which the majesty of buried Denmark
Did sometimes march? By heaven I charge thee, speak.
Marcellus: It is offended.
Barnardo: See, it stalks away.
Horatio: Stay. Speak, speak. I charge thee, speak.

[*Exit the Ghost.*

Marcellus: 'Tis gone and will not answer.
Barnardo: How now, Horatio? You tremble and look pale.
Is not this something more than fantasy?

And so we are taken into the world of *Hamlet*. It starts with the central question 'Who's there?' And indeed *Hamlet* is full of questions and riddles, and that very question is, in a larger sense, what the whole play is about. Notice how the first few lines are in prose, but when in verse, space is left for listening.

The half lines and questions at the beginning give us the sense of unease of a country on guard against invasion, but also a more particular sense of their own fear as if they are watching with their whole bodies. We are also made to question what is real and what is imaginary, and we sense that man is pitched on the battlements between heaven and earth, which is Hamlet's predicament. This opening beat has such a sense of music, it is as if hovering on the air.

I want to end this section with three practical reminders:

(i) Always bear in mind that the listener needs a little more time at the beginning of a scene to get tuned to both the characters and the situation, therefore it is good to play the first two or three lines of a scene at a fractionally slower tempo than the whole. Once you have established yourself vocally and established your vocabulary, the rest can bounce off quickly. And of course, as we have already seen, this is particularly important at the beginning of a play where there is so much to take in. However, this must never be laboured or sound heavy; it is a matter of keeping it buoyed up.

(ii) Never rush information. It is therefore very important to observe the structure of speeches which contain a lot of information, such as messenger speeches. It is particularly useful to do the exercise of moving between two markers at punctuation marks on these, as it helps you to clarify what is information and what is imagery and to find the right balance. Information should be quick but not rushed.

(iii) One-liners and short feeding lines must be as carefully poised as long speeches. This is often difficult when your part is small, for all your energy has to be ready for that one bit, and there is no time to build or recover if you get it wrong, so one feels a great deal of pressure to get it right. However, as you run the play, you become more able to judge the energy needed for those small speeches. Again, they must never seem rushed, for they are always important in that they add texture to the whole. They also need to be laid precisely for they often begin ladders of thought, and they need to be served well to the character who has to feed off them.

4 RECAP ON SPEECH STRUCTURES

All that we have talked about and looked at so far has been to do with just this: the structure within a speech or sequence of speeches. And we have found that this structure depends on:

(i) How the metre is disposed within a line, and how the sense stress works with the metre stress.

(ii) The through energies of line, thought phrase, and whole thought structure. We have to be aware of how each of those three contributes to the movement forward.

(iii) How the thoughts are broken up, be it in prose or verse, is directly related to the emotional state of the character.

(iv) The substance of the word — i.e., the number of syllables, the length of vowel and the quantity and type of consonants; all this within one line gives it its particular character, and this tells us of the quality of the thought.

(v) The use of antithesis, and how this sets up the parameters of the thought.

(vi) The logic of the imagery, and how the finding of the image is directly related to where the character is placed in terms of the laws and structure of his particular world, and of nature. And also how very often there is a ladder of imagery set up which leads us through a scene or part of a scene.

(vii) We have to be aware of word games and patterns. There is often for instance a double meaning to a word, and sometimes this is used overtly for its humour; at other times it is used more suggestively for subversive reasons.

(viii) How, nearly always, the statement of the premise is made at the beginning of the speech. The opening out of the theme then follows in a kind of debate, and some conclusion is reached.

(ix) The tempo of the whole, which is governed by the matter in hand, the debate.

Now of course every speech is totally individual, and it is only by doing the exercises that I have given and seeing what they throw up that we shall find the true nature of the speech, and how it relates to the character. As you become more informed by the exercises the less you will need to depend on them, because you will hear what is happening in the language more and more readily.

When you feel this structure behind you it will help to provide you with the energy and speed which is necessary. And here I want to repeat something I have already said, but which is so important, something which we understand intellectually but just do not trust enough when we are on the stage 'doing it'. It is that the listener understands better when the speaking is swift — I do not mean quick and rushed, but when, within the precise pointing of the text, the thoughts tumble out, impelled each by the one before. This means that we have to think more quickly, and when you feel the structure there inside, this is more likely to happen.

Another thing I want to repeat is that when we feel this structure we find we do not have to do all the work, all the thinking and feeling; we do not have to explain, because it is how the thoughts work that does that for you. The audience has to be let in to how the character ticks. This is what is interesting, and what finally moves them. The listener understands so much through the music of the thought.

And this leads nicely to the next point, which is that once we have found how the structure works, we need to reflect this musically in the voice. When we do the exercises of moving between two points on phrases and thought structures, we define for ourselves the shape of the speech and how the thought opens up, but this must be accompanied by a response in the tone — i.e., a shift of note. For just as the change of note at the beginning of a new phrase in music leads us into that phrase, so, when speaking, a change of thought requires a shift of note, very often a lifting of it, and we must not underestimate the need for that in the listener. Often it is in the change of note that our attention is grabbed. Now when you do the physical exercises you will notice that this will happen to an extent, but I think we have to consciously hear it musically as well. That is, on a musical level, we have to want to make it happen.

This sense of music in the structure has to be practised — some people are more instinctively aware of it than others. This has to do with involuntary responses, which I have gone into fully in *Voice and the Actor*. And it has to be a gradual process, for we do not want to sound artificial or to get into any hint of a declamatory style. We have to keep balancing the music with what is appropriate both for ourselves and for the time. Nevertheless we must not dismiss this musicality as being not to do with truth, for to deny it is also untruthful. So we have to practise using a little more range, and noticing how each thought needs to be begun on a different note, quite often lifted though not necessarily so, and how a speech needs to travel through a range of notes. Each speech will require a different breadth of range, but we have to listen for it and place it. But one has to say quite firmly that, for the listener, if we do not satisfy the need of the ear to be taken on, the speaking will seem dull and the attention will not be claimed. This is the skill then: to find the inner truth and present it with a certain musical awareness. The changes of pitch can be quite slight, and this will depend on the style of the production, but they must be there, and this is particularly true when we recognize how strongly based in rhetoric the text is. On a practical note, always begin low enough in pitch in order that you have somewhere to go vocally, and this is a simple note to give yourself.

With all this in mind, here are four speeches to look at:

Speech 1

Hamlet: To be, or not to be — that is the question;
Whether 'tis nobler in the mind to suffer
The slings and arrows of outrageous fortune
Or to take arms against a sea of troubles
And by opposing end them. To die, to sleep —
No more — and by a sleep to say we end
The heartache and the thousand natural shocks
That flesh is heir to. 'Tis a consummation
Devoutly to be wished. To die, to sleep —
To sleep — perchance to dream. Ay, there's the rub.
For in that sleep of death what dreams may come
When we have shuffled off this mortal coil
Must give us pause. There's the respect
That makes calamity of so long life.
For who would bear the whips and scorns of time,
Th'oppressor's wrong, the proud man's contumely,
The pangs of despised love, the law's delay,
The insolence of office, and the spurns
That patient merit of th'unworthy takes,
When he himself might his quietus make
With a bare bodkin? Who would fardels bear,
To grunt and sweat under a weary life,
But that the dread of something after death,
The undiscovered country, from whose bourn
No traveller returns, puzzles the will,
And makes us rather bear those ills we have

Than fly to others which we know not of?
Thus conscience does make cowards of us all;
And thus the native hue of resolution
Is sicklied o'er with the pale cast of thought,
And enterprises of great pitch and moment
With this regard their currents turn awry
And lose the name of action. Soft you now,
The fair Ophelia! — Nymph, in thy orisons
Be all my sins remembered.

Hamlet, III.1.

This of course is very familiar to us all, and just for that it is worth looking at quite specifically for the structure, for that makes us think of it afresh. These are some of the things you will notice:

The rhythm is fluid and easy, the thought sitting easily with the metre.

There are only about four lines which jump a little. In the first line the metrical stress is on 'is', whereas we would possibly want to stress 'that', though perhaps the stress on 'is' makes more significant sense. In the second line the first syllable of 'Whether has to be stressed, which immediately breaks the metre and hooks our mind on the question. It also leads us on to 'or' in the fourth line, which then makes us able to stress the two juxtaposed words 'take arms', giving them added force. On line 21 we would not stress 'With a' so that 'bare bodkin' can both have full stress; and four lines later the word 'puzzles' takes stress and jumps the metre, giving it a particular importance.

So it is very straighforward metrically. However, if you beat it out strictly for metre it puts us in touch with the discipline of the thoughts. And this is interesting because it forces us to stop thinking of the speech as coming from someone who is putting off making a decision; but rather from someone who is deliberately delaying action. It then becomes an active speech informed by his own particular rigorous thinking.

The whole speech is a perfect example of how the central question is first stated and then debated: the debate quickens — and this is where the sense of cadence has to come in, as the ideas tumble over themsleves.

Moving both on thought phrases and then on whole thought structures is very useful in this speech, and you will find it throws up very varied rhythms.

We get the sense that it is these thoughts which continually occupy his mind, but that the speaking clarifies them, and that the speaking is part of the delay in action, but not the weakening of resolve; for the current is there underneath, both in the firmness of the rhythm and in the imagery.

I think it is particularly useful with this to beat on the floor on all the words of physical strength and even violence. You will find the thinking to be surprisingly passionate and active.

Speech 2

King: But what of this? Are we not all in love?
Berowne: O, nothing so sure, and thereby all forsworn.
King: Then leave this chat, and, good Berowne, now prove
Our loving lawful and our faith not torn.
Dumaine: Ay, marry, there; some flattery for this evil!
Longville: O, some authority how to proceed!
Some tricks, some quillets, how to cheat the devil!
Dumaine: Some salve for perjury.
Berowne: 'Tis more than need.
Have at you then, affection's men-at-arms!
Consider what you first did swear unto:
To fast, to study, and to see no woman —
Flat treason 'gainst the kingly state of youth.
Say, can you fast? Your stomachs are too young,
And abstinence engenders maladies. . .
O, we have made a vow to study, lords,
And in that vow we have forsworn our books;
For when would you, my liege, or you, or you,
In leaden contemplation have found out
Such fiery numbers as the prompting eyes
Of beauty's tutors have enriched you with?
Other slow arts entirely keep the brain,
And therefore, finding barren practisers,
Scarce show a harvest of their heavy toil;
But love, first learnèd in a lady's eyes,
Lives not alone immurèd in the brain,
But with the motion of all elements
Courses as swift as thought in every power,
And gives to every power a double power,
Above their functions and their offices.
It adds a precious seeing to the eye:
A lover's eyes will gaze an eagle blind.
A lover's ear will hear the lowest sound
When the suspicious head of theft is stopped.
Love's feeling is more soft and sensible
Than are the tender horns of cockled snails.
Love's tongue proves dainty Bacchus gross in taste.
For valour, is not love a Hercules,

Still climbing trees in the Hesperides?
Subtle as Sphinx; as sweet and musical
As bright Apollo's lute, strung with his hair.
And when Love speaks, the voice of all the gods
Make heaven drowsy with the harmony.
Never durst poet touch a pen to write
Until his ink were tempered with Love's sighs.
O, then his lines would ravish savage ears
And plant in tyrants mild humility.
From women's eyes this doctrine I derive:
They sparkle still the right Promethean fire;
They are the books, the arts, the academes,
That show, contain, and nourish all the world;
Else none at all in aught proves excellent.
Then fools you were these women to forswear,
Or, keeping what is sworn, you will prove fools.
For wisdom's sake, a word that all men love,
Or for love's sake, a word that loves all men,
Or for men's sake, the authors of these women,
Or women's sake, by whom we men are men —
Let us once lose our oaths to find ourselves,
Or else we lose ourselves to keep our oaths.
It is religion to be thus forsworn,
For charity itself fulfils the law,
And who can sever love from charity?

Love's Labour's Lost, IV.3.

I have included this because it is so great to work on, both singly and in a group — it holds such pleasure. I do not want to go into it in detail because, once you have worked out the sense and the classical allusions, it is open and straightforward, and holds no hidden undercurrents of meaning. It is bookish, and rooted in the myths that he and his friends have committed themselves to study. When working on it you will notice:

It is metrically regular — i.e., the sense stress coincides with the metre stress. When the sense jumps the metre, it is quite clear and adds to the pleasure. Try it out by beating through the metre lightly.

The rhythm is always up-beat, and has wonderful syncopations — e.g., 'Courses as swift as thought in every power'. 'Courses' obviously breaks the metre and takes a lot of weight which can be made up for in the rest of the line.

Notice how you can lean on the long vowels, e.g., 'A lover's eyes will gaze an eagle blind'. So work it through on vowel sounds only and see what you find.

Notice too the tremendous variety of imagery, which needs to be meticulously accurate. The imagery is not there just because it is poetic, it is because he is an academic who delights in finding the exact word and the exact image. Yet it is feeling and sensuous, and so is excellent to get the voice moving on.

Also look for the different movement of the thoughts: first the individual thoughts and images, and then the reasoning of the whole thought structures.

Look at the wonderful shaping from:

> But love, first learnèd in a lady's eyes.

down to:

> Make heaven drowsy with the harmony.

He lists all the attributes of love and what it actively does to men, and we know of course, that he has not been excluded.

Notice the ladders through:

love . . . lady's eyes
not alone . . . in the brain
motion . . . elements
swift as thought
adds . . . seeing to the eye
A lover's eyes . . . eagle blind
A lover's ear . . . suspicious head of theft
Love's feeling . . . soft and sensible . . . cockled snails
Love's tongue . . . dainty Bacchus . . . gross in taste
For valour . . . Hercules
And when Love speaks . . . voice of all the gods

Then for four lines the thought calms and becomes more inward, and is to do with a writer's observation, before he starts on the last part of the speech, the culmination of his reasoning. This contains very precise forms of rhetoric — i.e., repetitions, word games, and the shifting of the sense around the words — word-play. And it ends with the intoxicated flourish of the last three lines. He wins his case.

An excellent exercise, by the way, is to go through a speech like this, either on your own or in a group, and say one word per line, the word which seems to take the thought on: it often clarifies how the thoughts build.

Speech 3

Joan: Look on thy Country, look on fertile France,
And see the Cities and the Towns defac'd,
By wasting ruin of the cruel foe,
As looks the mother on her lowly babe,
When Death doth close his tender-dying eyes.
See, see the pining Malady of France:
Behold the wounds, the most unnatural wounds,
Which thou thyself hast given her woeful breast.
Oh turn thy edged sword another way,
Strike those that hurt, and hurt not those that help:
One drop of blood drawn from thy Country's bosom,
Should grieve thee more than streams of foreign gore.
Return thee therefore with a flood of tears,
And wash away thy Country's stained spots.
Burgundy: Either she hath bewitch'd me with her words,
Or Nature makes me suddenly relent.
Joan: Besides, all French and France exclaims on thee,
Doubting thy birth and lawful progeny.
Who join'st thou with, but with a lordly Nation,
That will not trust thee, but for profit's sake?
When Talbot hath set footing once in France,
And fashion'd thee that instrument of ill,
Who then, but English Henry, will be Lord,
And thou be thrust out, like a fugitive?
Call we to mind, and mark but this for proof:
Was not the Duke of Orleans thy foe?
And was he not in England prisoner?
But when they heard he was thine enemy,
They set him free, without his ransom paid,
In spite of Burgundy and all his friends.
See then, thou fight'st against thy countrymen,
And join'st with them will be thy slaughter-men.
Come, come, return; return thou wandering Lord,
Charles and the rest will take thee in their arms.
Burgundy: I am vanquished:
These haughty words of hers
Have batter'd me like roaring cannon-shot,
And made me almost yield upon my knees.
Forgive me Country, and sweet Countrymen:
And Lords accept this hearty kind embrace.
My forces and my power of men are yours.
So farewell Talbot, I'll no longer trust thee.
Joan: Done like a Frenchman: turn and turn again.

Henry VI Part One, III.3.

All through these early Histories, the *Henry VI*s, *Richard III*, *King John*, *Richard II*, there are marvellous speeches, all worth looking at for their shape, the force of argument, and how the rhetoric informs the argument — the repetitions and patterns of words. This shape is absolutely integral with the thought, yet it is often very free and moves swiftly, as is the case here.

Just look at the shape of it:

> First, the statement of the subject at the beginning: 'Look on thy Country, look on fertile France'.
>
> Then notice the different tacks Joan takes to elaborate on that theme: the tender simile, 'As looks the mother on her lowly babe'; and the declamatory statements such as 'See, see the pining Malady of France', leading to the very reasonable and reasoning tone which begins the second speech.
>
> Then you have the very direct and provocative personal questions and all this builds up to a very persuasive argument, like any good political speech: to which all Burgundy can reply is 'I am vanquished' — the short line giving him time to feel as well as speak.

Now this very shape has a music, for you will see that each part requires a slightly different tone — both tonal quality and pitch, thus:

> The first speech builds quite steadily up, and the end is at the higher pitch than the beginning, and ends with the emotive two lines;
>
> > Return thee therefore with a flood of tears,
> > And wash away thy Country's stained spots.
>
> The second speech drops at the beginning in order that the argument can be presented reasonably. But then the two one-line questions sharpen the tempo and raise the temperature, and begin building almost to the end, up to 'slaughter-men'.
>
> The last two lines are unexpectedly warm and simple, and almost humorous: they drop in pitch though not in intention.
>
> It is not only the argument that is persuasive: it is the very music of it.

Also you will notice:

> It is very regular metrically, the pulse is strong and not particularly subtle.

The substance of the words is full, with no great variation in vowel length or consonant quantity, no dramatic changes — which also gives a certain regularity.

The ends of the thoughts coincide with the ends of the lines, and again this endorses the regularity of the pulse.

However, even with this regularity, there is still a lot of variety of texture, the images are rich and have to be fulfilled, for the concepts are big, and the names hold power.

This is just one example. I have earlier suggested you look at Burgundy's speech at the end of *Henry V*, Act V, Scene 1, with regard to movement of thoughts, and it is really a wonderful speech to look at. The way the argument is presented is so clear and has such variety of texture. The shaping is very formal, but within that formality the ideas are so precise, and often homely and there is in it such a caring for the ordinary in nature, yet the speech is politically strong and powerful. Also look at other speeches in the *Henry VI*s — Cade for example in Part 2, prose but wonderfully shaped. Also look at Anne's lament in *Richard III*, Act I, Scene 1, and indeed at any of Margaret's speeches later in the play — all excellent to practise on and find the formal building, the patterns and forms of words, plus the variety within the image.

Now for something more poetically subtle:

Speech 4

Aaron:

Now climbeth Tamora Olympus' top,
Safe out of fortune's shot, and sits aloft,
Secure of thunder's crack or lightning flash,
Advanc'd above pale envy's threat'ning reach.
As when the golden sun salutes the morn,
And, having gilt the ocean with his beams,
Gallops the zodiac in his glistering coach,
And overlooks the highest-peering hills;
So Tamora.
Upon her wit doth earthly honour wait,
And virtue stoops and trembles at her frown.
Then, Aaron, arm thy heart, and fit thy thoughts,
To mount aloft with thy imperial mistress,
And mount her pitch whom thou in triumph long
Hast prisoner held, fetter'd in amorous chains,
And faster bound to Aaron's charming eyes
Than is Prometheus tied to Caucasus.
Away with slavish weeds and servile thoughts!
I will be bright, and shine in pearl and gold,

To wait upon this new made empress.
To wait, said I? to wanton with this queen,
This goddess, this Semiramis, this nymph,
This siren that will charm Rome's Saturnine,
And see his shipwrack and his commonweal's.
Holla! what storm is this?

[*Enter Chiron and Demetrius, braving.*

Titus Andronicus, II.1.

The building of the music here is palpable, and readily felt:

It starts with the information in the first line.

He elaborates on this in the next three lines, as he relishes the idea.

In line 5, he further elaborates, taking us into an image of the sun to which he likens Tamora. This image colours the texture vocally but also he finds that image from within, and we know that it is precisely the position that he would like to be in — i.e., 'Advanc'd above pale envy's threat'ning reach'.

The image itself soars from line 5 to line 8, and comes to rest on the short line 'So Tamora'. That line can expand as much as you want.

Notice how the words 'Now', 'As', 'And', 'So' at the beginning of the lines hold up the lines and poise, adding to the suspension of the thought.

Lines 10 and 11 are calmer and more thoughtful, with the nice balancing of 'wit' and 'wait'. This slight respite gets us ready for the crux of the speech which is to do with his own actions.

Line 12 comes right back to him personally, with the initial word 'Then' leading us to the action of the following emotive words and the sexuality of the language.

This section mounts right through to 'Caucasus'.

We then discover something of his philosophy, how he sees the master-slave relationship, who is master and who is slave, and the play on the word 'wait' leading to 'wanton' and we know that he is ready to motivate the action.

And then the resolution, to see Saturnine's destruction — 'And see his shipwrack and his commonweal's'.

With regards to the exercises, of course do the ones moving

between thought phrases, and then the whole thought structures. This will make you feel how the thoughts move.

But, in particular, work on the vowels, and speak it through on vowels only. You will notice how the sense leans on them, and how their patterns add to the sensuality of the thinking.

I have taken four examples of speeches at random, and as you can see the shaping is important in all of them. But that sense of shaping does not generalize; it rather throws up the particular nature of each speech and makes it more specific. It makes us aware of the particular inquiry into the nature of that character's being, through the way he shapes the thoughts and through the choice of imagery.

5 SONNETS

I think that the sonnets are an extremely useful way into working on Shakespeare text. Just by speaking them and feeling them on the tongue, we make ourselves more easy with the rhythm of the language and how to manage it; and the fact that they are so very different in tone and texture makes us alert to the differences between play and play.

This quite brief look at them, then, is purely to do with what they can teach us about structure and a full commitment to the language, and is not in any way about them as pieces of literature. As you well know, so much has been written about them in terms of their biographical placing, to whom they were written, and so on. All this is both useful and interesting, for the more you know about them the fuller your understanding will be, and so the more layers of meaning you will find; and indeed actors have very successfully put them into a dramatic context and performed them. But here I want to look simply at the variety of rhythm that can occur in fourteen lines of iambic pentameter with a consistent rhyming pattern, and how we can investigate the language used, and how they can, in parallel, help the study of a part. In a sense we are 'using' them, but we are using them to find out about language, and in so doing we shall be tuning in to the attitudes and feelings of the writer. And for just this last reason, I would say that I personally believe they are more difficult for women to enter into than for men — they take us into a male world. I find this important to say.

I say all this because I think it is important to be clear as to how and why we are working on them. Yet the fact remains that they provide excellent material for the exploration of the language. It is useful to get hold of a well-annotated edition, and I find the one edited by W.C. Ingram and Theodore Redpath particularly useful.*

* Hodder and Stoughton.

The fact that the thought is given to us and argued in the space of fourteen lines is what is important, for we can feel that structure quite palpably, and get pleasure from the form of it. Basically it works like this:

> The subject is given in the first three or four lines as a general rule, but this varies hugely — it can be given in one line, for example:
>
> My love is strengthen'd, though more weak in seeming;
>
> or over two lines:
>
> Farewell — thou art too dear for possessing,
> And like enough thou know'st thy estimate:
>
> or it can happen over eight lines, and occasionally it takes up almost the whole sonnet.
>
> This subject is then elaborated on and given a general context, and this happens over the first eight lines, the octet.
>
> In the second half of the sonnet, the sestet, the theme becomes more specific and related to the writer. I would say more intense and inward.
>
> This last part is divided into two, with its first four lines exploring the theme at a deeper level. The conclusion comes in the final couplet, which in a way clinches the thought of the whole: sometimes it completely turns the thought round.
>
> So you have three quatrains, rhymed, a,b,a,b; c,d,c,d; and e,f,e,f; with the final couplet rhymed g,g.

For a perfect example of this pattern of thought and rhyme look here at this, probably the most famous sonnet of all:

Shall I compare thee to a summer's day?
Thou art more lovely and more temperate:
Rough winds do shake the darling buds of May,
And summer's lease hath all too short a date:
Sometime too hot the eye of heaven shines,
And often is his gold complexion dimm'd,
And every fair from fair sometime declines,
By chance or nature's changing course untrimm'd:
But thy eternal summer shall not fade
Nor lose possession of that fair thou ow'st,
Nor shall Death brag thou wander'st in his shade,
When in eternal lines to time thou grow'st:
So long as men can breathe or eyes can see,
So long lives this, and this gives life to thee.

Sonnet 18.

You will notice:

> The theme is stated in the first two lines in the form of question and answer.
>
> That answer is elaborated on through accumulated images of summer for the whole first half of the sonnet.
>
> At the ninth line it becomes more intense and more personal, and the tempo and tone changes as we approach the concluding thought.
>
> There is also a kind of riddle implicit in these lines as we wonder what can halt oncoming age.
>
> The answer comes in the final couplet, in the wonderful conceit that she, or whoever it is, will live as long as the sonnet is read.

So, whether the pattern is quite formal, as in this one, or whether the thought is more sprawling, one of the important things we learn from speaking them is how to place the main thrust of the thought and hold it in the mind of the listener, while digressing and going up side-alleys of imagery as it were — painting pictures incidental to the thought. In other words we learn how to phrase well.

But also we get from them something more difficult to define, which is to do with realizing the whole meaning of the words, and this relates directly to acting. And this ties up with something I said right at the beginning which is that we do not fully understand the meaning until we speak the words. We so often understand something intellectually, and make the words fit in to what we understand, rather than understanding through saying the words. Of course both processes have to go on, but we must not limit ourselves.

Now the language in the sonnets is so often to do with extremity of feeling: they are dealing with love which is obsessive and which recognizes excess, and because this extravagance is contained in a poem, I think we soften it and make it poetic. In fact it is this very extravagance that is important, and which often lets us into the humour, and even turns the thought round. The humour comes from being able to look at our predicament, recognize its depths, and yet be able to express it in words with a certain objectivity. If we can do this we will open up the ambiguity and ambivalence which so often they contain.

What we have to do then is clear our minds of misconceptions, take our time and go totally with the words. We have already seen in *Sonnet 138* how the layers of 'knowing' open up as you speak it, provided you allow yourself the time to explore it initially, and this will happen with all of them. You will find a continuing and surprising opening up of the meaning the more you allow the words to do their work — tread deeply in them. And this is precisely what makes them quite elusive, in that they seem on the surface often quite clear, but as you start to work on them and question them they become more complex and less definable, and so more interesting.

With all this in mind, let us take another familiar one and see what we find:

When, in disgrace with Fortune and men's eyes,
I all alone beweep my outcast state,
And trouble deaf heaven with my bootless cries,
And look upon myself and curse my fate —
Wishing me like to one more rich in hope,
Featur'd like him, like him with friends possess'd,
Desiring this man's art and that man's scope,
With what I most enjoy contented least:
Yet in these thoughts myself almost despising,
Haply I think on thee, and then my state
Like to the lark at break of day arising
From sullen earth, sings hymns at heaven's gate:
For thy sweet love remember'd such wealth brings
That then I scorn to change my state with kings.

Sonnet 29.

A straightforward sonnet about times of despair, not complicated to understand.

There is no initial statement of the theme, rather it unfolds steadily through the sonnet. You therefore have to be very sure about making the main thought clauses clear, hook them in your minds, so that you can hang the images on them. You might decide that the thinking goes roughly like this:

When
I beweep my outcast state
With what I most enjoy contented least
Yet myself almost despising,
Haply I think on thee, and then my state
sings hymns at heaven's gate:

That is the basic thread, but it is the images that tell us accurately of his state, and these are cumulative.

To understand something of his state you have to realize the language fully, so look at some of the words:

disgrace	outcast
bootless cries	curse
despising	contented least

All these are strong and we need to grasp their measure. We need to know what 'disgrace' is, and how we are affected physically by it.

But at the same time 'When' places it in time: so we know it is those moments when we feel in despair, and not all the time. This 'When' also leads us to 'then' — 'And then my state . . .'

All that follows is in antithesis to the first half. Therefore the more the first half is explored realistically, the greater will be the impact of the second half.

Through our own involvement with the words, we will glimpse the moments, which most of us have, of utter despair, and how they can turn, at a thought, to joy. The feelings are extreme.

The point is that the more seriously you take the words, the more you will understand the moments he is putting to us, which are real and are of suffering, and the more the humour will also surface.

This humour is to do with being able to look at yourself and understand those moments; and so the layers accumulate and the extravagance of the lark image bubbles up from inside.

So, when working on it for yourself, you will want to do all the exercises, such as moving between thoughts and making physical actions on words which are extreme, in order to feel the extravagance of the language physically, and this will make the comfort of the end more apparent.

And this is how we must look at them all; we must be totally specific with the words, for they alone take us into the particular state which is being expressed. I know that always this will be limited to our own responses; nevertheless, we must pursue them as accurately as we know how.

So, given that their structure, whether very tight or quite sprawling, is as a mirror of the speeches in the plays, how best can we work on them?

First, forget that they are poems and use them rather as direct speech — i.e., not as reflective poetic thought, but as if they were part of a play and you were either addressing someone personally, or actively working out your thoughts. For they are all addressed to someone; and sometimes you can imagine that person is present in the body, and sometimes in spirit only. But it is this immediacy which comes from directness which is essential, which gives them their vigour, and which clarifies them for you as you speak. And this is what is useful for the actor.

Group work

If you are using them in group work, then imagine your own scenario, not outlandish, but a situation that you can relate to personally, and out of which you can speak the text.

Then, having done your own work on the sonnet's rhythm and language, speak it to a member of the group, if that is appropriate.

If you can speak it to someone in the group, it will clarify it enormously by giving you the drive through — it will help you to communicate without explaining. Also that person's response will be interesting, and not always as you had expected.

If it is not appropriate to speak it to someone present in the room, then find your own way of making it direct. For instance, it can be useful to imagine that you are writing it in a letter, for this makes you particularly conscious of the need to find the right word; and this, in turn, points up the fact that there can be a joy in being articulate, in putting something exactly right. As in real life one can often clarify one's feelings by writing them down, and also get pleasure out of doing so precisely.

Or you can imagine that person is simply in another room. But whatever you decide on, the important thing is to have one person in mind and to make it as direct as possible.

The reaction of the group is most important: they must question everything they do not understand. This teaches us a lot about how audiences listen and understand. It also makes us aware of the possibilities of the meaning, for different people will pick up on different things.

It is important to be open to this ambiguity, and to resist what seems to me to be a prevailing attitude — that one line has to mean one thing. When we work on these sonnets we realize how much the meaning can shift as we put a slightly different emphasis on the thought.

We need to be after a sense of emotional involvement without pressure, for it is in this way that your listener will receive the most.

Solo work

You can work on a sonnet in exactly the same way as for group work, by imagining your own situation out of which you speak the text.

You may not have the benefit of a group response, but it is just as valuable in its own way; for you can become involved in personalizing the thought without the complication of interpreting a character, and at the same time you can work on breathing, on muscularity and on rhythm and cadence. This last is most important, for you can really explore the need to find a new note for a new thought and become aware of those changes

If you are working on a Shakespeare play, then it is excellent to find a sonnet which corresponds to the emotional quality of your character, and use it as a touchstone to tune into the language and rhythm of the character, and into expressing those ideas.

For instance, if you are playing one of the lovers in *The Dream*, or Jessica or Lorenzo in *The Merchant*, then the sequence of *Sonnets 43* to *47* would be good to look at, or *Sonnet 118*. Or for very much more complex characters, like for instance Angelo in *Measure for Measure*, *Sonnets 129* and *147* would be very useful to look at. You need to look through and find what speaks to you.

Suggestions for both group and solo work

I suppose the most valuable thing about working on sonnets is that we become acquainted with the metaphysical nature of the thought and how it is explored, and how the thought and the feeling are integral with each other. Here are four which I think are particularly interesting to work on:

(1) If the dull substance of my flesh were thought,
Injurious distance should not stop my way;
For then despite of space I would be brought
From limits far remote where thou dost stay:
No matter then although my foot did stand
Upon the farthest earth remov'd from thee;
For nimble thought can jump both sea and land
As soon as think the place where he would be.
But ah, thought kills me that I am not thought,
To leap large lengths of miles when thou art gone,
But that, so much of earth and water wrought,
I must attend Time's leisure with my moan;
Receiving naught, by elements so slow,
But heavy tears — badges of either's woe!

Sonnet 44.

Because I must limit the number of sonnets to look at, my choices here are to do with personal taste, as I am sure you will have realized.

I like this sonnet particularly because it looks at the idea of space, and how one can be imaginitively in another place: how one can be present in body in one place, but in spirit you can be living somewhere else.

This starts with the magic word 'if', and the longing that implies — that one can almost will the distance away. (How, in prison one must feel that if you could will six feet of wall away, you could be free.) The spirit is bounded by material facts, so the dull substance of flesh cannot overcome distance. So you will notice:

'If' sets up the premise.

You need to set up the antithesis of 'flesh' and 'thought': thought is made up of the elements of fire and air, but the writer is made up of earth and water and so cannot move like thought.

There is a wonderful humour in the extravagance of the lines:

> But ah, thought kills me that I am not thought,
> To leap large lengths of miles when thou art gone,

You also need to set up the antithesis of the 'I' of the speaker, and the 'thee' whom he is addressing.

Feel the different weighting of the words 'dull substance' as against 'nimble thought', and the length in 'leap large lengths of miles' or 'earth and water wrought'. There is a feeling of weight through the poem.

If you are working it in a group, then you can experiment with space. Set up a distance between the speaker and the one he wants to speak to, and make some kind of block so that he cannot get through — anything to find the reality of distance.

(2)

> Being your slave, what should I do but tend
> Upon the hours and times of your desire?
> I have no precious time at all to spend,
> Nor services to do, till you require:
> Nor dare I chide the world-without-end hour
> Whilst I, my sovereign, watch the clock for you,
> Nor think the bitterness of absence sour
> When you have bid your servant once adieu:
> Nor dare I question with my jealous thought
> Where you may be, or your affairs suppose,
> But like a sad slave stay and think of nought
> Save where you are how happy you make those.
> So true a fool is love that in your will,
> Though you do anything, he thinks no ill.

Sonnet 57.

Here again the idea of place is important, that somehow the centre is where the other person is.

It is interesting in that the rhythm is broken at the very beginning with the emphasis on the first word 'Being your slave . . .' There is no question, no 'if' to take us into the premise, that fact is the premise.

The sonnet hinges on the word 'slave' and all that it implies, and this idea he explores through the fourteen lines.

It is useful to tap out all the words which are to do with this master-slave relationship, and discover to what depths he goes to develop that theme.

It is also useful to explore it musically and find how, as each new thought occurs, it requires a slight lifting vocally, a heightening, until the concluding lines. Each 'nor' takes you slightly up the scale, until you come to 'But like a sad slave . . .', and this ties you into the beginning and leads you on to the conclusion.

And that conclusion of course has its pun on 'will', which can mean both the other person's waywardness, or the poet's name. 'will' also has the other meaning of 'carnal desire', though that is unlikely here; but the point is the word has its ambiguities which cannot be quite contained.

When you speak this allowing the words to have their full meaning, you will find humour comes out of the total surrender to the concept of 'Being your slave', and the responsibility that puts on the other person wherever they are, and whoever they are with — they may also be a slave to this idea.

All these layers open out as you investigate the language.

(3) Since I left you, mine eye is in my mind,
And that which governs me to go about
Doth part his function and is partly blind —
Seems seeing, but effectually is out:
For it no form delivers to the heart
Of bird, of flower, or shape which it doth latch;
Of his quick objects hath the mind no part,
Nor his own vision hold what it doth catch:
For if it see the rud'st or gentlest sight,
The most sweet favour, or deformèd'st creature,
The mountain, or the sea, the day, or night,
The crow, or dove, it shapes them to your feature:
Incapable of more, replete with you,
My most true mind thus maketh mine eye untrue.

Sonnet 113.

This is not a complicated sonnet; we simply have to set up the antithesis between what the eye sees and what the mind or heart sees. And this is what is intriguing about many of the sonnets; the idea that the heart and mind have a different reality from that of the world present around us — that there are two worlds, an inner and an outer one, each with its own truth. This is a good one to work on:

> The images are clearly defined, so go with them totally, for the humour will come out of their absurdity:
>
> > crow or dove
> > day or night
>
> Whatever is seen outwardly makes no impact but becomes the other person's feature.
>
> There is a slight ambivalence in the use of the word 'replete' at the end — perhaps almost too full?

In the same vein, look also at *Sonnet 27*:

> Weary with toil, I haste me to my bed,
> The dear repose for limbs with travel tir'd;
> But then begins a journey in my head
> To work my mind when body's work's expir'd . . .

Or at the sequence round *Sonnet 47*:

> Betwixt mine eye and heart a league is took,
> And each doth good turns now unto the other:

They are all excellent to do in that you have to set up the premise so clearly, and keep the antitheses hooked in your minds, latched there.

(4)

> My love is a fever, longing still
> For that which longer nurseth the disease,
> Feeding on that which doth preserve the ill,
> The uncertain sickly appetite to please.
> My reason, the physician to my love
> Angry that his prescriptions are not kept,
> Hath left me, and I desperate now approve
> Desire is death, which physic did except.
> Past cure I am now reason is past care,
> And frantic mad with ever more unrest;
> My thoughts and my discourse as madmen's are,
> At random from the truth, vainly express'd:
>   For I have sworn thee fair, and thought thee bright,
>   Who art as black as hell, as dark as night.

Sonnet 147.

This is more complex, the obsession is darker and more troubled.

> You have to set up the premise of love being as a fever, and all that that implies — discomfort, heat, restlessness. But it is not only that, for this fever feeds on what is causing the fever; in other words it is self-feeding.
>
> The images themselves are disturbing.
>
> It is quite complicated to make clear, which is why it is good to work on, for you have to handle the ideas skilfully. You have to lift 'My reason' and carry it through to 'hath left me' in order to make the meaning clear.
>
> And it is difficult also to make clear the line and a half that follows:
>
> and I desperate now approve
> Desire is death, which physic did except.
>
> which means something like: 'I now realize that, contrary to what physic proscribed, desire means death'.
>
> There is a wonderful restlessness in the rhythm and the way it is broken up which directly bears out the state of mind expressed. And you will find the more direct you are with it, the more you go with the wholeness of the ideas, the more it will clarify.

And this is so with all the sonnets: there is an extravagance in the ideas which is expressed through the imagery. And what they teach us is to be able to pursue the thought and the imagery and weld it together.

They are not all as complicated as this one — for instance, *Sonnet 143*, 'Lo, as a careful housewife . . .', just prior to this one, likens the poet's situation to a child with its mother, and pursues this one idea through. The image is surprisingly homely, yet, in its total surrender to the idea, it is extravagant. Or *Sonnet 97*: 'How like a winter hath my absence been From thee . . .', which contains the idea that, though he has lived through summer and autumn, it has all been as winter because of the absence of his love. Or *Sonnet 23*: 'As un unperfect actor on the stage . . .', where the idea of being unable to express his feelings is uppermost, and that because of this he is turned into something less than human. Yet all of them have the added awareness that they have been set down in a very exact literary form, and that they will continue to exist after the people concerned are dead. This in itself is ironic.

Do work on them. Do not be afraid of their complexity. They will help you to manage ideas and imagery together, and as such are a marvellous resource to work on alongside the plays.

Chapter 10

RELATING TO OTHER TEXTS

So we have to ask how all this work fits in with other text, and is it useful? I think yes.

We have to regard Shakespeare text as a touchstone: once you have become at ease with that language, other text falls into place. The jaggedness of Jacobean writing is more jagged because of our experience of the equilibrium of Shakespeare and therefore the jaggedness means more. The elaborate convolutions of Restoration writing seem more flowery because we miss a certain homeliness which is never far away in Shakespeare. And this is also true of modern text — however naturalistic and underplayed it appears, we use it better and know its colour because of the other work. We know its antithesis as it were.

Now apart from the work on metre, which will apply only perhaps to Jacobean writing, all the exercises we have used will work for other text, though of course very different qualities will emerge. But certainly all the exercises to do with moving at changes of thought, to do with group involvement and 'physicalizing' in any way, will be valuable.

Let us take a brief look at four different kinds of text — perhaps I should say a brief listen.

1 JACOBEAN TEXT

This is nearly always much more convoluted than Shakespeare, and certainly does not have the rhythmic flow, which is why it is often difficult to learn. But oddly, because it is difficult to understand initially, once you have found the thought line through, the flow and rhythm takes care of itself. I think perhaps there are not so many possibilities. You have to go with the syntax of the thought, which often jumps and is jagged, but it always works on a cumulative principal — the speeches open out and grow.

I think the texture of the language is heavier, and the images are darker, but it is generally forceful, and often very modern sounding.

First a speech from *The Duchess of Malfi* (Webster):

Old Lady: It seems you are well acquainted with my closet?
Bosola: One would suspect it for a shop of witchcraft, to find in it the fat of serpents; spawn of snakes, Jews' spittle, and their young children's ordure, and all these for the face. I would sooner eat a dead pigeon, taken from the soles of the feet of one sick of the plague, than kiss one of you fasting. Here are two of you, whose sin of your youth is the very patrimony of the physician, makes him renew his footcloth with the spring, and change his high-priz'd courtesan with the fall of the leaf: I do wonder you do not loathe yourselves. Observe my meditation now:
What thing is in this outward form of man
To be belov'd? We account it ominous,
If nature do produce a colt, or lamb,
A fawn or goat, in any limb resembling
A man; and fly from't as a prodigy.
Man stands amaz'd to see his deformity,
In any other creature but himself.
But in our own flesh, though we bear diseases
Which have their true names only tane from beasts,
As the most ulcerous wolf, and swinish measle;
Though we are eaten up of lice, and worms,
And though continually we bear about us
A rotten and dead body, we delight
To hide it in rich tissue: all our fear,
Nay, all our terror, is lest our physician
Should put us in the ground, to be made sweet,
Your wife's gone to Rome: you two couple, and get you
To the wells at Lucca, to recover your aches.

[*Exeunt Castruchio and Old Lady.*

I have other work on foot: I observe our Duchess
Is sick a-days, she pukes, her stomach seethes,
The fins of her eyelids look most teeming blue,
She wanes i'the'cheek, and waxes fat i'th'flank;
And, contrary to our Italian fashion,
Wears a loose-bodied gown: there's somewhat in't.
I have a trick, may chance discover it,
A pretty one; I have bought some apricocks,
The first our spring yields.

II.1.

And of course the trick is to give her apricots to make her sick, and prove that she is pregnant. How packed and wonderful that speech is. We have to be absolutely on top of the thought changes, for they do not flow easily out of each other. This is particularly good to look at because of the transition from prose to verse, and the difference is very marked. Although the language is not always easy to understand, the sound is quite modern.

2 RESTORATION TEXT

This has always to do with delight in being articulate and witty. It is quite self-conscious in a way, and we have to be aware of presenting it and of making the phrases turn right. We have to find a style which is both truthful and witty.

Here is a short passage from *The Country Wife* of Wycherley. Horner has had it given out that he is impotent in order that husbands will trust him with their wives:

Horner: Thou art an ass. Don't you see already, upon the report, and my carriage, this grave man of business leaves his wife in my lodgings, invites me to his house and wife, who before would not be acquainted with me out of jealousy?

Quack: Nay, by this means you may be the more acquainted with their husbands, but the less with their wives.

Horner: Let me alone; if I can but abuse the husbands, I'll soon disabuse the wives. Stay — I'll reckon you up the advantages I am like to have by my strategem. First, I shall be rid of all my old acquaintances, the most insatiable sort of duns, that invade our lodgings in a morning; and next to the pleasure of making a new mistress is that of being rid of an old one, and of all old debts. Love, when it comes to be so, is paid the most unwillingly.

Quack: Well, you may be so rid of your old acquaintances; but how will you get any new ones?

Horner: Doctor, thou wilt never make a good chemist, thou art so incredulous and impatient. Ask but all the young fellows of the town if they do not lose more time, like huntsmen, in starting the game, than in running it down. One knows not where to find 'em; who will or will not. Women of quality are so civil, you can hardly distinguish love from good breeding, and a man is often mistaken: but now I can be sure she that shows an aversion to me loves the sport, as those women that are gone, whom I warrant to be right. And then the next thing is, your women of honour, as you call 'em, are only chary of their reputations, not their persons; and 'tis scandal they would avoid, not men. Now may I have, by the reputation of an eunuch, the privileges of one, and be seen in a lady's chamber in a morning as early as her husband; kiss virgins before their parents or lovers; and may be, in short, the passe-partout of the town. Now, doctor.

I.1.

It is wordy, highly-shaped and elaborate. It needs to be swift, and you need the breath to get round the whole thought phrases, so that they can gather momentum as they go.

3 FORMAL MODERN TEXT

Here let us look at a speech from Shaw's *Man and Superman*. The style is very literary, and you have to invest it with your own truth, or it will sould like a tract. But any Shaw speech is wonderful to work on, it needs a great deal of range, and is both rhetorical and dry.

Octavius: What matter, if the slavery makes us happy?

Tanner: No matter at all if you have no purpose of your own, and are, like most men, a mere breadwinner. But you, Tavy, are an artist: that is, you have a purpose as absorbing and as unscrupulous as a woman's purpose.

Octavius: Not unscrupulous.

Tanner: Quite unscrupulous. The true artist will let his wife starve, his children go barefoot, his mother drudge for his living at seventy, sooner than work at anything but his art. To women he is half vivisector, half vampire. He gets into intimate relations with them to study them, to strip the mask of convention from them, to surprise their inmost secrets, knowing that they have the power to rouse his deepest creative energies, to rescue him from his cold reason, to make him see visions and dream dreams, to inspire him, as he calls it. He persuades women that they may do this for their own purpose whilst he really means them to do it for his. He steals the mother's milk and blackens it to make printers' ink to scoff at her and glorify ideal women with. He pretends to spare her the pangs of child-bearing so that he may have for himself the tenderness and fostering that belong of right to her children. Since marriage began, the great artist has been known as a bad husband. But he is worse: he is a child-robber, a blood-sucker, a hypocrite, and a cheat. Perish the race and wither a thousand women if only the sacrifice of them enable him to act Hamlet better, to paint a finer picture, to write a deeper poem, a greater play, a profounder philosophy! For mark you, Tavy, the artist's work is to show us ourselves as we really are. Our minds are nothing but this knowledge of ourselves; and he who adds a jot to such knowledge creates new mind as surely as any woman creates new men. In the rage of that creation he is as ruthless as the woman, as dangerous to her as she to him, and as horribly fascinating. Of all human struggles there is none so treacherous and remorseless as the struggle betwen the artist man and the mother woman. Which shall use up the other? That is the issue between them. And it is all the deadlier because, in your romanticist cant, they love one another.

Man and Superman, Act I.

This is a debate, wonderfully shaped and argued; and, as I say, all Shaw makes excellent practice, for it is both modern and formal, and makes us better able to recognize the shaping that occurs within quite naturalistic writing.

4 MODERN TEXT

This of course would make material for a whole book on its own, there is so much variety of approach that could be used. The point I would make clearly is that however naturalistic the dialogue, it still is presented speech, and as such you have to find its precise style. All good writing has a very specific rhythm, unique to itself, and we have to be alert to this for, just as in Shakespeare, that rhythm and form is integral to the meaning. There is however no iambic pentameter to measure it by, and so it is more difficult to pin down.

All the exercises that we use for Shakespeare will be useful: walking between thoughts or dialogue; speaking your own thoughts and then the dialogue. This last is particularly useful as so often the dialogue is only the top layer of the thought. The language often does not flow, and the moments in between speech are as important as the speech itself. But always the language is active and provoking the next moment, however casual it appears to be.

In this chapter I can only give a taste of the language patterns you may be working on, and so here is a random choice. Two pieces: one Chorus from the second of Bond's War Plays, *The Tin Can People*; and a short piece from *Sus* by Barrie Keeffe.

It seems to me very important that we look for the formal in modern writing, because in our own familiar speech we often fail to see the stylization, and this takes its life away. The Bond, then, is a piece of very formal writing, each line has to be pointed and phrased: the form is essential to its whole meaning. In the Keeffe play, Delroy is being interrogated by two policemen for the suspected murder of his wife — she has actually died because of a miscarriage. The suspense in the play is tremendous, and this piece of dialogue ends the first scene. Look at its pace and its formality.

FOURTH CHORUS

Why were the bombs dropped?
If that could be told simply they wouldn't be dropped
Suppose we said bombs were better food on one plate than
        on another?
Or money in an account while somewhere in the same city
        people are in debt for a few sticks of furniture?
Or one school in green fields and another for the poor
        on a waste lot?
That would be hard to understand

Injustice is harmful when its seen: when its unseen the disaster
 is terrible
To justify injustice words beliefs opinions faiths passions —
 all are corrupted
Soon people need an interpreter to understand the words that
 come from their own mouth and would have to be
 someone else to know the passions in their own
 breast!
That is even harder to understand

And so the bombs lie among the crumbs on your kitchen table and the
 books on the school desk
Are propped on the walls of lawcourts and workshops
Football fans wave them over their heads wrapped in team-scarfs
And every night they are locked in the safe by a junior
 cashier
You must create justice: and what chance do you have of that,
 you who must eat bread baked in the bomb-factory?

We make ourselves as much as we make the houses in which we live
But we make ourselves without plans: and even our tools we have
 to invent as we work
There you see the convulsions of history
Truly you live in a new age: as you enter your house to complete
 it you bring with you your new tool, the bomb
We can only tell you: you must create justice

The Tin Can People
from 'The War Plays', Part 2.

SUS

Wilby: Wife not well, you say. Ill?

Delroy: Not too well. Having a few upsets. The pregnancy. You know. She had it before. She stays in bed a lot and —

Wilby: And you went out, leaving her ill in bed?

Pause

Well, I mean to say, that was a bit callous, weren't it?

Delroy: The boys, the election and . . . It's OK. I put the kids to bed before I come out and I'll check she's OK before I go to the club. Any problem, she bangs on the floor and the kid downstairs, he comes in the boozer and tells me and two minutes later I'm back there, OK?

Pause. Karn sits.

Karn: So you last saw her . . . when did you last see her?

Delroy: When I got to the pub. Just before then. Sevenish.

Pause.

Karn: What was she wearing?

Delroy: Eh?
Karn: What was your wife wearing when you left her five hours ago.

Silence.

Delroy: She was in bed.
Wilby: Wearing?
Delroy: What do you mean . . . wearing?
Wilby: Describe what she was wearing.
Delroy: Well, she was wearing this nightie thing, like.
Karn: Like what?
Delroy: Like, sort of, down here and . . . long and . . . kinda made her feel nice, 'cause she weren't feeling too great and it was a bit cold, like she was and —
Karn: Colour?
Delroy: Colour? What do you mean colour?
Wilby: Colour of the nightdress.

Pause.

Delroy: Well, pink weren't it. Kinda pinkish and with white lacey bits round here and . . . no sleeves . . . She looked really good in it, you know, to cheer herself up, she looked really pretty, you know.
Karn: Wilby, would you get the —
Wilby: Of course.

Wilby goes.

Delroy: I'll be off now and all —
Karn: I'm afraid not, Mister Delroy. You see, there has been a crime tonight. This ain't sus.
Delroy: Yeah well, it ain't nothing to do with me 'cause I got witnesses that I weren't nowhere except —
Karn: Sit down, Mister Delroy.
Delroy: You've got nothing on me, I'm going home —
Karn: Sit down, Mister Delroy.
Delroy: Go fuck yourself, I'm going —

He goes to the door: it opens and Wilby enters carrying a plastic specimen bag. Pause. Delroy doesn't move. Wilby takes the bag to Karn, who looks in it. He looks at Delroy. Wilby stands in the doorway.

Karn: She died tonight.

Pause.

At eight fifteen . . . your wife died.

Karn stares at Delroy.

There was a great loss of blood. In fact, once we get the post-mortem result, I wouldn't be surprised to hear that she bled to death.

Silence. Then Delroy tries to laugh.

Delroy: Very good . . . very good . . . bit fucking cruel, bit sadistic, know what I mean. I ain't done nothing. My wife ain't . . . How can you say such an evil thing? What you trying to fucking fit me up for? Me confess to robbing gas meters or something, that what you want, you cunt.

Karn: What was she wearing?

Delroy: I told you.

Karn: Mister Wilby, open the door.

Pause. Then Wilby opens the door. Delroy hesitates.

Delroy: You're crazy, you know that? Crazy. That's . . . vicious, what you said.

Karn: As you like.

Delroy: So I go then . . . OK? That's right then, I'm going, out of this madhouse — I'm off.

Karn: Oh, one thing Mister Delroy —

Delroy stops at the open door and looks at Karn.

If you'd just have a look . . . if this was the nightie your late wife was wearing.

Pause. Karn tosses the plastic bag to Wilby, who opens it in front of Delroy. Pause.

Mind the blood stains. Still warm, almost.

Delroy looks in the bag. Silence. The phone rings. Karn lifts the receiver.

Karn *(listens, then to Wilby):* ITN predicting a 65 per cent majority . . . for the Thatch. (*He replaces the receiver.*) Sit down Delroy. Few things I want to ask you.

Delroy looks at Karn.

Oh yeah, she's dead.

Blackout.
Music loud: chorus of Bob Dylan's 'Baby Stop Crying'.

Sus, Scene 1.

Part 4

Voice Work

Chapter 11

PREPARATION

In this next whole section I want to look at the ways we can prepare the voice directly before performance, both in the group and on your own: and particularly I want to look at how to prepare for work in different spaces.

1 FINDING THE SPACE

Every place you go into has a different acoustic, therefore you have to be prepared to make adjustments quite objectively, which is in fact good because it keeps you vocally on your toes as it were, and that kind of challenge is good. To make these adjustments you are dependent a good deal on other people to give you feedback as to what is carrying and what is not, therefore it is good to work as a team. However, try to rely on your own judgement as much as possible.

I think it is important in the run-up to opening a play to do voice work in the space you are going to use; voice work as opposed to rehearsal work. So often something of a play gets lost between the last run-through in the rehearsal space and performing on stage, and I am sure it is only because time is not given for actors to get used to the space and experiment with it so that the necessary expansion happens organically. Instead, actors are told that they are not carrying to the back and that they must be bigger. The immediate reaction is then to be louder, and almost unawares we start to push and perhaps go up slightly in pitch, and that is when something of the spirit of the play gets lost — we stop talking to each other. Now of course we have to reach to the back, which may mean increasing volume, but this is very seldom the most important thing; and to find out what is really needed we have to work with each other as a group, and listen.

First, here are some pointers in terms of the space you may be using and the adjustments that may be needed. Then we will look at some work that you can do usefully in the space.

(i) **Size:** whatever size space you are working in, it is essential to investigate all the areas for clarity, for each space has its own idiosyncrasies; and that is just as true for the small studio areas.

Large spaces: Not all large spaces are difficult; sometimes they can be bright, and easy to use and kind. However, watch out for dead spots. In a conventional theatre space you will often find the area at the back of the stalls quite difficult. The fact that it is under the circle deadens the sound, and because it is not so easy to see, people often feel they cannot hear.

Often the sound in the top balcony is good, though you must stay conscious of the height, and so be careful not to direct the voice downwards.

Some spaces are deceptive, in that you feel your voice is carrying better than it is, and here is where you need another's opinion.

Alternatively, but more rare, some spaces are particularly unkind in that you do not get feedback from your voice — you lose its sound as you speak. This is most likely to happen when the auditorium is wide and the stage open. It can be dangerous, because when you cannot hear your own voice you start to push — with the same effect, only not as extreme, as talking in the open air when you tend to shout because you cannot hear what is happening. This is when you can damage the voice, so resist the temptation to be louder. Rather sit back on the voice, find as much resonance as you can, and let it sing. This kind of space needs resonance more than volume.

If a space is bright acoustically, and the sound very resonant, then cut down on the volume and make the consonants very firm.

Medium and small spaces: these are often tricky and need care. They may not need the volume, but they are deceptive and make us over-comfortable and just too intimate.

Thrust stages often feel very good and open, but very often there is difficulty in hearing round the sides.

(ii) **How to adapt:** Now to reach out to a large space you often need a little more sound, up a decibel or two. But much more important is greater accuracy and attention to consonants, allowing for their length and honouring them so that their vibrations are fully given and never drop away — all the things in fact that we have talked about regarding verbal energy.

So do not just sharpen the consonants because that will only emphasize the beginnings of words and you will get blasts of tone but no finished words. Feel through them and be aware of the time it takes for them to carry.

And it is this time element that is important. To be aware of the time it takes for words to reach the back, and to do this without slowing the language up, takes great concentration, and this is where the phrasing and the rhythm become crucial.

Pitch and tone: Pitch is important in that different spaces react differently. One space will like a low resonant voice and it will carry, but in another space those notes will get lost and swallowed.

So you will find different notes carry and others get lost. It is always only a question of half a tone or a tone, but it is important to find the right middle pitch for the space, and to be comfortable.

And this is where you are dependent to a certain extent on others, though you can help yourself a lot by going into the auditorium when you are not on stage, and listening to fellow-actors and judging for yourself. A good time of course to do this is during the technical, where you can notice precisely where the set is helpful, or perhaps where the voice gets lost when turning up-stage.

Always the more forward the tone is, the more the language is right on the lips, the better it will carry.

In small spaces it is essential to keep the discipline of the verbal energy. Because we do not need the volume, the tendency is to become just over-naturalistic, and the ends drop and get lost. This happens most particularly with modern text. And so, as I have said before, we have to find the right style, the right placing, however demotic the language and intimate the space.

So really all this has to do with common sense. But it is perhaps quite useful to know that that is what you have to depend on, that there is no one way of doing it right, but that you have to feel out each space and make your own judgement.

What is so important is not to allow yourself to be pushed or rushed, and to realize that a) volume alone is not the answer — people may hear but will not necessarily understand; and b) all the work you have done on the text, all the work to do with verbal energy and phrasing, is what will make the text drop in. We just have to become very sensitive to the time and flow that each space needs to make that happen.

Group work in the space

(i) First, do some warm-up exercises as given in the following chapter, on the stage or in your acting space, so that everyone is tuned up.

Then get in a circle and set up a hum, each person feeling the vibrations in the chest, back, head and face.

When that hum feels satisfactory, then everyone go into the auditorium, spreading round as much as possible, and set up the hum again. Continue that hum until you feel it just as strong and vibrant as when you were close together.

And setting up that hum is important: it obviously should not be in unison because everyone needs to find their own comfortable note, but when a group is in tune with each other and confident, the resulting note is good — it has an identity. When you feel that, then move it up a little in pitch.

(ii) Come back together on stage and set up a hum again in a circle.

When that is good, let each person in turn sing a word from the play on any note you like. The group must listen and then sing it back accurately.

Do this a second time round the circle, and this time the group can slightly exaggerate what they hear — even make some kind of gesture as they sing. But always be accurate to the quality of the person initiating the word.

You can develop this and sing phrases round.

This is good to do before a performance, because it keeps you in tune with the play, but it gets both sound and energy going and is very freeing.

(iii) Take a piece of text, not from the play but something similar in style, and work it through together on the stage for breathing, for verbal energy and relaxation.

Then take a line or a line-and-a-half round in order, giving a moment for each person to get familiar with his own bit. Then move round into the theatre, as far apart as possible, and speak it through.

This is excellent for noticing the different qualities that carry, how easy it is to drop the end consonants, and how so often a text needs lifting — something we must be continually aware of, for we cannot always quite believe how necessary it is.

Experiment with the volume. See how quiet you can go and yet still be comfortable to listen to.

Whisper it round — useful for noticing just what different times words take.

Everyone must say exactly what they cannot hear.

It is important to choose the right piece of text to work on, and this you can only judge by what you are going to perform. Try and relate it as much as possible.

However, speeches like those of Berowne in *Love's Labour's Lost* are excellent to do, as is Burgundy in *Henry V*. Also poetry is excellent if you can find something that relates, for instance a few verses of the *Rape of Lucrece*, or verses from Spenser's *Epithalamion* are all good.

But you do not necessarily need to take period text. Sometimes it is good to do something quite different and modern. It must be what feels right for the group.

(iv) What I do very often, and which I find most useful and exhilarating, is to take a poem and cut it up into short phrases of one or two lines, of a length that is easy to remember, and give one piece in order to each person in the circle. Make sure each person knows who they come after.

Give them a moment to get familiar with the text.

Then spread round the theatre and speak it through in turn.

The benefit of this is that no-one knows what anyone else is going to say; and this reminds us afresh that this is exactly where the audience is at, and that that is why we must be so aware of giving the language.

Our own familiarity with the text so often dulls that extra sense, that third ear.

Now, if you are going to do this, one member of the group has to find a poem and cut it up. I have set out poems that I like to use in the next section, so you will see the kind of text I mean. It must not be too difficult in language, but it is good if the text is a little off-beat, for then it makes us take sharper note.

Also, and this is crucial, when you pass the lines on, you will notice how they have to be lifted, or our interest in them drops away.

This is particularly useful for modern naturalistic text, for all the reasons that I have said.

The group must be really honest with each other and say exactly what they cannot hear comfortably.

(v) Finally, take select scenes from the play, and work them round the theatre.

This is particularly useful for scenes which are one to one, and fairly intimate. But do not be afraid of them; move them round the space and get comfortable in it. Be reassured that you can keep talking to each other yet reach over the space that you are in.

Solo work

This is very important to do, so that you find your own level and are confident with it. So often the adjustment you need to make is small, yet it can make a huge difference to what people receive.

Simply work a piece of text from the stage, and get someone to go and listen in different parts of the theatre, and get their reactions.

Experiment with the volume first, and find what is comfortable to listen to.

Then experiment with the pitch, and really be open to the need to lift the new thoughts and to keep the ends open.

Experiment also with different positions on the stage.

Make the other person tell you exactly what they do not hear easily. This way you will get the confidence to use both skill and intuition.

2 USING POETRY

I just want to say a few things here about using poetry, which I have always found excellent as preparation, and which I have written about quite fully elsewhere.

Not only the sonnets, but so much poetry is wonderful to use, for it makes us aware of rhythm and texture, and how to use language that is dense, and how to manage the poetic and the ordinary within the space of one line. Above all it teaches us about the associations of words and images, and that we cannot just be literal. The literal meaning is always only the tip of the iceberg.

So explore as much poetry as possible. Some of the simpler Donne poems for instance are excellent to work on. If you are studying a romantic part, what better than one of his love poems, for they teach us so much about metaphysical thought, and help us into that frame of reference. Take the following:

SONG

Sweetest love, I do not goe,
  For wearinesse of thee,
Nor in hope the world can show
  A fitter Love for mee;
    But since that I
Must dye at last, 'tis best,
To use my selfe in jest
  Thus by fain'd deaths to dye;

Yesternight the Sunne went hence,
  And yet is here to day,
He hath no desire nor sense,
  Nor halfe so short a way:
  Then feare not mee,
But beleeve that I shall make
Speedier journeyes, since I take
  More wings and spurres than hee.

O how feeble is mans power,
  That if good fortune fall,
Cannot adde another houre,
  Nor a lost houre recall!
    But come bad chance,
And wee joyne to'it our strength,
And wee teach it art and length,
  It selfe o'er us to'advance.

When thou sigh'st, thou sigh'st not winde,
  But sigh'st my soule away,
When thou weep'st, unkindly kinde,
  My lifes blood doth decay.
    It cannot bee
That thou lov'st mee, as thou say'st,
If in thine my life thou waste,
  Thou art the best of mee.

Let not thy divining heart
  Forethinke me any ill,
Destiny may take thy part,
  And may thy feares fulfill;
    But thinke that wee
Are but turn'd aside to sleepe;
They who one another keepe
  Alive, ne'r parted bee.

John Donne

The poem is about the oneness of their souls, and of absence; and it puts us in touch with a way of debating love, and inquiring into its spiritual rather than material essence. It is good to work on because:

You have to manage the short and the long lines and make them balance. You also have to keep the sense opening out from line to line through the verse.

Each verse deals with a slightly different angle of the argument, and therefore requires a new starting-point — a new note.

It has such a very particular music and rhythm, and we have to honour that without losing track of the thought; we have to keep it talking as direct speech.

It is excellent for two people to work on together, either taking a verse each, or half a verse, but keeping it moving both rhythmically and musically.

Experiment with as much range as possible.

Another great one to work on is his *A Valediction: forbidding mourning*, in which you get these three verses:

Dull sublunary lovers love
  (Whose soule is sense) cannot admit
Absence, because it doth remove
  Those things that elemented it.

But we by a love, so much refin'd,
  That our selves know not what it is,
Inter-assured of the mind,
  Care lesse, eyes, lips, and hands to misse.

Our two soules therefore, which are one,
  Though I must goe, endure not yet
A breach, but an expansion,
  Like gold to ayery thinnesse beat. John Donne

And this continues the debate about love of such refined quality that their souls are together whatever the distance between. And this is precisely the kind of thinking which informs our understanding of the lovers in any of the Shakespeare plays. And I think it is salutary for us to realize that we so often emphasize the feeling as opposed to the thought, when really they are together — it is the thought in both these poems that is exciting.

For other poetry, Yeats, Eliot, Hopkins, Auden are all excellent to work on. All have a different sound, a different way of mixing the poetic and the demotic. Also sometimes good to work on in a group is a ballad, to keep a sense of story-telling going in the voice. This opens up inflections.

Here I am including six modern poems, very different, but all good to use in a group, handing them round line to line. They are ones that I am particularly fond of, but they are really just to start you off finding your own material.

(i) QUESTIONS OF A STUDIOUS WORKING MAN

Who built Thebes of the Seven Gates?
In the books you find the names of kings.
Was it the kings who hauled chunks of rock to the place?
And Babylon, many times demolished,
Who raised it up again so many times? In what houses
Of gold-glittering Lima did the builders live?
Where, the evening that the Great Wall of China was finished,
Did the masons go? Great Rome
Is full of triumphal arches. Over whom
Did the Caesars triumph? Had Byzantium, much praised in song,
Only palaces for its inhabitants? Even in fabulous Atlantis,
The very night the ocean engulfed it,
The drowning still roared for their slaves.
Young Alexander conquered India.
Was it he alone?
Caesar defeated the Gauls.
Did he not have a cook at least in his service?
Philip of Spain wept when his armada
Had sunk. Was he the only one to weep?
Frederick the Second won the Seven Years War. Who
Else won that war?

Every page a victory.
Who cooked the feast for the victors?
Every ten years a great man.
Who paid the bill?

So many accounts
So many questions.

Bertolt Brecht

This divides up very well, and is perfect to do in a space as preparation for performance. As indeed are these two of Bond:

(ii) TO THE AUDIENCE

You sit and watch the stage
Your back is turned —
To what?

The firing squad
Shoots in the back of the neck
Whole nations have been caught
Looking the wrong way

PREPARATION

I want to remind you
Of what you forgot to see
On the way here
To listen to what
You were too busy to hear
To ask you to believe
What you were too ashamed to admit

If what you see on the stage displeases
You run away
Lucky audience!
Is there no innocence in chains
In the world you run to?
No child starving
Because your world's too weak
And all the rich too poor
To feed it?

On the stage actors talk of life and imitate death
You must solve their problems in your life
I remind you
They show future deaths.

(iii) ON LEAVING THE THEATRE

Do not leave the theatre satisfied
Do not be reconciled

Have you been entertained?
Laughter that's not also an idea
Is cruel

Have you been touched?
Sympathy that's not also an action
Corrodes

To make the play the writer used god's scissors
Whose was the pattern?
The actors rehearsed with care
Have they moulded you to their shape?
Has the lighting man blinded you?
The designer dressed your ego?

You cannot live on our wax fruit
Leave the theatre hungry
For change

Edward Bond

Another, also very good to hand round:

(iv) VENDING MACHINE

he puts four dimes into the slot
he gets himself some cigarettes
he gets cancer
he gets apartheid
he gets the king of greece
federal tax state tax sales tax and excise
he gets machine guns and surplus value
free enterprise and positivism
he gets a big lift big business big girls
the big stick the great society the big bang
the big puke
king size extra size super size

he gets more and more
for his four dimes
but for the moment all the things he is getting himself
disappear

even the cigarettes

he looks at the vending machine
but he doesn't see it
he sees himself
for a fleeting moment
and he almost looks like a man

then very soon he is gone again
with a little click
there are his cigarettes

he has disappeared
it was just a fleeting moment
some kind of sudden bliss

he has disappeared
he is gone
buried under all the stuff he has gotten
for his four dimes

Hans Magnus Enzensburger

(v) A WORLD IN EACH HUMAN BEING

Each human creature is a world that's peopled
by blind inhabitants in dark rebellion
against the I set over them as king.
In every soul a thousand souls are prisoned
in every world a thousand worlds are hidden
and these blind worlds, these lower worlds are real
and living, though they never come to birth,
real as the I is real. And we the kings
we princes of the possible within us
we too are subjects, prisoners ourselves
in some great being whose essential I
we grasp as little as our master can
his master. And our own emotions
have taken colour from their love and dying.
As when far out a liner passes, under
the horizon, lying smooth and clear
in the evening light. And we know nothing of it
until a wave swells towards us on the beach,
first one, and then another, and then more
that break and climb and break till everything
is as it was again. Yet nothing
is as it was again.

And so we shadows shake with strange unrest
when something tells us that a voyage has started,
that something of the possible is freed.

Gunnar Ekelof
(Trans. Ann Draycon)

This is more complicated to divide up, but it is still possible, and it has a very good feeling of inquiry running through it, which is useful for the actor to feel. The inflections are not positive, but always opening out.

This next, of Ferlinghetti, is particularly helpful: hand it round in each part of the line, each layer, for then the phrases suspend, for the lines are left in the air and cannot be dropped. There are several others of his which are excellent to use. The wit is in how the lines are suspended:

(vi) CONSTANTLY RISKING ABSURDITY

Constantly risking absurdity
and death
whenever he performs
above the heads
of his audience
the poet like an acrobat
climbs on rime
to a high wire of his own making
and balancing on eyebeams
above a sea of faces
paces his way
to the other side of day
performing entrechats
and slight-of-foot tricks
and other high theatrics
and all without mistaking
any thing
for what it may not be
For he's the super realist
who must perforce perceive
taut truth
before the taking of each stance or step
in his supposed advance
toward that still higher perch
where Beauty stands and waits
with gravity
to start her death-defying leap
And he
a little charleychaplin man
who may or may not catch
her fair eternal form
spreadeagled in the empty air
of existence

Lawrence Ferlinghetti

I think that is a valuable one to use: it has a gaiety in it and a wit and a wonderful poise to the lines from which you can learn a lot.

A great deal of T. S. Eliot is good to use because of how it shifts from the formal to the colloquial in the space of a few lines. I like particularly to use the poem *Triumphal March*, from 'Coriolan', because of its shifts in style and time, and its historical perspectives.

All this work is invaluable, for it makes us aware of form, and how the form is part of the sense, and how we have to allow each line its own time and pointing. I particularly like the Brecht and the Bond; they are both passionate and unforced. But there is plenty of material which is suitable, and which you can match to the needs of the group.

3 CADENCE AND NOTE

Just a word about cadence. This is not simply inflection, which implies sense and emphasis. Rather it is the musical flow of a line within which stress happens incidentally. Of course inflection is part of it, but cadence happens because of the musical flow of the language, and because of the underlying drive of the thought and the shape of the whole.

I am not talking about being rhetorical or sounding poetic, but we need to tune in to the musical possibilities in the language, to know that the flow of the thought can be helped by changing the note; and that more often than not, it is a new note that will grab the listener's attention, rather than an increase of volume. Use poetry to help you to find this.

Chapter 12

FURTHER VOICE EXERCISES

Finally, here are some exercises, and they are so important. For never forget that it is the breath that makes us able to get pace, relaxation and unforced sound, and by which we can encompass a long thought and so illuminate the sense.

The following are an extension of the ones given in *Voice and the Actor*, for, since writing that, I have become more interested in developing the breath as deep into the stomach as possible. I was taught to put my hand on the abdominal muscles above the waist, and allow those muscles to control the movement of the diaphragm. I feel now that this is limiting, and that it makes us over-conscious of a muscular impulse to the breath; whereas we can in fact take it deeper and draw the breath in because of the impulse to speak, rather than rely on a muscular movement to draw it in.

I also believe that the further down into the centre we take the breath, the more in touch the breath is with our feelings, and therefore the more the voice will respond to the texture of the language. This shift of emphasis also helps to let the voice sit down inside to give you more of a feeling of your own weight, and therefore to get a firmer body of tone.

However, I want to emphasize that there is no one right way, and different people have different methods. Try the exercises my way, but ultimately do what is comfortable and feels best.

These exercises can be done both solo and in a group. You may not want to do the whole sequence each time, though try and do as much of it as you can. Sometimes however time is short, so select what is useful.

It seems to me that it is always beneficial for a company to do voice work together for a short time before a performance. Obviously you cannot do it necessarily every time, but some time should be set aside at least twice a week for this to happen. There is great benefit from making sound together. Always end up speaking a short piece of text together, and then humming and singing on an open vowel.

A suitable piece of text would be the following poem by Dylan Thomas. It has good firm voiced consonants which take time to honour fully. It can be clearly broken up into breath phrases. First breathe on each thought phrase — i.e., on semi-colons and full-stops. Then breathe in three lines and two lines, that is on full-stops; let the vowels be open and free. Also, though you may not understand it completely, you can relate to the images quite quickly.

THE FORCE THAT THROUGH THE GREEN FUSE DRIVES THE FLOWER

The force that through the green fuse drives the flower
Drives my green age; that blasts the roots of trees
Is my destroyer.
And I am dumb to tell the crooked rose
My youth is bent by the same wintry fever.

The force that drives the water through the rocks
Drives my red blood; that dries the mouthing streams
Turns mine to wax.
And I am dumb to mouth unto my veins
How at the mountain spring the same mouth sucks.

The hand that whirls the water in the pool
Stirs the quicksand; that ropes the blowing wind
Hauls my shroud sail.
And I am dumb to tell the hanging man
How of my clay is made the hangman's lime.

The lips of time leech to the fountain head;
Love drips and gathers, but the fallen blood
Shall calm her sores.
And I am dumb to tell a weather's wind
How time has ticked a heaven round the stars.

And I am dumb to tell the lover's tomb
How at my sheet goes the same crooked worm.

Dylan Thomas

A pantheistic philosophy. Nevertheless the strength and drive through is rich for the voice.

The important thing is to do the exercises, and not worry about whether you are doing them right. When you are doing them alone, one is so often put off by worrying how you are doing them. You cannot really go wrong, and certainly you cannot do harm. So do them as clearly as you can, and gradually they will become easy and fall into place.

Also what often holds one up is the idea in the mind that it takes longer to breathe deeply. This in fact is not true, but we have to get used to the idea. Once you feel that it is the easier way and that it gives you the freedom and strength you want, you will use it naturally.

THE EXERCISES

1 On the floor

Lie on the floor and feel your back as much in touch with the floor as possible.

First, find out how you feel most comfortable, whether with your legs crooked or flat.

If you prefer them crooked up, then make sure they are crooked high and steady, with the feet and knees about six inches apart. If flat, make sure your body is straight.

Adjust the angle of your seat, so that the whole of your seat is flat to the floor. This will help to keep the middle of the back from arching.

Try to get the back as flat as possible, but without tensing it or pushing it down. Feel the floor supporting your back.

You may find that your head drops too far back, so making tension in the front of the neck. In which case put a book under your head — not too thick, but just thick enough to make an easy alignment between your head and shoulders. The head should feel level with the shoulders, so that you can feel it lengthening out of the neck.

Feel your shoulders widening across the floor so that the arm joints are easing out of the shoulder joints, and the top of your back feels spread.

Feel your back lengthening along the floor, each vertebra slightly lengthening out of the one below. Feel your neck lengthening out of your back. Feel the elbows and wrists free.

Turn your head gently to one side, and then to the other side, then back to the middle. Press the head gently back into the floor, feeling the tension in the back of the neck, then release it and feel the difference. Repeat this once. And repeat again once or twice during the floor exercises.

Take time to feel your back spread.

Breathing: Ribs. We want to get the ribs moving to their optimum capacity without lifting at all in the upper chest, and without tension in the neck or shoulders.

> Put the backs of your hands on the ribs at the side — where the rib-cage bulges most, and so where there is most room for movement.
>
> Feel the ribs quite firmly with your hands — i.e., put some pressure on the ribs.
>
> Keep the wrists and elbows free.
>
>> Breathe in through the nose — hold a moment — feel the shoulders and neck free — open your mouth and sigh out — making sure the throat is open and free — empty — feel the lungs empty of air — wait a moment — and then repeat once.
>
> For the rib exercises it is good to breathe in through the nose as this stimulates the ribs.
>
> When you breathe out the throat should be open and there should be no sound there, for there should be no holding on to the breath, however slight. If there is a sound, even just a slight compression of the breath, it means that there is energy being employed in the throat — which is exactly what we want to avoid. Energy in the throat means that our vocal focus is there, instead of with the breath.
>
> Set up a steady rhythm of breathing as follows:
>
>> Breathe in — hold and free shoulders and neck — open your mouth — and breathe out for 10 counts — empty — wait a moment so that you feel the need to breathe — and then repeat.
>
> Sometimes tension comes at the moment when you have breathed in and are changing gear, as it were, ready to breathe out. Try not to hold in the throat — the holding should happen in the ribs. If you keep as free as possible this sense of holding will gradually go.
>
> The same applies at the moment when you are emptying the lungs.
>
> Once this rhythm has been set up and has become familiar, both these moments will become smoother. However, it is important that you are always aware of the need to breathe — so take time for that.
>
> In. . . free. . . hum out gently for 10, feeling the vibration in the chest— quite unforced — empty.

In. . . free. . . hum slightly louder for 10, moving the lips around to feel the vibration there — empty.

In. . . free. . . hum quite loudly for 10, making sure the jaw is free and the throat open. There should be no more tension than when you were humming gently. Simply feel the breath making the sound — empty.

In. . . free. . . sing out gently on OO, making a defined shape with the lips.

In. . . free. . . sing out a little louder on OH, filling the cheeks with resonance — also for 10 — empty.

In. . . free. . . sing out on AW for 10, shaping the vowel firmly on the lips, keeping the jaw loose and the throat free.

In. . . free. . . sing out on AH for 10, jaw open and loose, tongue flat, quite loud.

In. . . free. . . sing out on AY for 10, feeling the movement of the tongue as you make the diphthong. Feel the tongue moving the sound out.

In. . . free. . . sing out on EE, feel the jaw and throat open. Shape the sound with the front of the tongue while keeping the back of the tongue as free as possible. Try to feel some vibration on the tongue.

While singing out on these vowels, put your hand sometimes on the chest to feel the vibration there.

Relax a moment. Turn your head from side to side as before.

Now take time to feel your throat open.

Drop your jaw and exercise the back of your tongue:

First — Ke
then — kekeke

You feel the muscle in the back of the tongue meeting the soft palate. Feel the pressure in the two sets of muscles. Notice the little spurt of air as the muscles release the sound.

Now the same with

ge
and gegege

You will feel no spurt of air as it is all made into vibration. Put your hand on your chest and feel the vibration there.

Repeat these two sounds, but this time with conscious tension in the throat. Feel the throat pushing and the consonant very explosive. You will notice how this cuts out all the chest resonance.

Then repeat without tension keeping the sound firm but free. Feel the exact movement of the muscles.

Now repeat these two sounds and open on to a vowel. First find a spot on the ceiling so that you send the sound to that spot like a dart.

ke — AH
ke — AY

ge — AH
ge — AY

Back to the breathing sequence — increasing the count out to 15.

In. . . free. . . hum out for 15. During the hum out tense and free the back of the tongue twice, then open on to AH.

In. . . free. . . sing out on AH for 15 touching your toes once as you do so.
Repeat, putting your feet over your head once.

Then go through the same sequence of vowels as before to the outgoing count of 15.

If you wish you can increase the outgoing count to 20 for part of the time.

These exercises will have opened the ribs out well. They are not for controlling the breath — for control will come through thought. They are specifically for increasing the capacity of the ribs.

If you find it difficult to last the counts to begin with it does not matter — the fact that you need the breath will serve to stimulate the ribs, and the important thing is to get through the sequence of exercises without worrying how well you are doing them, or whether you are doing them right! In the end, the doing of them will bring strength.

The rib breath gives you solidity of sound and freedom in the upper chest. When you are doing the exercises pat the chest from time to time to check the vibrations there; you will hear the resonance.

Having found this freedom in the ribs, you will be able to focus on the energy which you will find in the stomach breath. Often people have plenty of breath, but it is just not organized to give the best use.

Exercises are simply to focus our energy on the best way possible, but are never an end in themselves.

Breathing: stomach. People have obviously been taught different ways of breathing — perhaps to keep the ribs out while using the breath from the diaphragm. This is not wrong, though I personally think it becomes too contrived and makes the use of the breath too conscious.

I think the deeper we can take the breath into the stomach the better, so we release the breath from as deep within ourselves as possible. This roots you down to the centre, and gives the sound energy and freedom. Further, it puts us in touch with our deepest feelings.

You have exercised the ribs, so do not worry about them — they will remain flexible.

Put one hand on your stomach below the waist.

Fill down . . . and let the breath out through V. Feel the vibration on the lower lip.

Fill down . . . and out through Z, vibrating the tongue tip.

Fill down . . . sing gently out on OO, feeling the steady flow of breath from the stomach.

Repeat with AH.

Try to feel the connection of the breath with sound. The throat should be quite free.

Now, to get the very specific feeling of the sound starting in the stomach:

Fill down . . . touch the sound out three times on AH — spoken.

For the following exercises try to feel there is nothing happening in your body — just the breath working for you.

Feel the sounds being touched off in the stomach, not by muscularly pushing them — there should be no jerk — nor by being too soft, and therefore breathy. Speak the vowels quite ordinarily on one outgoing breath, with a space between each. You will then notice how the breath stops and starts the sound, and you will feel exactly where the sound starts. Firm but free.

It is useful to start each vowel with a very slight H. This ensures that the throat is open and there is no glottal stop.

Again, get a rhythm going, so that you do not think about each sound too intensely. Feel the breath letting the sound go — touching it out.

Fill down . . . touch the sound out three times on OO

Fill down . . . on OH

Fill down . . . on AW

Fill down . . . on AH

Fill down . . . on AY

Fill down . . . on EE

Fill down . . . on I.

As you go on you will feel the connection between the breath and the sound. It will be effortless, yet firm.

You can repeat this sequence by singing the vowels.

When the exercise becomes familiar, it is always good to focus the vowels on to a spot on the ceiling, so that the sounds are like three darts. This helps to release the sound without pushing or jerking it.

To stand·up: roll first on to your side, so that you keep the sense of length and width in your back; do not get up too quickly. Give yourself a moment before you start to get up to feel the spread of your back.

2 **When standing**

Feel your weight placed equally on your feet, feet not too far apart. Take time to feel your back long and wide.

Bounce gently down on your knees to get the sense of weight in your body — i.e., the bounce should be a downward bounce and not an upward one.

To get the sense of length in your back it is useful to imagine a string coming down from the ceiling and attaching to the middle of your head (not to the front or back of the head as that will pull the wrong way). Let the string pull you up to the ceiling, up on your toes, and then let you down to the normal position. Do this two or three times. Then let the string let you down so that your knees bend down and out. Take care not to let your back bend. Keep it straight, then let the string lift you up to a normal position. Repeat twice.

You will find this endorses the feeling of length that you had on the floor. Always keep free.

In this good standing position, long but not tense:

Drop your *head* forward and feel the muscles in the back of the neck stretching. Pull up slowly with those muscles.

Do the same thing once the wrong way — i.e., drop your

head forward and turn it up quickly. You will not feel the muscles working.

Again drop your head forward and feel the muscles pulling. Then pull the head up slowly keeping the chin in.

Drop the head to the side, stretch and pull up.

Drop to the other side, stretch and pull up.

Roll the head slowly letting it fill every position (be careful not to turn it, as this will not stretch the muscles).

Roll it round the other way letting it drop right forward, and then pulling up slowly with the muscles in the back of the head.

Nod it gently still feeling the muscles in the back of the neck.

Lift your *shoulders* gently about an inch, drop them, and let them go. You will find there is a deeper relaxation — deep in the muscle which you will be able to feel if you take the time. It is very important that you notice this feeling; then you will be able to repeat it at will.

Repeat a couple of times.

Breathing. Put one hand on your stomach below the waist. Fill down and out through a continuant F.

You can go through the same sequence of stomach breath exercises as on the floor.

Focus the vowels on a particular point in the room.

Start by bouncing gently on your knees. Then if you want you can move in between each set of vowels. Jump or run, but always be still when you take the breath down.

You can speak them first, then sing them, then call them, then shout them.

Always feel the breath connected with the sound.

3 Sitting on the floor

Put your hands in front of your mouth. Fill down into your stomach, slightly rocking back on your seat so you feel your own weight. This also releases tension in the neck. Open your mouth and sigh out through the open AH position. Listen to the open breathed vowel as it hits your hands.

There should be no holding in the throat, and you can hear the pure breathed resonance from your body. The vowel should be open and free.

Breathe down again, and touch the sound out three times with sound. As you breathe out let the weight come forward to the normal position.

Repeat this last sequence on the open AY vowel, and be sure to feel the movement of the tongue in the making of the vowel.

Taking the sequence of vowels that we have already used, find a spot on the floor about two feet in front of you and release the vowels — like three darts — to that spot.

Touch the sound off with the breath. You will feel the sound has a floor inside you. Every so often rock a little, to feel your own weight.

It is useful always to rock. Lean back quite far, almost until you fall over, then you can feel your weight going down into the floor. It is good to speak a piece of text like this.

When you feel the vowels centred take the three voiced continuant consonants — v — z — th — and speak them to the spot in front. Then go through the sequence of vowels with those consonants in front. You will feel the weight of the vowel in balance with the vibration of the consonant.

4 Standing again

Put the work you have done into practice on a piece of text, a piece that sounds good and has long phrases so that it needs plenty of breath. Pin it up to the wall in front of you.

A good sequence of work is this:

> For the first few lines swing each arm round alternately, windmill-fashion. This gets the breathing free.
>
> Continue with the next few lines, bouncing heavily on your knees, finding the vocal weight.
>
> Standing still, continue with the next few lines, living through the vowels so that you transfer the body weight that you have felt into the weight of the vowel.

It is useful on a piece of text to isolate the vowels sometimes — i.e., speak the text as you would attending to the sense, yet only verbalizing the vowels. This makes you conscious of how much the vowels carry the sense (we tend to think of the consonants only as doing this) and also of how much they vary in length so that their weight is always changing.

You can also do this with the consonants.

Again, with the same piece of text, sing it through and make up a tune as you go, like a piece of recitative. This releases the energy of the words separately from the logical meaning.

Always finish by speaking the text straight, but allow the work you have done to influence it, and to keep open the possibilities.

Further Perspectives

Almost as soon as you define anything about voice—you want to change it. I suppose that is the nature of the work. This is not only because one is working with different people who bring different energies and perceptions to text: it is also because the way we speak, and therefore the way we interpret, is subject to considerable change, and we must constantly be alert to this.

The modes of speech, the cadences we use, the prevailing standard pronunciation and its implications, all these change from one generation to another, from one decade to another: and the influences that promote the change are always societal. So—it is very good to have the opportunity to add some thoughts that I have had since writing the book.

What seems to me important is that we in the theatre retain the power to excite people with language; it should not be owned by the educated and/or those who rule, so we must awaken peoples' ears to the pleasure of verbal communication—to its music and to its cultural diversity, for I do believe that there is a generation now which has not experienced this, and I think that this is because the culture has more to do with visual than with aural stimuli.

When I directed *King Lear* at The Other Place in Stratford in 1988 the production was linked to our education programme: and as part of this programme there was a workshop attached to many of the performances, as my main concern was to engage our audiences actively with the language. The workshop which we ran most frequently was one called 'Our Changing Language': as a starting point we took a short piece of dialogue from Act II Sc. 4 of the play between Lear and his two daughters Goneril and Regan. Our aim was that the audience would hear it in four ways:

i. a Shakespeare scholar read the passage in as near Elizabethan as was possible;

ii. we then played a record of the same passage as recorded only 25 years ago;

iii. we then played it ourselves as if for a modern television drama, as intimately as possible;

iv. lastly we played it as we had rehearsed it.

It was interesting to hear. The first, of course, was difficult to understand, and therefore in the end, alienating; the second, although good, already sounded dated and therefore did not feel truthful, or appropriate for now; the intimacy of the third way was not appropriate, because in its naturalism the energy of the language was overlooked, and therefore you could not perceive the underlying passion and violence; the fourth way was the result of how we had worked to embrace the rhythm and energy of the text, to honour the image, and yet to make it sound as if it was for now. It was obviously a slightly self-conscious exercise, but it brought home very strongly just how much fashions of speech change, and just how much work we have continually to do to adjust the balance; the balance between rhetoric and naturalism: between what is ordinary and what is extreme; between entering the image in its extravagance yet not sounding false or melodramatic. How do you enter the myth, the violence, the love in that play.

In 1984 I went to work in China: I went there at the invitation of their Ministry of Culture to work with actors from all parts of the country. My brief was to work on voice and text from a Western perspective—very interesting to do in another language. The main reason I was given was that because so many skills had been lost during the period of the Cultural Revolution, resonance and expressiveness etc., actors needed to relearn some of those basic skills. And I was shown many films showing the work of actors in pre-Cultural Revolution times: work which incidentally was heavily influenced by the Moscow Arts Theatre: the voices were rich and full of texture.

The time I spent there was fascinating: but I could remember thinking 'how can skills which have developed over centuries be lost in so short a time?' But, do we see some evidence of loss of skill here: we live in a product-oriented society where the chief function of language seems to be to give information in some way. We watch television, we watch videos, we listen to commercial jingles—often the only poetry we hear: language has become either passive and literal, or to do with selling a commodity—(perhaps yourself!). The prevailing mode seems to be either so positive that speech becomes almost aggressive which cuts out any possibility of self-enquiry or doubt, any sensibility to the language. Or it is minimal, monosyllabic, undercut and 'cool'. Whichever it is, there is little personal imagery, only technological indifference to the emotional roots of language. And we must ask—has all this affected the way we present language in the theatre, and made us less able to hear and transmit the texture/substance that is in the word. If violence is a symptom of loss of speech, then we need desperately now to create a more verbal society—one which is not shy to express feelings—or doubt.

Arising from this, there are two perspectives I want to look at: first a historical one, which has to do with where I have come from.

English theatre has always been language-based and consequently dependent on verbal and vocal dexterity. The tradition of Shakespeare, of Jacobean and Restoration writing has influenced not only the acting styles, but also what the audience has expected from the actor. This emphasis on rhetorical style obviously influenced the voice work done with actors: in the last century this was very much based on a singing technique—with gesture and good articulation—elocution—also being part of the work. The 'voice beautiful', subtly allied to upper class speech, was a popular concept, though there were those who did not subscribe to it. There were a number of professional voice teachers—Gustave Garcia was perhaps the most famous—he published a book called *The Actor's Art* in 1882—and he was probably the first who concentrated on the specific needs of the actor as opposed to the singer. However, it was not until 1934 when the Central School of Speech Training and Dramatic Art was founded in London by Elsie Fogerty, that voice training for actors was taken seriously as a separate skill. She was first an actor, and then became interested in training. She was perhaps the first person to look realistically at the needs of the actor, and to turn attention from this 'voice beautiful' with its accompanying rhetorical style and gesture, and focus instead on the meaning and texture of the spoken word: it was still, of course, the English middle-class accent that was the norm.

By the time I went to the Central School to train, Gwynneth Thurburn had taken over: it was run very much on the lines of a drama school today, with Movement, acting methods etc. being taught, and was open and modern in its outlook—Gwynneth was a most progressive and radical figure. What was so good from my point of view was the emphasis on text work in both the actor and the teacher training. There was the opportunity to work on every kind of text, prose and verse, and be excited about it in a way which was not self-conscious, but which genuinely tried to keep the truth of everyday speech while still honouring the specific rhythms, imagery, and cadence of the writing. I think that how we hear poetry now is quite different, as it should be, for there are many different voices and idioms in terms of culture and dialect to encompass; but what was important for me then was the time taken on the groundwork; groundwork in terms of metre, verse form, figures of speech etc., which opened the ear to the possibilities of formal language, and gave one the confidence to listen—and also to appreciate what was formal and what broke rules—in other words what was 'other', and therefore interesting in another way.

But other forces were at work; in the '50's a different kind of play was being written—a new style of writing. In the US there was Miller, Williams, Odets etc.; and in England there was Osborne and Wesker, among others, who finally broke through the stranglehold of class and demanded a new kind of realism—I think that the realism was different from the American one in that the emphasis was still very much on text, for the development of the play happened more through language than through situation.

At the same time, in the States, a new approach to acting took root—the Method, influenced by Stanislavsky; and this radically changed the actors' perception of language and how it should be presented. Under great teachers and directors such as Berghof, Clurman and Kazan, the emphasis was on finding the physical attributes of a character, on inter-character relations and the motivation of a scene; communication through language almost became secondary. This approach underpinned much of the work of film and television in the States; and because it had such quality and power, its influence on this side of the Atlantic was considerable—it made us want something different. The result was that the actor's position regarding text shifted: because motive and inner feeling did not always coincide with structure and rhetoric, no longer was the way to speak classical text a clear-cut process. Not only did the actor have to make choices regarding the presentation of language, those who went to listen also had to make choices: the audience was divided in that some people went to the theatre wanting to hear the play the way it used to be/sound—others began to want to hear something new.

When I started to teach in the late '40's, my work was geared to 'voice production' in a quite conventional way: this meant the training of the voice to be clear and interesting, to release tensions, and make sure the speech was articulated 'correctly' —i.e. acceptable to class standards. But two things had a great bearing on the work I did: one was an interest in language and how it could be communicated, and the other was the effect of Method work on the approach to acting and how that was interpreted here: I wanted to find out how these could interrelate. In this respect I was influenced by the work of my husband, Harry Moore, an American actor and teacher who had trained in the Method studio in New York: I began to seek ways of making language relate in a different way to motive and feeling without losing its music.

I was particularly lucky therefore, in 1970, to come to work with the RSC, a) because working in a Company situation gave me the opportunity to work in detail on text and on the actor/text relationship with some continuity; and b) the fact that, though the main work was Shakespeare and classical text, the Company was also putting on a great deal of exciting and radical new writing, and this juxtaposition of the old and the new was incredibly rich—and illuminating. Now the Company obviously did not use a Method approach, nor was it declamatory—although the form of the verse writing was strictly adhered to, but it was always searching after the reality of the text, and its truth for now.

Parallel with this we were beginning an education programme in the Company—a programme which has since developed into a forceful unit of its own. Over the years I have run countless workshops on Shakespeare in schools, in community groups, and also many weekend workshops for English and Drama teachers: this taught me a huge amount, and gave me a further perspective.

I nearly always worked on Shakespeare, and my task with the students, or members of a group, was to back up the work of the teachers by getting them actively involved with the language. For myself, I wanted every member of the group not just to understand literally what they were saying, but to feel something as they spoke—I wanted them at some point to feel the text going through them. To speak words should alter you—this was something I learned from Peter Brook—only he would put it better! I wanted them to be rid of any received idea of how it 'should' be spoken, and the notion that there is a particular way: I think when language is written down we almost respect it too much, we make it 'behave' as we think it should—and this happens to actors too—and so we put it in a strait-jacket in some way which makes it impossible to respond to instinctively.

So, in the desire to get a group to understand something of the emotional depth under the language, I found physical analogies to help them enter it. I have already given an example of this on page 113, where I described the work I did with a group of Sixth Formers on a speech from Othello. But I would like to elaborate on this a little, for it took quite a long time to set the exercise up so that they understood what was wanted, and for them to pull each other hard enough to suit the purpose; when they finally did it however, they felt so strongly the chaos underlying the words, that sense of being pulled by something stronger than they could manage and being momentarily out of control, that they were able to apprehend something beyond the literal meaning—something perhaps of Othello's nature—i.e. that he was quite literally drowning in his feelings, helpless. As Theseus says in *A Midsummer Night's Dream* they were able:

to apprehend
More than cool reason ever comprehends.

V.i.

Some of the exercises I happened on by chance—sometimes out of my desperation to get such a kind of response—but every time an exercise evolved, I found it confirmed my belief that if you release people from the constraints of making only literal sense, making the words behave intelligently, you release a deeper and more subconscious response, which is of course in the end more intelligent, more imaginative. A further comment: quite often the response to imagery was more fertile and imaginative among the 'lower-ability' students than with those studying for advanced exams. So does too much analysis and reading round the subject inhibit the essentially active nature of dramatic text: do we lose some part of the very precious quality of finding pleasure in language? The answer surely must be that we find an interaction between the two—we must find a balance: for it is only by speaking the language aloud, and with purpose, that we can begin to gauge the depth of feelings involved.

Now, obviously, most of the exercises in the book were worked out with actors, either in rehearsal or in individual sessions, in order to work through the specific needs of the text. However, the work that I did with students sharpened my perceptions, and helped me begin to find a bridge between naturalism and extravagance.

But before I leave this area I want to talk a little about work in closed institutions. I have done a great deal of work in top-security prisons, and the following is an account of a session I particularly remember in HM Prison: Long Lartin.

First, as always, I began with some simple voice work, some relaxation and breathing; working the breath into sound, and feeling the shape of vowels and the energy of consonants. This sense of finding their own voice and their own vibrations is essential—listening to the inner voice—the concentration of energy then becomes quite different. We were looking at *A Winter's Tale*, and to begin with we all sat round to read the first scene, and a few pages of the second scene down to Leontes' first soliloquy. We read it once round in a circle as best we could, some more ably than others—it took a little time to build up confidence. We then talked around the scene to discover what was happening in the story, the emotional state of the characters, the effects of jealousy, what we understood of the structure of the society etc.: I then asked for volunteers to read it again taking the different parts. We read it this time with the characters speaking in the middle, and the rest of the group sitting round them in a circle; and I asked the group to repeat the words which were to do with love—either in the sense of affection or admiration, or, as happens later in the scene, in the sense of sexual desire—to do this as they were spoken. In doing this they began to choose words for themselves, and in a way to own them. They were surprised by the quality and texture there; how in the first scene Archidemus and Camillo openly compete with each other over the quality and richness of their hospitality. But they were even more surprised at the sexuality they found in these words of Hermione:

Hermione: What? Have I twice said well? When was't before?
I prithee tell me. Cram's with praise, and make's
As fat as tame things. One good deed dying tongueless
Slaughters a thousand waiting upon that.
Our praises are our wages. You may ride's
With one soft kiss a thousand furlongs ere
With spur we heat an acre. But to th'goal:
My last good deed was to entreat his stay.
What was my first? It has an elder sister,
Or I mistake you. O, would her name were Grace!
But once before I spoke to th'purpose? When?
Nay, let me have't; I long.

I.ii.

They began to feel that they knew something about the play. We continued to work, and next took this speech of Leontes in the same scene:

Leontes: Inch-thick, knee-deep, o'er head and ears a fork'd one'!
Go play, boy, play; thy mother plays, and I
Play too—but so disgraced a part, whose issue
Will hiss me to my grave. Contempt and clamour
Will be my knell. Go play, boy, play. There have been,
Or I am much deceived, cuckolds ere now;
And many a man there is, even at this present.
Now, while I speak this, holds his wife by th'arm,
That little thinks she has been sluic'd in's absence,
And his pond fished by his next neighbour, by
Sir Smile, his neighbour. Nay, there's comfort in't
Whiles other men have gates, and those gates opened,
As mine, against their will. Should all despair
That have revolted wives, the tenth of mankind
Would hang themselves. Physic for't there's none;
It is a bawdy planet, that will strike
Where 'tis predominant; and 'tis powerful, think it,
From east, west, north, and south. Be it concluded,
No barricado for a belly. Know't:
It will let in and out the enemy
With bag and baggage. Many thousand on's
Have the disease and feel't not. How now, boy?

I.ii.

We first worked on it together in different ways to get them familiar with the taste of the words: I then asked them to move round the room while speaking, changing the direction on the punctuation marks to find the sudden violent turns of thought. We continued to look at this violence by repeating the words that express/contain disgust in some way—e.g., contempt, cuckold, sluiced, bawdy, fished etc.—the list is long: and as they spoke the words I asked them to do something physical like kicking chairs, or banging on the floor, always making sure that the exercise did not get out of control. We did this to open up the hidden agenda of the language and reveal the ambivalence and complexity of the feelings underneath; it also made clear how the words themselves were self-feeding, and lead to action. They began to comprehend/imagine something of the structure of that society through the vocabulary used.

The group, all with first-hand knowledge of the possibilities of violence, had a realisation that formal, articulate language had the power to uncover/explore hidden or violent feelings—they are not afraid of its extremes: their response was not sophisticated or tarnished by pre-knowledge of what it was about, rather they found something volatile and explosive within its form—all the things that Leontes is. We were then ready to go on to look for language which uncovered delicacy of feeling, a discovery of love perhaps, which is to be found later in the play through Perdita and Florizel.

This was a particularly good session I remember: near the end one of the group was so excited that he said something like—'you see, they didn't need scenery in those days—it's all in the words.' That was a revelation for him.

When we do exercises like this, words take on different shapes and lengths, vowels become extended and consonants more muscular: the movement of the words becomes one with the movement of the inner self, and the word becomes active in every sense. It also becomes subversive, for it does not behave quite as you expect. And so this work allowed me to see how text can be explored objectively, yet with a purpose to open up the individual to the possibility of defining themselves through language. I think that the majority of people have so little self-esteem when it comes to expressing their inner self, that they then resort to accepted clichéd responses: and the thought then crosses one's mind as to what extent do we then define ourselves in this way. The work then confirms for me that, from a modern perspective, motive and feeling can tie directly to the word—and this, in any country with any speech pattern.

So far, two perspectives with very different starting points—perhaps I should say retrospectives: but I hope it explains a little about what I have tried to tie together in the book. The first puts us in touch with the sound and the music, for each language has its own, and is of itself capable of arousing our emotions. The second perspective, the rough end as it were, puts us in touch with the need to speak. Edgar again:

The worst is not,
So long as we can say 'This is the
worst.'

But more than this: words are a healthy sign, a sign of life, a sign that we know who we are.

But—there is a third perspective which has to do with accent and the bringing together of cultures: a practical question for now, and a very different issue from when I started teaching—and one that is complex.

In January of this year, I organised a meeting of Theatre Voice Teachers which was held at The Other Place in Stratford, and we devoted one of the days to the issue of accent. We started the day with a look at how Received/Standard Pronunciation has developed in different parts of the UK, plus its standard equivalents in other countries. Representatives from each part of the UK, and from Australia, New Zealand, the US and Canada talked about how it is used, how they deal with it, and, perhaps, most important, the different cultural influences. We looked at how it is taught now, and whether it is still useful or relevant. We debated the sociological and emotional implications of standardising speech—i.e., how do we teach some kind of standard speech which is useful for an actor's career, without sacrificing either personal or cultural identity, and therefore integrity—and what is standard speech anyway. There were as many levels to the answer as there were regions, countries, cultures represented. Certainly all of them had to do with some form of class or culture dominance, a ruling mode of speech which was either complied with or rebelled against. And we found that every region, every country had reacted in a particular way, and had a very definite prevailing attitude to it.

We also had interesting contributions later in the week from teachers in Poland, Bulgaria and India, talking about how the prevalent political situation affects the way you speak. From Bulgaria we heard something of the effect of a repressive regime on language, and how you need to hold on to your own way of speaking in order to keep your sense of identity; more than this—how you have to bend your language so that you can speak truth without compromising or endangering yourself or your family. From India we heard of the effects of colonialism on your voice: to what extent it splits you away from your roots, and therefore how important it is to recover your sound memory.

From my own experience of working in India recently with actors and acting teachers, who worked mostly in English, I realised afresh just how difficult it is to feel an emotional connection with another language, and the effect that has on the voice. Although I chose to work with Hindi texts, that was often their second language, and for all the reasons we know about of wanting to make your voice behave, of making sense of a language that does not quite belong to you, it was very difficult for them to find the root of their voice. This was in India—but this cultural displacement with regards language happens everywhere.

I have digressed a little, but I think this is all part of the central question at the moment, for our accent and/or cultural entry affects how we perceive text, how we hear it, and therefore in the end how we interpret it. It must also be a political question, for we have to open theatre out to everyone. Some of this of course has to do with casting choices and policies. If a play is written in a particular dialect there is no problem, for then the actor must observe that in order to retain the credibility of the world of the play. But in classical text it is so much more complex, for an accent in itself makes some kind of statement, either to do with region or culture, and so it comes down to choice—for which we must take responsibility.

What is important is that we open our ears to the differences, because that is the way to keep the vitality in the language. And we have to train ourselves to listen; to listen for the rhythms, the cadence in the writing, the muscularity and energy which is there in every piece of text. We have to honour the intrinsic music without damaging our own truth.

People need the music of language, for it both provokes and comforts; we must work for it.

Finally, two things—to do with style and with image. We have talked a good deal about the shifting balance of a declamatory style and how it can fuse with modern sensibilities; and I suppose most popular theatre is some kind of mix of these. I have talked a little in the book about Brecht and Brechtian style: this happens to suit my taste because it requires us not only to be involved in the characters and their predicaments, but also to view their human position—but that is not at the moment in fashion. There is now a movement towards storytelling: this is good in that it opens out conventional Western forms to a more multi-cultural approach, though I think it lets us off the hook in terms of taking some kind of objective view. What is essential is that we continually redefine both our ways of working on text and how we present it: and this of course relates as much to directors as to actors. We must continually ask—what is right for now.

Every piece of theatre we perform has its own style, form and space—I mean space in the language: this form, i.e., the sentence structure and rhythm, holds very specifically the writer's intention and gives it meaning beyond the actor's individual interpretation or motive, call it what you will. So, it seems to me we not only have to make the audience feel, we also must give them the space to hear something beyond just what we say, and to be aware of another dimension—and this dimension has to do with our reason for doing the work.

Secondly, we must never short-change the image, for it is the image which is the surface indication of the earth-shift that may be going on under the character.

When I was directing *King Lear,* Edward Bond sent me some notes about the play: these were, of course, wonderfully illuminating. One of the things he mentioned was the fact that, at the end of the play when the worst has happened and he has borne the dead Cordelia in his arms, in the middle of his last speech Lear says—'Pray you undo this button'—how seemingly ordinary, yet momentous. And this set me to enquire what is happening underneath—and that words are often the calm surface of an underlying volcano. This applies equally to modern writing though the idiom is different, and the image may simply be contained in the movement of the language—just look again at the speech from *Streetcar* on page 43. Whatever the cultural idiom, the writing and the image must be given its right space and weight.

Lear: And my poor fool is hanged! No, no, no life!
Why should a dog, a horse, a rat have life
And thou no breath at all? Thou'lt come no more;
Never, never, never, never, never.
Pray you undo this button. Thank you, sir.
Do you see this? Look on her! Look, her lips!
Look there! Look there! He dies.

This has been a very personal account of the various strands of work that have influenced me, which I hope will inform what is already in the book. There are many ways into working on voice and text, and you have to use what is most helpful.

Language in theatre should be about entering into another person's world, but in doing so we must always relate to the whole world of the play.

I hope all that we have looked at in the book will help towards finding a freedom and an excitement in language; for the reiease of thought into words should be as exhilarating as dance, and the exercises will help us to achieve this. Words are always a life-force, always a provocation: they are the opposite of silence. And so we should always be concerned with the predicament and not the feeling—that will take care of itself. There should be no pressure on the audience to make judgements—that will come out of the story itself.

And lastly, it is through humour that the human position is perceived, and so, with this in mind, I would like to finish with this poem of Auden, of which I am particularly fond:

MUSEÉ DES BEAUX ARTS

About suffering they were never wrong,
The Old Masters: how well they understood
Its human position; how it takes place
While someone else is eating or opening a window or just walking
 dully along;
How, when the aged are reverently, passionately waiting
For the miraculous birth, there always must be
Children who did not specially want it to happen, skating
On a pond at the edge of the wood:
They never forgot
That even the dreadful martyrdom must run its course
Anyhow in a corner, some untidy spot
Where the dogs go on with their doggy life and the torturer's
 horse
Scratches its innocent behind on a tree.

In Brueghel's *Icarus*, for instance: how everything turns away
Quite leisurely from the disaster: the ploughman may
Have heard the splash, the forsaken cry,
But for him it was not an important failure; the sun shone
As it had to on the white legs disappearing into the green
Water; and the expensive delicate ship that must have seen
Something amazing, a boy falling out of the sky,
Had somewhere to get to and sailed calmly on.

W.H. Auden

Index of Quotations

OTHER PLAY TEXTS

Quotes by Subject

The following is a list of the main headings in the book together with the quoted texts which refer to them: as so many of the points are interrelated it is intended only as a rough guide in order to help in following through a particular train of enquiry. Not all quoted texts are listed, and references to exercises are not included.